PATTERN CUTTING FOR LINGERIE, BEACHWEAR AND LEISUREWEAR

ANN HAGGAR

b

Blackwell Science

Blackwell Science Ltd
Editorial Offices:
Osney Mead, Oxford OX2 0EL
25 John Street, London WC1N 2BL
23 Ainslie Place, Edinburgh EH3 6AJ
350 Main Street, Malden
  MA 02148 5018, USA
10, rue Casimir Delavigne
  75006 Paris, France

Other Editorial Offices:
Blackwell Wissenschafts-Verlag GmbH
Kurfürstendamm 57
10707 Berlin, Germany

Blackwell Science KK
MG Kodenmacho Building
7–10 Kodenmacho Nihombashi
Chuo-ku, Tokyo 104, Japan

First published by BSP Professional
  Books 1990
Reprinted 1992
Reprinted by Blackwell Science
  1993, 1995, 1996, 1997, 1999

Set by Setrite Typesetters, Hong Kong
Printed and bound in Great Britain at
The Alden Press Limited, Oxford and Northampton

DISTRIBUTORS

Marston Book Services Ltd
PO Box 269
Abingdon, Oxon OX14 4YN
(*Orders:* Tel: 01235 465500
        Fax: 01235 465555)

USA
Blackwell Science, Inc.
Commerce Place
350 Main Street
Malden, MA 02148 5018
(*Orders:* Tel: 800 759 6102
           617 388 8250
        Fax: 617 388 8255)

Canada
Login Brothers Book Company
324 Saulteaux Crescent
Winnipeg, Manitoba R3J 3T2
(*Orders:* Tel: 204 224-4068
        Fax: 204 837-3116)

Australia
Blackwell Science Pty Ltd
54 University Street
Carlton, Victoria 3053
(*Orders:* Tel: 3 9347 0300
        Fax: 3 9347 5001)

British Library
Cataloging in Publication Data

Haggar, Ann
    Pattern cutting for lingerie, beachwear and
    leisurewear.
    1. Lingerie, Making, Manuals
    2. Swimming costumes. Patterns.
    Making
    I. Title
    646.4'204

    ISBN 0–632–02033–4

For further information on
Blackwell Science, visit our website:
www.blackwell-science.com

Contents

Preface

This book originated as a response to a request for written instruction in the techniques of pattern cutting for lingerie.

As the boundaries between lingerie, beachwear and leisurewear continue to become less distinct I decided to extend the scope of this book to cover all three subjects. The design, cutting and sewing technology being interrelated is used in fact to great advantage by manufacturers across a wide range of garments.

Well-balanced, perfected patterns are not achieved in minutes even by experienced pattern cutters. Therefore one of the most important attributes of a good cutter is the skill of manipulating such patterns to extend their use. This skill can be paralleled with designers using their favourite shapes several times over in one collection, differently detailed to vary the theme. Suggestions are therefore made where appropriate for using perfected patterns as a basis for other styles – a time-saving practice widely used professionally but not widely taught.

Another area infrequently covered in text books is that of choosing the correct type of fabric for the design. This can have a profound effect on the cut of the pattern and therefore suggestions for suitable fabrics are included, specifically to help beginners.

This book is written for all those who wish to increase their knowledge and understanding of these subjects. They may be students, enthusiastic creative dressmakers, teachers or professionals, including those usually engaged in dress production who wish to add these categories of clothing to their ranges. The book is suitable for the following courses of study:

Fashion Degree Courses
Higher National Diploma
City and Guilds of London Institute

Acknowledgements
I would like to thank:
Louise Cleminson, colleague and mentor, for help with proof reading.
Caroline Savage of Blackwell Science for the design of the layout.
Katherine Dowling for modelling and practical assistance.
Elizabeth Stevens for her help in typing the manuscript.
The Library staff of the London College of Fashion and the British Library.
My husband, Henry for his advice coloured by an unending quest for perfection.

Introduction

Lingerie, beachwear and leisurewear have all taken an increasing share of the fashion market in recent years. This is a direct consequence of women taking a greater interest in *everything* they wear, an increase in leisure time generally and the current fashion for active leisure pursuits in particular.

There is no mystique about cutting patterns for these related types of clothing. The same principles apply as when cutting for separates, dresses or coats − in some cases even the same block patterns may be used as a basis. The only real differences lie in the design, choice of fabric (which can affect the cut of the pattern) and in greater variations of fit.

Patterns for underwear and swimwear are often close fitting. It is therefore essential to have a thorough understanding of the differences between measurements of the actual body and measurements of the garments that fit over the body. To promote this understanding the reader's attention is drawn to the comprehensive size chart on page 6 which lists separately the body measurements *and* the standard amounts of ease built in to patterns, allowing resulting garments to fit easily over the body. It is the systematic removal of this ease (sometimes called 'tolerance') that gives the skin-tight fit required for many items of underwear and swimwear. Conversely, increasing the amount of ease loosens the fit for certain types of leisurewear garments.

Flat pattern methods are used throughout the book, producing results quickly. It is, however, advisable to test the more fitted patterns, e.g. corsets, swimsuits, one-piece playsuits and stretchwear, by cutting a trial garment (toile) in a similar, less expensive fabric. For the experienced cutter this will either confirm the pattern's good fit and shape or show where adjustments need to be made. For the student or aspiring pattern cutter there is no better way of developing an eye capable of visualising a three-dimensional shape whilst looking at a flat pattern. Experience is also gained in judging good proportion and line. All these assets are far more important than the ability to calculate mathematically.

Although pattern cutters do not have to be experienced dressmakers, they need to know how garments are put together as this so often affects the way a pattern is made. The fabric chosen for a design and the way it is used (grain) also greatly affects the cut of the pattern; to make the reader aware of this important consideration, fabric suggestions are given in each section.

All patterns in this book originate from the basic blocks constructed in Chapter 1. These blocks are cut nett, i.e. without seam allowances, in order to avoid confusion when they are subdivided as they would be for a Princess line style. They appear in the diagrams at $\frac{1}{5}$ of their full size. Unworkable figures should be rounded up to the nearest millimetre or part of a centimetre. This commonsense approach should be used throughout the book. Any similar fitting set of blocks may be substituted for those offered here; to compensate for small differences, slight adjustments may be necessary when following the instructions.

The book is arranged with the simpler patterns at the beginning and the more complex at the end of each section. Those with little or no experience are advised to work in sequence in order that they may understand the relationship of one pattern to another.

The instructions take you through from the planning stage (basic draft) to finished pattern pieces. The addition of seam allowances is not usually included unless in a particularly interesting situation; this allows more emphasis to be placed on technique and methods.

Measurements for parts of patterns such as skirt length, collar width and pocket size/position, etc. are very much a matter for the designer/pattern cutter's own judgment. After the basic shape and fit of the garment, it is the combination of such dimensions that gives each design its individual appearance. Specific measurements have been suggested to assist the novice.

Straight grain lines should always be marked along the full length (or width) of the pattern; when a long pattern piece is marked with only a short grain line in the middle, the ends of the pattern are in danger of being placed 'off grain' when cutting out.

The inclusion of balance marks on pattern seams is vitally important. Without them the garment may not be assembled correctly or swiftly; areas of fullness, e.g. easing, gathers or pleats, may not be properly controlled. Their positions on the seam lines should be decided at the planning stage and not when the pattern is completed. For perfect matching place balance marks at right angles to seams or in line with any unusually angled seams, e.g. a wing seam running into the armhole.

As with most skills, pattern cutting can be constantly reappraised. I would appreciate constructive comments from readers.

PART 1 PRINCIPLE PATTERNS
from
BRAS to BATHROBES

1 THE BASIC BLOCKS

THE BASIC BLOCKS

Lingerie, beachwear and leisurewear are extremely diversified in their degrees of fit. They range from the skin-tight − corsets, swimsuits and leotards − to the loose and casual − French knickers, bathrobes and beach pyjamas. The efficient production of patterns for such a wide variety of garments depends on a comprehensive set of blocks suitably constructed to deal with the varying degrees of fit.

The blocks that follow form the basis for all the garments featured in this book. These blocks have been designed to fit the body with the normal dress ease allowances (see size chart on page 6) which will help the pattern cutter who usually produces patterns for top clothing to correctly judge the resulting fit of lingerie and beachwear patterns. As an additional bonus these blocks could of course be used to provide a full range of patterns for top clothes.

The Basic Blocks may be used without substantial changes to their size to produce patterns for the more fitted ranges, for example, underwear. For looser, more casual fitting garments such as nightwear and some items of leisurewear, use the Dartless Bodice Blocks − either the closer or looser fitting version depending on the degree of fit required. Clear instructions are given in the following chapters for the development of these basic blocks into the specialised patterns needed for lingerie, beach and leisurewear styles and garments made from stretch fabrics. All blocks are constructed without seam allowances to avoid confusion when they are subdivided.

The diagrams of the blocks, as you see them on the pages of this book, are miniatures at one fifth scale. This enables you to trace from them and use the resulting block patterns for trial pattern making and experimentation. Remember that any changes or design details applied must also be at one fifth scale. Although full scale pattern making is always preferable, the use of fifth scale blocks allows you to work at drawing pad size when access to a large cutting table is restricted, quickly solving problems at something like a fifth of the time.

Underwear patterns are usually cut from fitted blocks.
Nightwear patterns can be based on either close or loose fitting blocks, depending on the fabric used − stretch or non-stretch.
Beach and leisurewear patterns can be cut from close or loose fitting blocks, depending on the style.
Stretchwear patterns may require a close or loose fitting base, depending on the style. This book concentrates on close fitting stretchwear which is thought (often mistakenly) to present more difficulties.

NOTE ON THE USE OF THE WOMEN'S STANDARD SIZE CHART

The extensive size charts on pages 6 and 8 contain not only the usual body measurements (in column 1) used for dress production but also supplementary information for designing and cutting patterns for very fitted garments. When cutting for special fitting requirements, a thorough understanding of the differences between body and pattern size is essential. Note therefore that the ease allowances (in column 2) made for movement over and above the body measurements when constructing a block or pattern, are listed separately from the bare body measurements.

This enables the pattern cutter to easily determine the degree of fit in the early stages of pattern making. The final column contains an example of the full measurements used to draft the Basic Blocks for a size 12 figure. Before drafting other sizes calculate the drafting measurement by adding the ease allowances, which remain constant for all sizes, to the body measurements for the required size.

The measurements are divided into the horizontal and the vertical. When taking personal measurements working in sequence will help to avoid omissions.

WOMEN'S STANDARD SIZE CHART
Horizontal Measurements

Size	Body Measurements						Ease Allowances on Basic Dress Blocks and Trouser*	Total Block Drafting Measurement, i.e. body plus ease Example for size 12
	8	10	12	14	16	18		
(1) Bust**	80	84	88	92	96	100	10	98
(2) Waist	60	64	68	72	76	80	1 cm on skirt 4 cm on bodice 1 cm on trouser	69 72 69
(3) Hips (20 cm from waist)	86	90	94	98	102	106	5	99
(4) Top hips (10 cm from waist)	80	84	88	92	96	100	4/5	92/93
(5) Back width (X back)	34	35	36	37	38	39	1.6	37.6
(6) Chest width	31.5	32.5	33.5	34.5	35.5	36.5	0.6	34.1
(7) Shoulder	12.4	12.7	13	13.3	13.6	13.9	—	13
(8) Bust separation	16.8	18	19.2	20.4	21.6	22.8	—	19.2
(9) Neck base circumference	35.5	36.5	37.5	38.5	39.5	40.5		37.5
(10) Chest circumference	74	78	82	86	90	94	*	—
(11) Rib cage	67	71	75	79	83	87	*	—
(12) Top arm	26	27	28	29	30	31	5	33
(13) Elbow	22.2	23.6	25	26.4	27.8	29.2	minimum of 5	—
(14) Wrist	15	15.5	16	16.5	17	17.5	6.5 to fit over hand	22.5
(15) Thigh	48	51	54	57	60	63	—	—
(16) Knee	32.2	33.6	35	36.4	37.8	39.2	minimum of 6 for bending	55
(17) Ankle	21.8	22.4	23	23.6	24.2	24.8	minimum of 9 to fit over foot	43

* Ease automatically included on Dress Blocks; information given for individual patterns as appropriate.
** Minimum measurement for a garment to pull over head and shoulders = body bust measurement.

Women's Standard Size Chart

Horizontal Measurements

- (1) Bust
- (2) Waist
- (3) Hips
- (4) Top hips
- (5) Back width (X back)
- (6) Chest width
- (7) Shoulder
- (8) Bust separation
- (9) Neckbase circumference
- (10) Rib cage
- (11) Chest circumference
- (12) Top arm
- (13) Elbow
- (14) Wrist
- (15) Thigh
- (16) Knee
- (17) Ankle

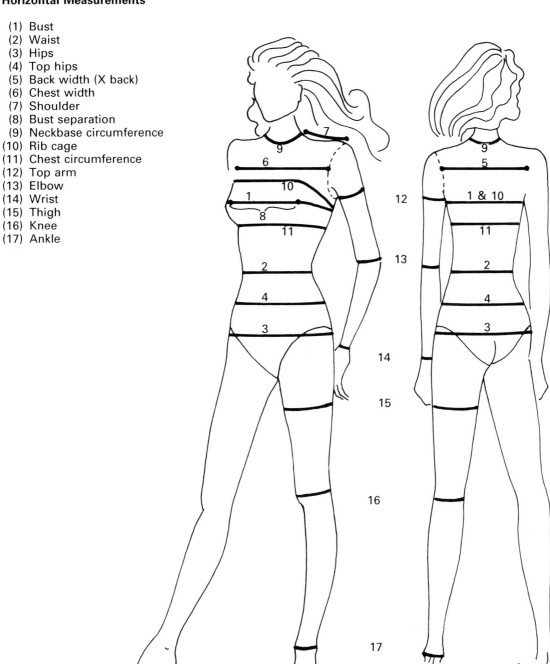

WOMEN'S STANDARD SIZE CHART
Vertical Measurements

Size	Body Measurements						Ease Allowances on Basic Dress Blocks and Trouser	Total Block Drafting Measurement, i.e. body plus ease Example for size 12
	8	10	12	14	16	18		
(18) Nape–Waist	40	40.5	41	41.5	42	42.5	—	41
(19) Nape–Bust	24	24.2	24.4	24.6	24.8	25	—	24.4
(20) Nape–Armhole depth	21	21.2	21.4	21.6	21.8	22	—	21.4
(21) Nape–ground	140.4	142.2	144	145.8	147.6	149.4	—	144
(22) Bust height (from nape–nipple)	33.5	34	34.5	35	35.5	36	—	—
(23) Top sleeve length	56.4	57.2	58	59.6	60.4	61.2	—	58
(24) Waist–Hip	19.4	19.7	20	20.3	20.6	20.9	—	20
(25) Waist–Knee	58.4	59.2	60	60.8	61.6	62.4	—	60
(26) Waist–floor	100.4	101.7	103	104.3	105.6	106.9	—	103
(27) Full height	159	161.5	164	166.5	169	171.5	—	—
(28) Body rise (depth of crutch)	26.4	27.2	28	28.8	29.6	30.4	automatically included due to method of taking body measurement	28
(29) Crutch length (CF–CB through legs)	61	63.5	66	68.5	71	73.5	depends on style	used only for checking
(30) Trunk length	136.5	140	143.5	147	150.5	154	depends on style	used only for checking

Additional Vertical and Through-Body Measurements

(28) Body rise
(29) Crutch length
(30) Trunk length

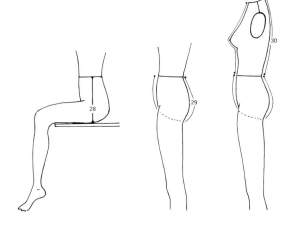

Women's Standard Size Chart

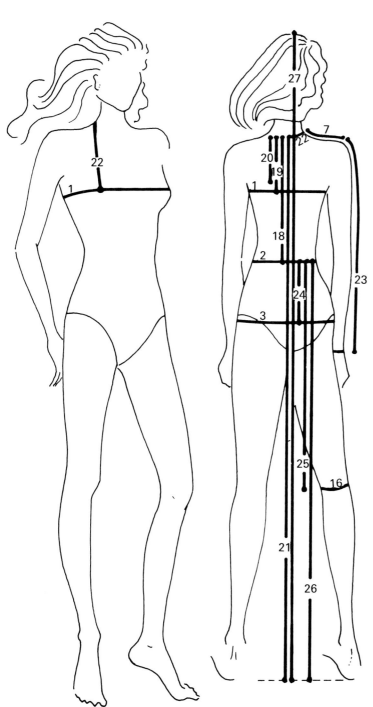

Vertical Measurements

(18) Nape—waist
(19) Nape—bust
(20) Nape—armhole depth
(21) Nape—ground
(22) Bust height, from nape—nipple
(23) Top sleeve length
(24) Waist—hip
(25) Waist—knee
(26) Waist—floor
(27) Full height

THE BASIC DRESS BLOCKS
The Straight Skirt Block

Three main measurements are required to draft the skirt block:

(1) Waist to knee length.
(2) Total hip measurement − i.e. hip circumference plus 5 cm ease allowance.
(3) Total waist measurement − i.e. waist circumference plus 1 cm ease allowance.
    Drafting paper size − 70 cm wide × 80 cm long.

Square lines out from 0
0−1 = waist to knee length plus 1 cm. Mark CB.
0−2 = half total hip. Square down for CF.
0−3 = 1.5 cm back waist drop. Square a short line at 3.
2−4 = 1 cm front waist drop. Square a short line at 4.
4−5 = waist to hip length. Square across to CB.
  6 = midway CB and CF.
  7 = midway 4−5. Square across to CB. Mark point 8. Top hip line.
3−9 = one quarter total waist plus 4.6 cm.
4−10 = one quarter total waist plus 4 cm. Connect 3−9 and 4−10 with lightly drawn lines.
8−11 = one quarter total hip minus 0.8 cm.
7−12 = one quarter total hip minus 1 cm. Connect 9−11−6 and 10−12−6 for hip curves.

To reduce top of skirt to fit total waist measurement, i.e. body waist plus 1 cm ease which will produce a close fitting skirt waist.

Calculate the waist dart allowance as follows:

Measure 3−9 and 4−10. Record measurements on draft and add together (43.2 cm for size 12). From this measurement subtract half total waist measurement (34.5 cm for size 12).
43.2 cm minus 34.5 cm = 8.7 cm dart allowance.

Note on size of waist darts
The purpose of a dart is to remove excess material and thereby make the garment fit the body. Obviously, the more shapely areas of the body need larger darts, e.g. the bust as one of the most prominent parts of the body requires a large dart to take away the excess from the surrounding area. The shoulder blade being considerably less prominent, a smaller dart is sufficient to perform the same task.
    To consider the area between waist and hip, the back is hollowed beneath the waistline and is actually quite shapely. Larger darts are required here than in the corresponding front area which is relatively flat. Therefore, divide the calculated dart allowance (8.7 cm for size 12) as follows:

back dart(s) = 5.2 cm[1]
front dart   = 3.5 cm[2]

[1] The back dart allowance should be further divided into two darts as a single large dart will 'poke' if used in this area of the body.
[2] Equal to one tenth of *half* total waist measurement, a useful point to remember when drafting other sizes or to personal measurements. What remains of the allowance is allocated to the back darts.

To position the darts on lines 3−9 and 4−10
Back: 3−13 = one third of 3−9 plus 0.7 cm
      3−14 = two thirds of 3−9 plus 0.7 cm
      Square down from line 0−2 through points 13 & 14, to 1.5 cm below top hip line.
These squared lines form the centres of two darts. The dart nearest CB should be slightly smaller than that nearest side seam, e.g. 2.5 cm and 2.7 cm.
Front: 4−15 = two thirds of 4−10. Square down from line 0−2 to top hip line. This forms the centre of a 3.5 cm dart.

To complete block, see small diagram opposite
Fold out darts and connect 3−9 and 4−10 with smooth curves. (As an alternative to folding the pattern, see Figs 9(a)−(c) on page 45.)
Keep CF and CB waist lines right angles for approximately 3 cm − this ensures no points or dents when patterns are doubled over.

Straight Skirt Block

Example, size 12

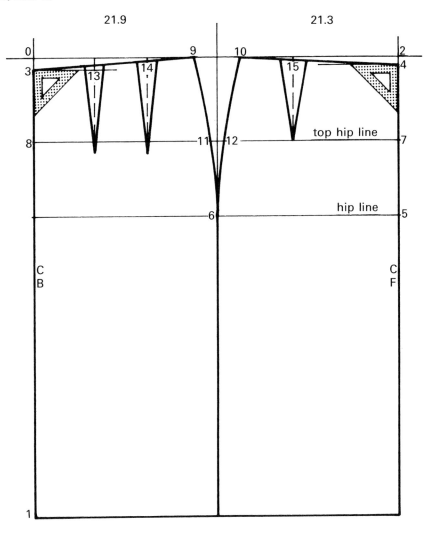

21.9

21.3

21.9
+ 21.3
43.2
− 34.5
8.7 WR

top hip line

hip line

scale 1:5

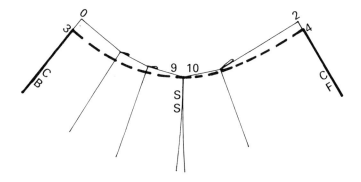

The Bodice Block

Six main measurements are required to draft the bodice block:

(1) Nape to waist length.
(2) Total bust measurement − i.e. bust circumference plus 10 cm ease allowance.
(3) Total back width − i.e. back width plus 1.6 cm ease allowance.
(4) Shoulder.
(5) Total chest width − i.e. chest width plus 0.6 cm ease allowance.
(6) Waist measurement − i.e. waist circumference plus 4 cm ease allowance.

Drafting paper size − 70 cm wide × 60 cm long.

Square lines out from 0

0−1 = nape to waist plus 2 cm. Mark CB. Square across from 1.
0−2 = half total bust measurement plus 0.5 cm (for drafting gap at side seam). Square down for CF line. This completes the rectangle.
0−3 = 2 cm. Square across.
3−4 = half of 1−3 plus 4 cm toward waist. Square across for bust line.
4−5 = 3 cm. Square across for underarm line (depth of armhole). Mark 6.
5−7 = half of 5−3. Square across for X back line.

For back neck:
0−8 = one fifth neck base circumference minus 0.2 cm. Square down.
        Curve neckline 1.5 cm diagonally from corner.

For front neck:
2−9 = one fifth neck base circumference minus 1.6 cm. Square down.
2−10 = one fifth neck base circumference plus 0.2 cm. Square across.
        Curve neckline 2.5 cm diagonally from corner.
7−11 = half total back width. Square down to underarm line. Mark 12 midway.
3−13 = one third of 3−7 minus 0.4 cm. Square across.
13−14 = 7−11 plus 2.4 cm (for dart allowance and shoulder shaping).
8−14 = Connect for provisional back shoulder.
14−15 = half shoulder length plus 0.5 cm.
15−16 = 1.4 cm dart.

15−17 = Squared from provisional shoulder line and 2 cm up from X back line. Connect 15−17−16 extending dart lines above provisional shoulder line.
10−18 = half 10−6 plus 2 cm toward waist. Square across.
18−19 = half total chest width plus 2.2 cm bust dart allowance. Square down to underarm line.
10−20 = 18−19 plus 4.3 cm for dart allowance and shoulder shaping.
20−21 = 0.3 cm. See enlarged diagram.
9−21 = Connect for provisional front shoulder.
22 = bust point − half bust separation, applied from CF.
21−23 = 14−15 on back shoulder. Connect 22−23 extending beyond provisional shoulder.
23−24 = one eighth of half total bust measurement minus 0.3 cm.
        Connect 22−24 extending beyond provisional shoulder.
25 = midway 5−6. Square down for provisional side seam. Mark 26 at side waistline and 27 at CF waistline.
27−28 = 1.3 cm extra front waist length allowed for bust prominence.
        Connect 1−27 for provisional waistline.

To shape armhole
Back: rule dotted guide line from 14−11. Midway 14−11 and 11−12 hollow armhole line 0.2 cm. Connect 14−25 curving through a 2.5 cm diagonal point from corner.
Front: rule dotted guide line from 21−19. Midway 21−19 hollow armhole line 0.8 cm. Connect 21−25 curving through a 2.3 cm diagonal point from corner.

Bodice waist reduction − to fit body waist measurement plus 4 cm ease which will produce an average dress fit. Calculate as follows:
Measure 1−28 (49.5 cm for size 12). From this subtract half total waist (see total drafting measurements in Size Chart, page 6).
49.5 cm − 36 cm = 13.5 cm waist reduction.
    Plan this reduction where it will have most effect, i.e. under the most curveaceous areas of the body:
    under shoulder blades
    at side seam
    under bust

Bodice Block

Example, size 12

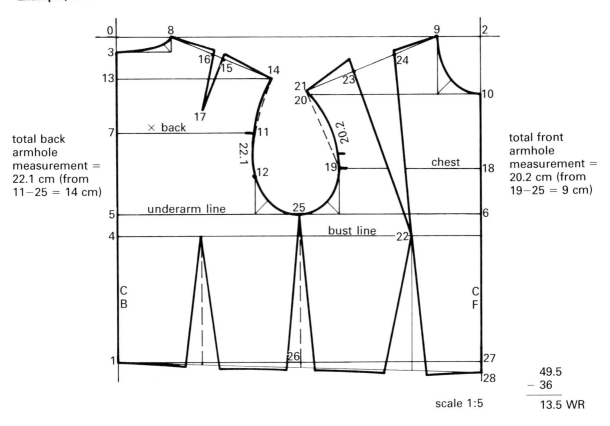

total back armhole measurement = 22.1 cm (from 11−25 = 14 cm)

total front armhole measurement = 20.2 cm (from 19−25 = 9 cm)

× back

underarm line

bust line

chest

C B

C F

scale 1:5

$$\begin{array}{r} 49.5 \\ -\ 36 \\ \hline 13.5\ \text{WR} \end{array}$$

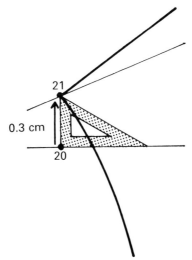

0.3 cm

A smoother fit will result if the side seam shaping is kept smaller than the back and front waist darts. Therefore, divide the amount of waist reduction as follows:

back dart = 4.5 cm
side seam = 3.5 cm
front dart = 5.5 cm

To position darts on line 1−28

Back: square down from end of shoulder blade dart (17). This line forms the centre of the dart, which extends to the bust line.

Side: squared line 25−26 forms the centre of the side seam reduction.

Front: square down from bust point (22). Measure one third of the front dart toward CF and two thirds toward side seam.

To complete block

Fold out back and front shoulder darts and rule final shoulder lines from 8−14 and 9−21. Fold out waist darts and side seam reduction. Connect 1−28 in a smooth curve, dropping slightly below line in order to round off points made by darts and seam.

Trace off block, leaving draft intact for possible future reference. Check that neck and armhole form a continuous curve by placing shoulder seams together. Make sure that block is labelled with its size and any other useful information, e.g. bust line, underarm line, chest and X back lines and CB and CF.

Note 1 Make sure the 'corners' are square at base of neck (3 & 10) and CB and CF (1 & 28).

Note 2 The front bust and waist darts meet on the bust line for the purposes of:
(a) easy block construction
(b) easy dart manipulation
(c) correct and easy division of front bodice, e.g. Princess line seams.

In subsequent pattern making, shorten darts at least 2.5 cm from the bust point and re-draw back to the base.

Note 3 Refer to Sleeve Block section, 'Positioning of sleeve in armhole' on page 15, for information on armhole balance points.

The Sleeve Block

Four main measurements are required to draft the sleeve block:

(1) Armhole circumference (also called scye), carefully measured from the bodice block, using the tape measure on its edge.
(2) Top sleeve length.
(3) Total top arm measurement − i.e. top arm circumference plus 5 cm ease allowance.
(4) Total wrist measurement − i.e. wrist circumference plus 6.5 cm ease allowance to fit over hand.
Drafting paper size − 50 cm wide × 80 cm long.

Square lines out from 0
$\begin{array}{ll} 0-1 & = \text{crown height} = \text{one third armhole} \\ & \quad \text{circumference, measured from bodice} \\ & \quad \text{block.} \\ 1-2 & = \text{top sleeve length (also centre/straight grain} \\ & \quad \text{line). Square a short line at 1 and a longer} \\ & \quad \text{line at 2.} \end{array}$

$\left. \begin{array}{l} 0-3 \\ 0-4 \end{array} \right\} = \begin{array}{l} \text{half total top arm measurement. Mark} \\ \text{underarm line. Connect } 1-3 \text{ and } 1-4 \text{ with} \\ \text{straight guide lines.} \end{array}$

To shape sleeve head
Back:
$\begin{array}{ll} 3-5 & = \text{one third } 3-1 \\ 6 & = \text{midway } 5-1 \\ 7 & = \text{midway } 3-5 \text{ and } 0.5 \text{ cm in from guide line.} \\ 8 & = 2 \text{ cm out from } 6 \\ & \quad \text{Connect } 3-7-5-8-1 \end{array}$
Front:
$\begin{array}{ll} 4-9 & = \text{half } 4-1 \text{ minus } 1.8 \text{ cm} \\ 10 & = \text{midway } 9-1 \\ 11 & = \text{midway } 4-9 \text{ and } 1.5 \text{ cm in from guide line.} \\ 12 & = 2 \text{ cm out from } 10 \\ & \quad \text{Connect } 4-11-9-12-1 \end{array}$
Elbow level from $0 = 25-26$ on bodice draft.

Wrist shaping
$\left. \begin{array}{l} 2-13 \\ \\ 2-14 \end{array} \right\} = \begin{array}{l} \text{Total wrist measurement plus } 5.5 \text{ cm dart} \\ \text{allowance} \div 2. \text{ Elbow point is midway} \\ \text{underarm seam } (3-13) \text{ and centre grain line} \\ (1-2). \end{array}$
$\begin{array}{ll} 13-15 & = \text{half } 13-2 \text{ plus } 0.8 \text{ cm. Connect to elbow} \\ & \quad \text{point. This line forms the centre of a } 5.5 \text{ cm} \\ & \quad \text{wrist dart.} \end{array}$
To complete wrist:
Fold out dart. Midway $2-13$ drop 0.5 cm. Midway

$2-14$ raise 0.5 cm. Connect wrist curve through all these points. Check this curve with sleeve seam closed.

Sleeve head easing
When a set-in sleeve is inserted into an armhole it has to fit and mould over the prominence of the shoulder bone. To do this satisfactorily the sleeve head must be slightly larger than the armhole. The extra is eased in, mainly over the shoulder area and, to a much lesser extent, into the lower part of the armhole where, instead of providing shape and form, it ensures that the sleeve is not strained into the armhole. It is this division between shoulder area and lower armhole which decides the positions for the balance points, and the sleeve head easing allocated between these points.

On this block the sleeve head easing amounts to approximately 3 cm, i.e. 1.5 cm on both back and front − an average amount for a basic block. However, this amount may be quite unsuitable in certain circumstances − for example:

(1) Jacket, coat and dress sleeves styled with high heads, perhaps exaggerated with rolled padding and therefore requiring a large amount of sleeve head easing.
(2) Shirt sleeves − where the use of a flattened sleeve head is traditional, which requires very little sleeve head easing.
(3) Open woven, pliable fabrics, e.g. soft woollen tweed − where it may be insufficient.
(4) Closely woven, incompressible fabrics, e.g. cotton shirting, taffetas − where it would be excessive.

As seen from the above examples, many factors can combine to influence the required amount of sleeve head easing. *Style and type of fabric must be considered together.* There are no hard and fast rules and no substitute for your own experience. Some mistakes are inevitable in the early stages; most are correctable and with sensitive observation experience is quickly gained.

Positioning of sleeve in armhole
To help with the correct placement of sleeve in the armhole, the main balance points are located thus:

on back armhole − at point 11 on X back line
on front armhole − at point 19 on chest line

An extra balance point marked on the front armhole, 2 cm above 19, ensures that the sleeve cannot be

Sleeve Block

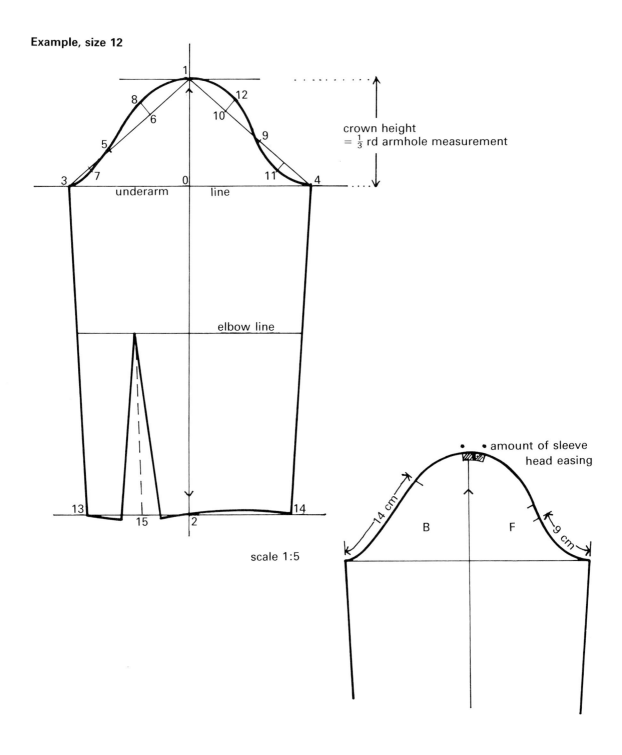

Example, size 12

crown height
= $\frac{1}{3}$ rd armhole measurement

underarm   line

elbow line

scale 1:5

amount of sleeve
head easing

B   F

inserted back to front. In addition to these, the underarm and shoulder seams serve as further matching points.

Important All curved lines must be carefully measured with the tape measure on its edge.

(1) Measure back armhole from underarm point (25) to balance point (11).
Record this measurement on the block. Continue on up to shoulder point (14), recording the whole back armhole measurement as well.
(2) Measure front armhole from 25−19 and, ignoring the second balance point for the time being, continue measuring up to 21. Note measurements down as for back armhole in preparation for transfer to sleeve head.

Establishing the amount of sleeve head easing

(1) Apply the whole back armhole measurement to the back sleeve head curve, starting at 3. The measurement will register slightly left of the centre/grain line. Mark this point.
(2) Repeat this procedure on the front sleeve head, using the front armhole measurement. The front register point will be further from the centre/grain line.

The gap between these shoulder points is the sleeve head easing. This is divided in two − *the centre point being the balance mark that matches the shoulder seam.* The sleeve head easing is now equally divided between back and front and recorded on the block for future reference.

Transfer and correct positioning of balance marks to sleeve head

(1) Add 0.2 cm to the lower back armhole measurement (11−25). Apply this measurement along lower back sleeve curve from underarm point (3). Mark balance point.
(2) Add 0.2 cm to the lower front armhole measurement (19−25). Apply this measurement to the front sleeve curve from underarm point (4). Mark first balance point, and then another 2 cm above.

The One-Piece Dress Block

(adapted from the Basic Bodice and Skirt Blocks)

BACK DRESS

(1) Rule a dress length line down left side of a sheet of paper large enough to take the back and front Bodice Blocks side by side with a small gap between, and the Skirt Block underneath. On this line place the CB bodice – outline and include shoulder and waist dart (lightly), X back, underarm and bust lines – all useful when adapting the block to different styles. Square a line from CB to side waist point and beyond, to reach CF.

(2) Place the back Skirt Block below with its *side waist point touching the squared waist line*. There will be a gap between CB waist points. Outline the skirt in this position, lightly between side waist and top hip; include the hip and top hip line but not the darts.

(3) The side seam will have a 'step' in it at waist level caused by the difference in ease over bust and hip. Re-draw from bodice side waist point to just below top hip level. *Complete the waist shaping by drawing the dress dart*: reduce the bodice dart volume by 0.5 cm on either side. Draw a line through centre of dart, continuing it down to midway between top hip and hip line, completing the dart at this point.

FRONT DRESS

(1) Place front Bodice Block on a dress length line parallel to CB. *The back and front underarm levels must be aligned and the front side waist point must sit on the squared waist line*. Outline the bodice in this position. Mark shoulder and waist darts (lightly), chest, underarm and bust lines.

(2) Place front Skirt Block below with *its side waist point touching the squared line*. There will be a smaller gap between CF waist points and the side seam will have a slightly larger 'step' than the back (on account of the extra width allowed for the bust prominence over that allowed for the less prominent shoulder blade). It must be re-drawn to match back side seam. (This may be done by measuring or by tracing the back side seam and laying it on top of the front as a guide.) Reduce the front waist dart by 0.5 cm on each side and complete the dart as for back dress.

Example, size 12

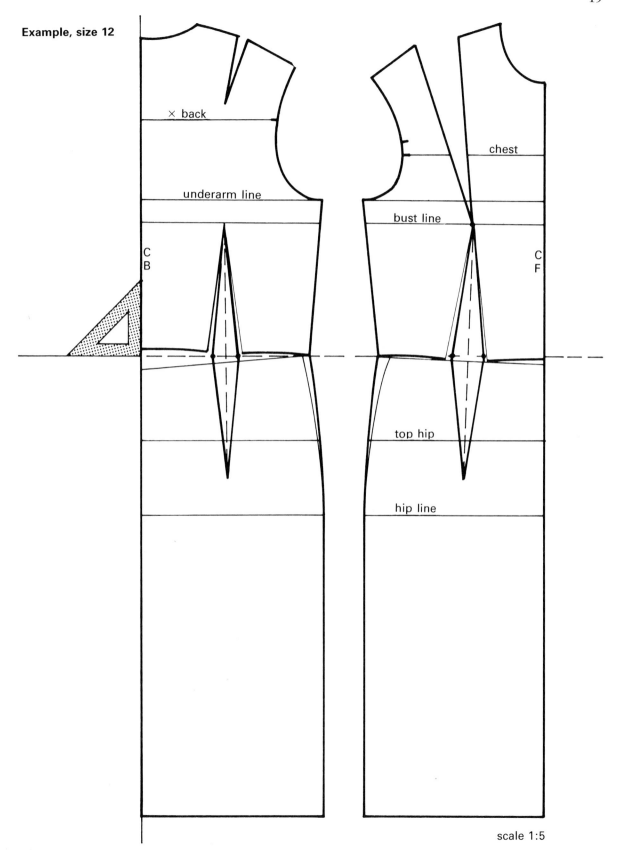

× back

chest

underarm line

bust line

C
B

C
F

top hip

hip line

scale 1:5

The block is now ready to use. Since the CB and CF lines are perfectly straight, both may be placed on the fold. If, however, a CB seam is permissible the opportunity arises to refine the fit of the back dress. The gap between CB bodice and skirt causes a few wrinkles across the back waist; by reducing the gap the wrinkles will disappear. Therefore, slash through squared line on CB waist, stopping just short of the side seam, and overlap 1.5 cm at CB off to nothing at side seam in an 'invisible horizontal dart'. In this instance a 1 cm gap will remain between CB bodice and skirt waist points, just enough for a smooth fit on the average figure. Increase the amount of overlap for hollow-backed figures and decrease for stooping (round-shouldered) figures. Draw a straight grain line parallel to the skirt CB.

Note While simpler methods of obtaining the One-Piece Dress Block are available, they do not give such comprehensive instructions in the correct placement of the blocks, nor in the later refinements of fit, and are therefore unlikely to produce such a well-fitting block.

One-Piece Dress Block with a CB seam — alteration to improve fit

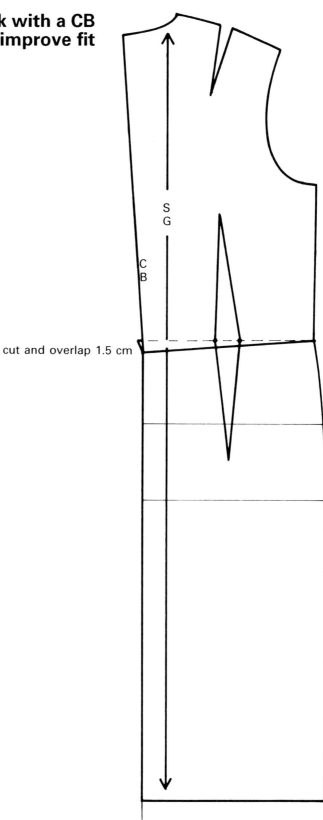

cut and overlap 1.5 cm

The Trouser Block

Seven main measurements are required to draft the trouser block:

(1) Waist to floor length.
(2) Body rise (depth of crutch).
(3) Waist to knee length.
(4) Total hip measurement − i.e. hip circumference plus 5 cm ease allowance.
(5) Total waist measurement − i.e. waist circumference plus 1 cm ease allowance.
(6) Total knee measurement − i.e. knee circumference plus 20 cm ease allowance.
(7) Total ankle measurement − i.e. ankle circumference plus 20 cm ease allowance.
For (2) see note 1.
For (6) and (7) see note 2.
Drafting paper size − 80 cm wide × 120 cm long.

Square lines out from 0

$0-1$ = waist to floor length plus 1 cm. Mark provisional waist and side seam. Square across at 1.

$0-2$ = waist to hip length plus 1 cm. Square across. Mark hip line.

$0-3$ = body rise (depth of crutch). Square across. Mark crutch level.

$0-4$ = waist to knee length plus 1 cm. Square across. Mark knee level.

$2-5$ = quarter total hip measurement plus 1.2 cm.

$2-6$ = quarter total hip measurement minus 1 cm.

7 = squared from 5.

8 = squared from 6.

$7-9$ = one tenth total hip plus 0.5 cm. Drop 1.2 cm for back crutch point. See note 3.

$8-10$ = one tenth total hip minus 2.5 cm = front crutch point.

$7-11$ = 2.8 cm diagonally.

$8-12$ = 3.3 cm diagonally.

$0-13$ = quarter total waist plus 5.5 cm. Connect 5−13 continuing line above provisional waist line. Mark 14 (CB waist point) 1 cm above. Connect 5−11−9 for seat curve.

$0-15$ = quarter total waist plus 5.5 cm. Connect 6−15. For CF waist point (16) drop 1 cm. Connect 6−12−10 for crutch curve.

$14-17$ = quarter waist plus 4 cm.

$16-18$ = quarter waist plus 3.2 cm. Connect 14−17 and 16−18 with lightly drawn lines.

19 = midway 6−16. Square across (using side seam) for top hip line.

20 = CB/top hip line.

$20-21$ = quarter total hip minus 0.5 cm.

$19-22$ = quarter total hip minus 2 cm. Connect 17−21−2 and 18−22−2 for hip curves.

$2-23$ = one sixth total hip minus 0.5 cm. Square up to waist and down to hem for crease/grain line and centre of lower back leg.

$2-24$ = one sixth total hip minus 1.5 cm. Square up to waist and down to hem for crease/grain line and centre of lower front leg.

Back knee width = half total knee measurement plus 1.3 cm. Divide in two and apply half to the left and half to the right of crease line.

Front knee width = half total knee measurement minus 1.1 cm. Apply as for back.

Back ankle width = half total ankle measurement plus 1.5 cm. Apply as for knee.

Front ankle width = half total ankle measurement minus 1 cm. Apply as for knee.

Connect ankle to knee points, continuing up to 3 − all with straight lines.

To shape inside leg seams connect 9 and 10 to knee points with dotted lines.
Quarter each line.
Back: quarter way down from 9 = 1.2 cm
     halfway   = 1.5 cm
     three quarters   = 0.8 cm
     Connect 9 to knee line through these points.
Front: quarter way down from 10 = 0.5 cm
     halfway   = 0.3 cm
     three quarters   = 0.2 cm
     Connect 10 to knee line through these points.

To reduce top of trouser to fit total waist measurement, i.e. body waist plus 1 cm ease which will produce a close fitting trouser waist
Calculate the waist dart allowance as follows:

Measure 14−17 and 18−16. Record measurements on draft and add together (e.g. size 12 − 41.7 cm). Subtract half total waist measurement (e.g. size 12 − 34.5 cm) = 7.2 cm dart allowance.

Before calculating trouser darts, read comments on size of waist darts in the Skirt Block section, page 10.

Example, size 12

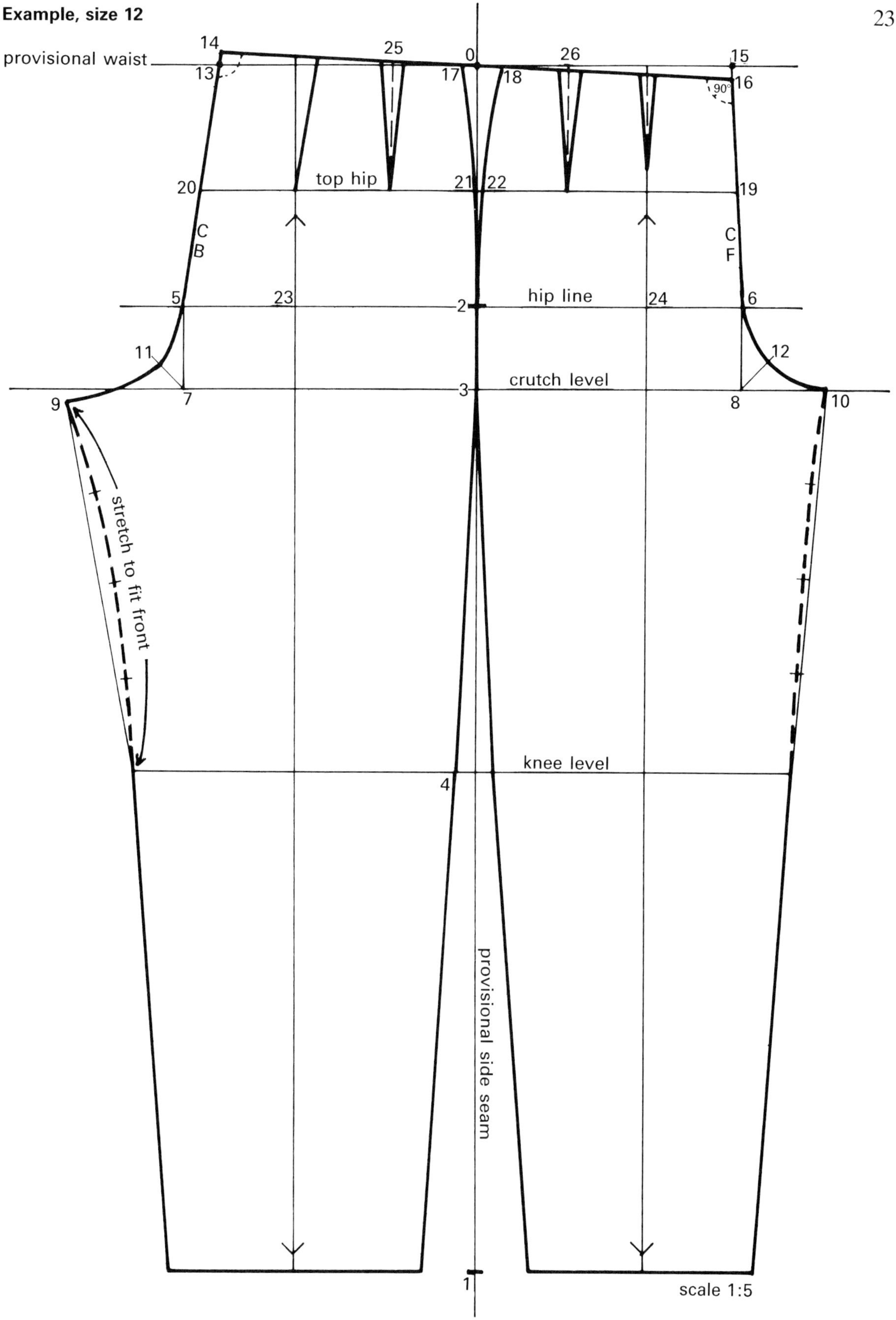

provisional waist
14
13
25
0
17
18
26
15
16
90°
top hip
20
21
22
19
C
B
C
F
5
23
2
hip line
24
6
11
12
crutch level
9
7
3
8
10
stretch to fit front
knee level
4
provisional side seam
1
scale 1:5

24

Divide the waist dart allowance as follows:
Back: 4 cm, further divided into two 2 cm darts
Front: 3.2 cm, further divided into one 2 cm dart and
one 1.2 cm dart

To position the darts on lines 14−17 and 16−18
Back: the crease/grain line forms the left side of
the first dart.
14−25 =   two thirds of 14−17 plus 1 cm. Square down
from line 13−17 for the centre of the second
dart.
Length: both finish on the top hip line.
Front: the crease/grain line forms the centre of the
first dart. Length = 2 cm above top line.
16−26 =   two thirds of 16−18 plus 1 cm. Square down
from line 15−18 for the centre of the second
dart. Length finishes on top hip line.

To complete block
Fold out darts and connect 14−17 and 16−18 with
smooth curves. Make CB and CF waist lines right
angles for approximately 3 cm (ensures no points or
dents when seams are joined).

Note 1 In trousers a high or low cut crutch is as much
of a fashion indicator as leg width and shape. This basic
block, constructed in between the two extremes, is
easily adjusted one way or the other to suit the design.

Note 2 The amount of ease allowed over knee and
ankle can be varied to suit the current silhouette. When
wide trousers are fashionable, increase the suggested
amount. For narrow trousers, decrease the amount *but
not below 6 cm over knee* (minimum for bending) *and
9 cm over ankle* (minimum for foot to pass through).

Note 3 By lowering the back crutch point, the back
inside leg becomes slightly shorter than the front. At
the sewing stage, stretch the back inside leg between
crutch and knee before stitching to the front, thereby
promoting a smoother wrinkle-free fit on the back
trouser.

SUPPLEMENTARY BLOCKS

These blocks are specifically designed as alternatives to the Basic Dress Blocks, which are fitted. Two supplementary blocks form the basis for a range of patterns of simpler shape. Less moulded and clinging to the figure, these blocks are therefore more appropriate for development into more generously cut, casual clothing.

- **The Dartless Bodice Block with Sleeve** — a good starting point for tops, vests, small jacket shapes and some more fitted items of beach and leisurewear. Being such a simple shape, the bodice is easily lengthened into a narrow tube or shift dress if required, for cutting in medium to lightweight fabrics.

- **The Loose-Fitting Dartless Bodice Block** is basically the same shape but enlarged generally to provide a proportionately increased block suitable for easy fitting clothing such as pyjamas, bathrobes, negligées, beachwraps and big shirt shapes.

  Two sleeves are provided with this block. The first on page 31 is drafted with a shorter crown height (flatter head); this automatically produces a wider sleeve. Lower crown heights and wider sleeves are both features of casual clothing. The second sleeve on page 32 is an exaggerated version of the first, with an extra flat head and even greater width at the underarm level, resulting in an authentic 'shirty' appearance at the top part of the sleeve.

- **Note: Before you cut your first pattern** ...

While it is accepted good practice to label all patterns with such of the following information as is relevant, when working with enlarged patterns it is *essential* to label with size (e.g. 'to fit 88 cm bust' or 'size 12') as their measurements will no longer be a guide to the garment size.

(1) Size
(2) Straight grain lines
(3) CB and CF
(4) Number to be cut from each pattern piece
(5) The names of any pattern pieces not instantly recognisable
    i.e. bra cup, pocket bag etc.
(6) Any sewing information which will help the sample machinist

---

The Dartless Bodice Block

The object is to flatten and loosen the Bodice Block on page 13 to make it more suitable as a basis for casual styles. The darts exist to fit the fabric to the contours of the body, and since flatter clothes need less fitting it makes sense to transfer the front and back shoulder darts into the armhole, enlarging it in readiness for a looser shirt-type sleeve.

Note   This type of block works better with centralised side seams. If you are using the Bodice Block there is no need for any alteration, but if using your own blocks check the width of the front and back at underarm level. Halve any difference between them; add the amount to the smaller and take it from the larger block.

FRONT BODICE BLOCK

(1) Outline front Bodice Block, lightly in the area of bust dart, end of shoulder and armhole, including both balance marks. Transfer bust dart into armhole at the lower balance point (19) either by pivoting from the bust point or using the slashing and overlapping method.

(2) Re-shape the armhole – work to a point approximately 2 cm inside lower 'dart' line. *The dart, instead of now being used as such merely contributes extra length to the armhole. Its lines, now obsolete, may be erased to avoid confusion.*

BACK BODICE BLOCK

(3) Outline back Bodice Block in the same way as the front, transferring the shoulder dart into the armhole at the X back level (point 11).

(4) Re-shape the armhole, filling in the lower half by 0.5 cm, providing additional back width.

Note Measure the new enlarged armhole and note the amounts on the block for future reference and when drafting a sleeve to fit.

SLEEVE FOR DARTLESS BODICE BLOCK

Due to the transference of the larger bust dart and the smaller back shoulder dart into the armhole, the two halves of the armhole are not only enlarged but also more equal. This provides a good basis for a looser sleeve block, more suitable for casual styles.

Draft the Sleeve Block on page 15 but with the following changes to the instructions to fit the enlarged armhole:

(1) 0–1 = *enlarged armhole measurement* divided by three. This will heighten the crown to suit the longer armhole.

(2) 0–3, 0–4 = half total top arm measurement *plus 1.5 cm*. This will widen the crown and provide a looser fitting sleeve (except at wrist level).

To complete the sleeve block ready for use
Having checked that sleeve head fits into armhole correctly (with sleeve head easing included), transfer the armhole balance marks onto the sleeve head measuring up from underarm points.

Dartless Bodice Block

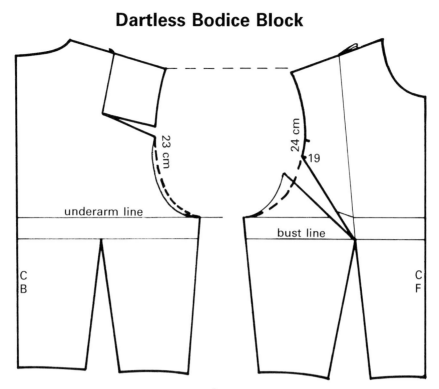

scale 1:5

Example, size 12

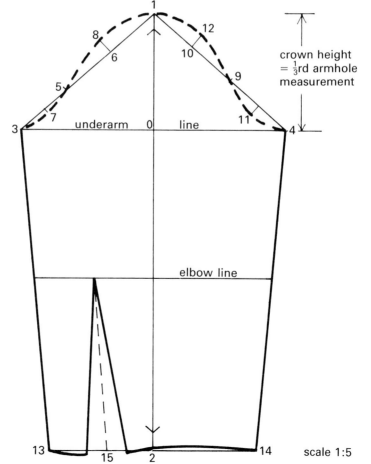

scale 1:5

To complete the sleeve block
ready for use

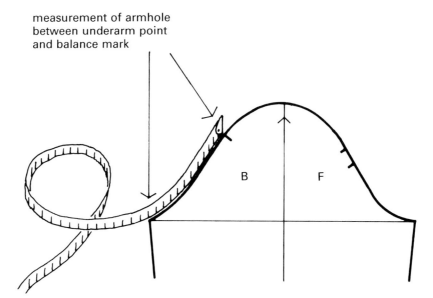

measurement of armhole
between underarm point
and balance mark

The Loose-fitting Dartless Bodice Block

In order to get closer to some styles that will be cut from the Dartless Bodice Block (e.g. negligées, pyjamas, beach-wraps), it needs to be enlarged to something resembling a large shirt block. This will provide an easy fitting body and sleeve with plenty of room for movement and for wearing over other clothes if appropriate.

(1) Place the Dartless Bodice Block (page 27) with the back and front underarm lines carefully positioned on a horizontal line. Allow 5 cm between underarm points, ensure that CB and CF lines are parallel and outline the blocks. (This extra 5 cm now gives a total of 20 cm ease over the whole bust measurement − a more suitable amount for loose styles than the 10 cm allowed on the Basic Dress Bodice Block.) Square down from underarm line midway between blocks for the new side seam.
(2) Lengthen 22 cm (or as required) below CB waist point. Square across to CF.
(3) If the shoulder remains at its present length it could look out of proportion with the newly widened body area. Therefore lengthen shoulders in the following way.
    Square lines from CB and CF through shoulder points. Measure out 2.5 cm along squared lines and mark new shoulder points. Connect new shoulder points to neck points. This method allows a small height addition as well as extra length, both appropriate for looser styles.
(4) **To lower the armhole**   Since the armhole is now wider (due to the 5 cm allowed between underarm points) it should also be lengthened a little to give an overall increase in size. Therefore, lower underarm point 1.5 cm and label UP.
(5) **To re-shape armhole**   Measure out 2.5 cm at approximately halfway around the armhole. Curve lines through these points up to SPs and down to UP; the new back armhole will just tip the original back UP; the new front armhole will run 2.5 cm inside the original front UP, measured along the underarm line. Complete the armhole by carrying the balance marks through to the new armhole lines, on the same levels.

SLEEVE FOR THE LOOSE-FITTING DARTLESS BODICE BLOCK
The main principles applied when drafting the Basic Dress Sleeve Block on page 15 can be used to provide a looser, more casual fitting sleeve block; three of the four main measurements used in the original draft will have to be adjusted in accordance with the changes made to the armhole:

(1) Armhole circumference, carefully measured from the Loose-fitting Dartless Block. In instruction 0−1 this measurement is divided into three to give the crown height. *In this sleeve the crown height should be reduced by 2.5 cm to give a flatter head* more suitable for casual clothing and to compensate for the longer shoulder.
    e.g. size 12

$$\text{back armhole} = 24 \text{ cm}$$
$$\text{front armhole} = 25$$
$$\text{total armhole circumference} = 49 \text{ cm} \div 3$$
$$= 16 \text{ cm} - 2.5 \text{ cm}$$
$$= 13.5 \text{ cm crown height}$$

(Odd millimetres are rounded off to make figures easier to work with.)
(2) Top sleeve length remains unchanged.
(3) Top arm circumference plus 5 cm ease allowance (as on Basic Dress Sleeve), plus underarm width addition of 5 cm, plus twice the amount the armhole was lowered (1.5 + 1.5)
    e.g. size 12

top arm circumference	28 cm
ease allowance	5
underarm width addition	5
lowering of armhole	1.5
	1.5
	41 cm total top arm measurement

(4) Wrist circumference plus 15 cm ease, a more appropriate amount for a looser sleeve.

Substituting these adjusted measurements, follow the instructions for the Basic Dress Sleeve Block, page 15. All other measurements remain the same.

Note   An elbow dart is unnecessary in this type of loose-fitting sleeve, but an opening may be required if the sleeve is to have a cuff. This should be positioned halfway between the back sleeve seam and centre line and a minimum of 10 cm long. Remember to check wrist curve whilst sleeve seam is closed.

Loose Fitting Dartless Block

Body

Example, size 12

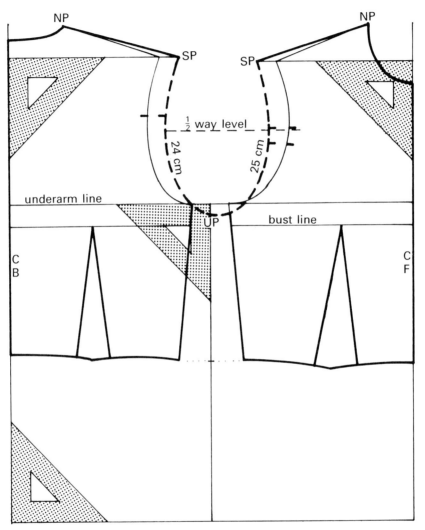

scale 1:5

31

Loose Fitting Dartless Block

Sleeve

Example, size 12

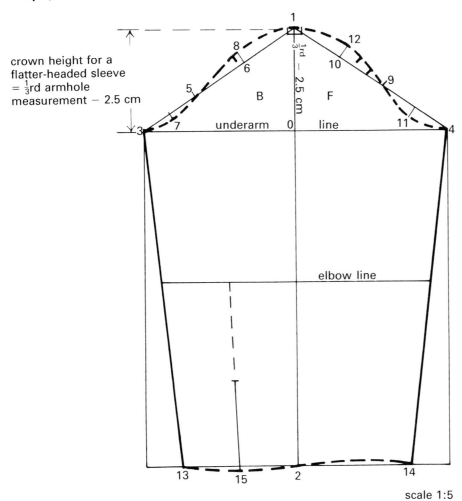

crown height for a
flatter-headed sleeve
= $\frac{1}{3}$rd armhole
measurement − 2.5 cm

scale 1:5

EXTRA FLAT HEADED SLEEVE
As an additional aid it is useful to have a really flat headed sleeve block, rather like a man's shirt sleeve, when designing very loose casual clothes. This saves a lot of time adjusting the ordinary block before you can begin cutting patterns from it, and it is ready to use whenever the need arises.

(1) Outline the sleeve belonging to the Loose-fitting Dartless Block. Include the underarm and elbow lines and the centre (grain) line.
   Measure 1−3 and 1−4 and record on block.
(2) 0−1 = crown height, reduced to 10 cm (approximately 1/5th armhole measurement).
   1−2 = top sleeve length, measured from lowered crown.
   Apply measurements of 1−3 and 1−4 from lowered crown point until they touch underarm line.

(3) **To shape lowered sleeve head**
   Divide back line 1−3 as follows:
   3−5 = one third 3−1.
     6 = midway 5−1.
     7 = midway 3−5 and 0.5 cm in from line.
     8 = 1.5 cm out from 6. See note 1.
   Connect 3−7−5−8−1
   Divide front line 1−4 as follows:
   4−9 = half 4−1 minus 1.8 cm.
    10 = midway 9−1.
    11 = midway 4−9 and 1 cm in from line.
    12 = 1.5 cm out from 10. See note 1.
   Connect 4−11−9−12−1

Note 1   Sleeve head shaping does not need to be so pronounced on flat headed sleeves.
Note 2   These adjustments automatically produce a lessened amount of sleeve head easing, essential for a professional look when inserting a flat headed sleeve into an armhole.

Extra Flat-headed Sleeve
for Loose Fitting Dartless Block

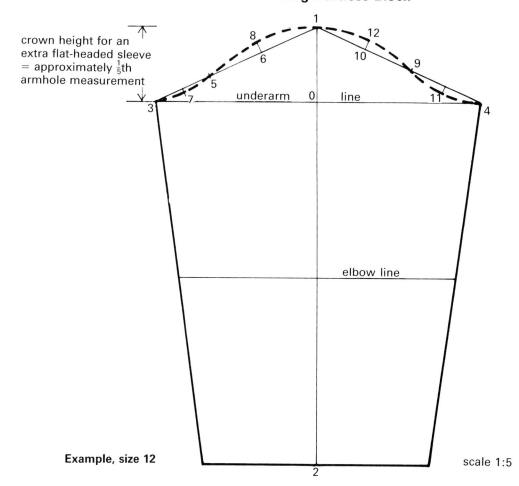

crown height for an extra flat-headed sleeve = approximately $\frac{1}{5}$th armhole measurement

underarm 0 line

elbow line

Example, size 12

scale 1:5

2 LINGERIE — UNDERWEAR

PETTICOATS

Petticoats protect the wearer from scratchy or irritating dresses or skirts. According to their fabric and shape they act either as a lining for the garment worn on top or they may provide support for certain styles of skirt, e.g. circular, tiered, 'balloon'.

Waist Petticoats

These vary in type and shape to suit the clothing worn on top.

(1) A tight-fitting underskirt can prevent straight skirts from 'bagging' at the back. These should be cut in a firmly woven fabric. Instead of an elasticated waist they are often darted or soft pleated into an unstiffened waistband with a simple placket opening, providing a smooth fit just under the waist. Side slits make striding easier, especially if petticoat length is below knee.

(2) In their fullest form they can provide support and shape under full-skirted styles; they may be cut in soft or stiff fabrics depending on the effect required. The attachment of frills and flounces can enhance the fullness. The use of a fitted yoke under the waist reduces bulk in that area and contrasts with the fullness introduced into the lower part of the petticoat. This type requires a fastened waist, e.g. buttons, hooks or ties.

Note When designing petticoats with elasticated waistlines, make sure the pattern waist size is equal to the hip measurement plus at least 5 cm so the garment will pull on easily whether over hips or shoulders.

STYLE 'A' – SLIM AND STRAIGHT
May be cut from the Straight Skirt Block but with a few adjustments. Since the waists of these styles are nearly always elasticated and pulled on over the hips, a suitable width increase must be made at waist level.

The width at hip level should not be less than the Straight Skirt Block unless designing a close-fitting foundation slip requiring a firm fabric, darting at the waist and a placket opening. For all other cases, and especially when using fine, soft fabrics, extra width should be added to avoid strain on the fabric, e.g. 5–10 cm extra ease at hip level.

Refer to Fig. 1
(1) Trace back and front Straight Skirt Block. Shorten hem 2.5 cm. Add 1.5 cm onto CB and CF and 1 cm onto side seams, providing an extra 10 cm width over the hip.

(2) Measure the enlarged waist (ignore waist darts – these will contribute to the extra width needed) and check that the waist measurement will fit easily over the body hip measurement. If not, further adjust the side seams in waist area only.

(3) Curve waistline from CB to CF through new side seam point. (This is best done with the tops of the side seams placed together – see Fig. 2.) Dart shaping should be smoothed off.

(4) Side seams may be slit for easier walking and lace trimmed if required. Make slit 18 cm or longer for visual proportion, and to perform its task properly.

Note As a general guide to length of elastic for waist, allow waist measurement minus 8 cm but check before cutting as stretchiness of elastics vary.

Slim, straight waist petticoat – Style A

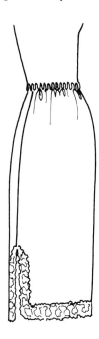

Slim, straight waist petticoat − Style A

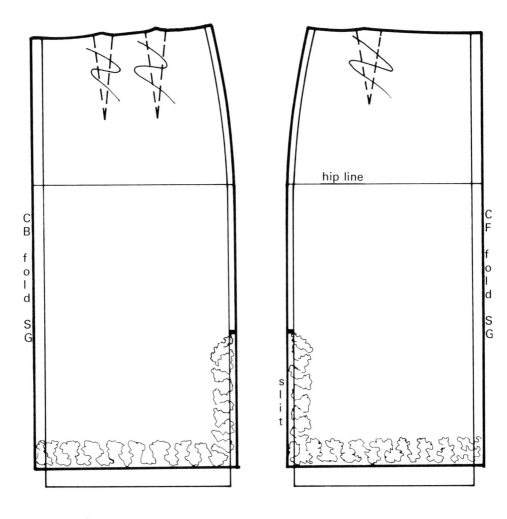

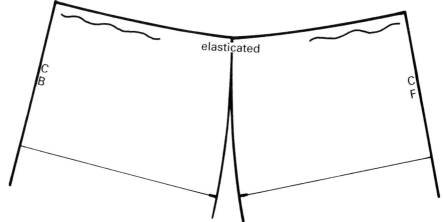

36

STYLE 'B' – FLARED AND FRILLED
As the correct waist size has now been established on
Style 'A', use that pattern as a basis for this
fuller-skirted style.

Suitable fabrics: fine cottons, medium or lightweight
silks or their man-made equivalents. If the purpose of
this full slip is to hold out a skirt worn on top it may be
cut in a crisp fabric, but remember the elasticated waist
and avoid too much bulk in that area.

Refer to Fig. 3
(1) Decide on final hem circumference. (The wider it
becomes, the more likely it is to be thought of in
terms of metres, e.g. 2 m, 3.50 m, etc.) Then
measure the hem circumference of Style 'A' to
judge the extra width needed.
(2) Decide on depth of frill and mark a line parallel to
hem.
(3) Divide pattern into three at hip level. Cut through
on frill line, then up to but not through waistline.
Spread cut sections equally (and add approximately
half spread amount onto side seams for good
balance) until required hem circumference is
reached; the same effect can be achieved by
carefully pivoting the pattern from the waist.
(4) Measure flared hem exactly. Cut a straight pattern
for the frill. Its length can be anything from $1\frac{1}{2}-3$
times the newly flared hem measurement,
depending on the fabric and effect required. The
frill pattern may be cut on either:
(a) The warp or lengthwise grain when it may be cut in
one piece, seamed at CB; or
(b) The weft or crosswise grain where joining seams
will be necessary. In this case the position of the
seams should be considered in conjunction with the
fabric width. See also comments on negligée frill on
page 136.
However the frill is cut, divide the whole into four
with balance marks for attachment to bottom of
slip, matching marks to CB, sides and CF for even
distribution of gathers, as in Fig. 4.

Flared, frilled waist petticoat – Style B

Flared, frilled waist petticoat – Style B

Fig. 3

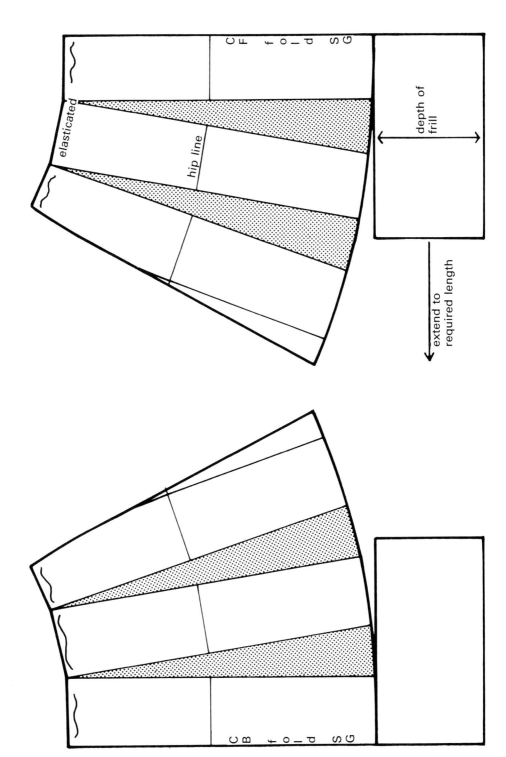

Fig. 4

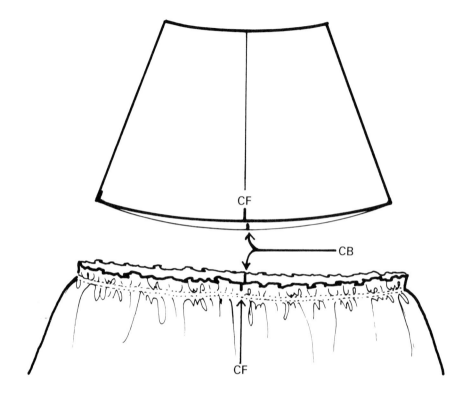

Full-skirted, yoked waist petticoat − Style C

STYLE 'C' − FULL-SKIRTED AND YOKED
The yoke is based closely on the Straight Skirt Block and the lower part has fullness introduced by means of gathers into the yoke seam, providing 'bounce' at this level.

Suitable fabrics: crisp or even stiff fabrics are best, or a combination, e.g. soft firmly woven cotton or silk for the yoke and stiff net for the skirt. The stretch fabrics often associated with petticoats are unsuitable for this style.

Refer to Fig. 5

(1) Trace back and front Straight Skirt Block, pivoting darts into hem line (or folding out darts and slashing up from hem line).

(2) Draw yoke line parallel to waist at the level of the dart ends. Divide lower skirt into three with dotted lines; it helps to number each piece to ensure the correct order after cutting. To control gathers, place balance marks at CB, CF and midway centres and sides on both yoke and skirt patterns.

Refer to Fig. 6

(3) Trace off the lower skirt, cut on dividing lines and add as much fullness as required. The additions in this example are equal at yoke and hem. This widens but does not change the shape of the pattern; for extra flare, add more at hem than at yoke line. Trace back and front yoke patterns separately from the plan in Fig. 5.

(4) The petticoat will need a narrow, unstiffened waistband and a fastening on yoke seam at CB.

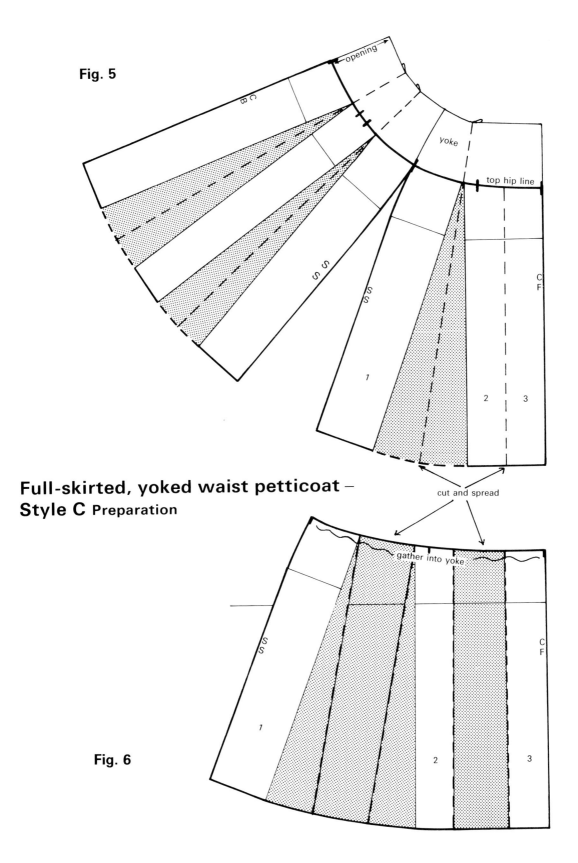

41

Fig. 5

opening

C B

yoke

top hip line

S S

S S

1

2 3

C F

cut and spread

gather into yoke

**Full-skirted, yoked waist petticoat –
Style C Preparation**

S S

1

2 3

C F

Fig. 6

Full Length Petticoats

Full length petticoats are used chiefly as a lining for the clothing worn on top and should be as inconspicuous as possible. Therefore they are cut in soft fabrics which, if woven and non-stretch, are best combined with bias cutting so that they cling and mould to the figure with the minimum of darts and seams. This combination is still indicative of the more expensive lingerie ranges. For the majority of mass produced petticoats, bias cutting has been largely superseded by the use of modern synthetic lingerie fabrics which have 'built-in stretch'.

Note that on full length petticoats the waistline is traditionally set slightly higher than normal to give a more proportionate look to the reduced size of the garment.

PETTICOAT BLOCK − adapted from the One-Piece Dress Block

Refer to Fig. 7

(1) Outline the back and front One-Piece Dress Block with at least 10 cm between hip points. Ensure that CB and CF are parallel and hip lines are level. Include the chest, underarm and bust lines, the squared waistline (raised 1.5 cm above the dress block waist) and the hip lines. The dress waist darts may be included for use with styles that have an opening but for pull-on styles their use is much restricted. Mark bust and shoulder darts lightly. Shorten hem by 2.5 cm.

Back

(2) Tighten side seam 1.2 cm on bust line, 0.5 cm on waistline, touching dress outline on top hip line and flaring 5 cm at hem. Check that hem is level at flaring point by measuring down dress side seam (from the point where it touches petticoat) and apply the same measurement to the new flared seam line. See Fig. 8.

(3) To shape top of petticoat, lower underarm by 1 cm and connect to CB on bust line with a gentle curve. The shoulder strap is positioned midway between CB and underarm point.

Front

(4) Re-shape side seam as for back.

(5) Double the bust dart on the armhole side only, to ensure a snug fit in an area usually loose fitting on account of the sleeve. *Altering the dart on armhole side only will ensure that any future division of the front (e.g. Princess line seams) will be correctly positioned.*

(6) **To shape top of petticoat**, lower underarm by 1 cm (to match back). For a good line when bust dart is sewn, fold out dart and draw line from CF to underarm point. For an alternative (professional) method which avoids creasing pattern, see Fig. 9(a). Use transparent paper and trace over the chest line from CF to the CF side of the bust dart. Then refer to Fig. 9(b); pivot paper from bust point over onto armhole side of dart. Complete line in a good curve down to underarm point; draw the side seam and a balance mark at bust line. Apply this tracing of the top of the petticoat minus its dart to the back Petticoat Block (matching side seams and balance marks) to check the curve from CF to CB, as in Fig. 9(c).

Return to Fig. 7

(7) **For shoulder strap**, measure from the pattern shoulder down to the new top edge on back and front and add together for complete strap length. (In practice the strap is often shortened, but for safety cut the full length initially and adjust at fitting.) Finished width, e.g. 1 cm.

(8) The contour of the petticoat improves if the waist darts are tightened slightly (0.5 cm) on each side midway bust and waistline. The bust and waist darts are frequently joined into a Princess line seam. In this case round off the bust point on the side panel to suit the shape of the figure.

Petticoat Block — adapted from the One-Piece Dress Block

43

Fig. 7

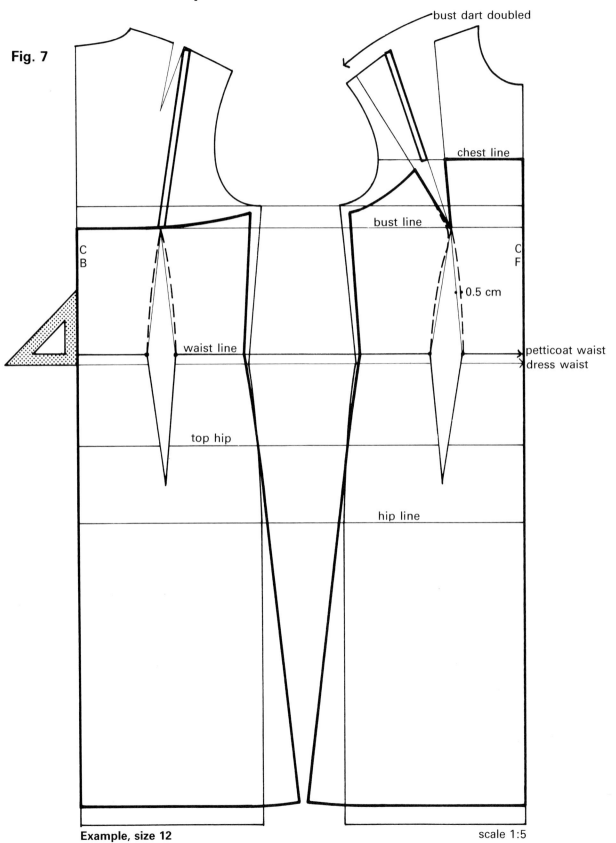

bust dart doubled

chest line

bust line

C
B

C
F

0.5 cm

waist line

petticoat waist

dress waist

top hip

hip line

Example, size 12

scale 1:5

44

Fig. 8

To illustrate Petticoat Block side seam adjustment

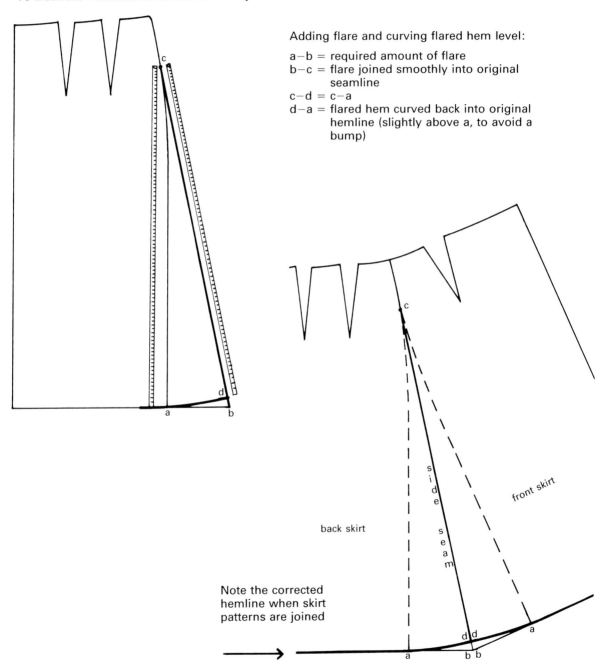

Adding flare and curving flared hem level:

a−b = required amount of flare
b−c = flare joined smoothly into original
        seamline
c−d = c−a
d−a = flared hem curved back into original
        hemline (slightly above a, to avoid a
        bump)

Note the corrected
hemline when skirt
patterns are joined

back skirt

side seam

front skirt

45

Fig. 9

To illustrate Petticoat Block shaping of top edge

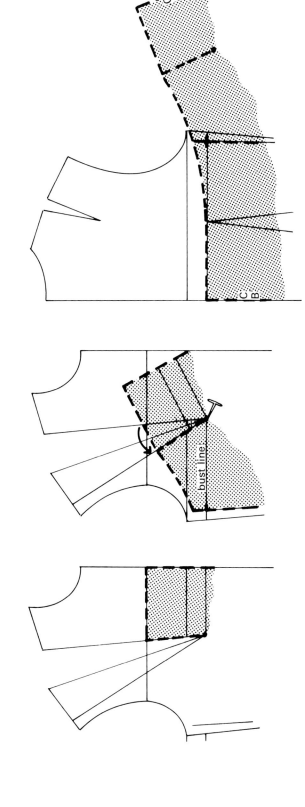

Fig. 9(a)

Trace over CF from just below bust line, up to required top edge and down CF side of bust dart.

Fig. 9(b)

Pivot transparent paper to the left, excluding the whole enlarged dart.
Complete top edge down to underarm point and draw side seam. Place a balance mark at bust line.

Fig. 9(c)

Place tracing of front next to the back, matching petticoat side seams and bust line balance marks. Draw top edge on back in accord with the front.

STYLE 'A' – PRINCESS LINE, PULL-ON
PETTICOAT (in non-stretch fabric)
As this petticoat must be pulled on over the shoulders,
the waist measurement must be increased to match the
body bust measurement (the minimum girth required
for a pull-on garment).

In a Princess line style some shaping at least between
bust and waist is desirable. In the case of a pull-on
petticoat it may not be possible to utilise the whole of
the waist darts as a minimum waist size must be
maintained; it may even be necessary, as here, to
decrease the dart volume slightly and add a little to the
side seams. One should aim for balanced seam shaping.

The panel seams provide the opportunity to add
extra flare to the skirt whilst retaining the closest
possible body fit.

Refer to Fig. 10
(1) Outline the Petticoat Block and include bust, waist
and hip lines and the waist darts, lightly drawn.
(2) In this example for non-stretch fabric, keep the
waist darts for shaping but reduce each one at waist
level by 2 cm so as not to over-tighten the waist on
a pull-on style. Then, to make the waist
measurement up to the body bust size, add 1.5 cm
to each side seam.
(3) **Add the required amount of flare** to the lower skirt
either by simply continuing the dart lines for a
moderate amount as in Fig. 10, or by flaring from
the waist or hip point (or even lower), depending
on the design, as in Fig. 11.

Refer to Fig. 11
(4) Curve the seams above the waist level to suit the
body contour. Re-shape the top edge according to
the style – here it is lowered to 2.5 cm above the
bust line and rounded slightly (above a straight
guide line).
(5) **Apply balance marks at right angles to seam** for
perfect matching when sewing; this is best done at
the early stage, before pattern pieces are traced off
separately (see Fig. 10). *If seam angles are changed
(as when adding flare as in Fig. 11) balance marks
must be repositioned with a set square, to ensure
their correct angle to the new seam.*

With panelled styles it is advisable to balance
mark the pattern pieces differently, i.e. one mark
on back panel, two on side seams etc. so that
garment will be made up in the correct order.

Princess line, pull-on petticoat – Style A

Refer to Fig. 11
(6) If adapting the style to a stretch fabric, use the SG
lines as in Fig. 10. For a non-stretch fabric, bias
cutting (SG lines shown in Fig. 11) will provide
more 'give'.
(7) Petticoat is lace trimmed at the top edge and hem
and in addition a lace trimmed frill is attached near
hem to maximise skirt fullness. **To make frill
pattern**, measure skirt circumference at level where
frill will attach and refer to Waist Petticoat, Style
'B' for more details.

For shoulder straps, see Petticoat Block,
paragraph 7, on page 42.

Princess line, pull-on petticoat − Style A

Fig. 10

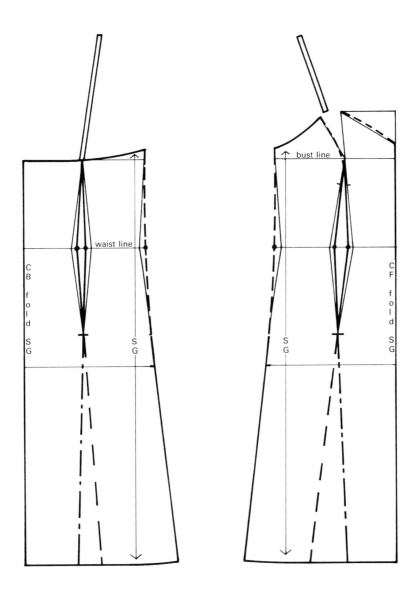

48

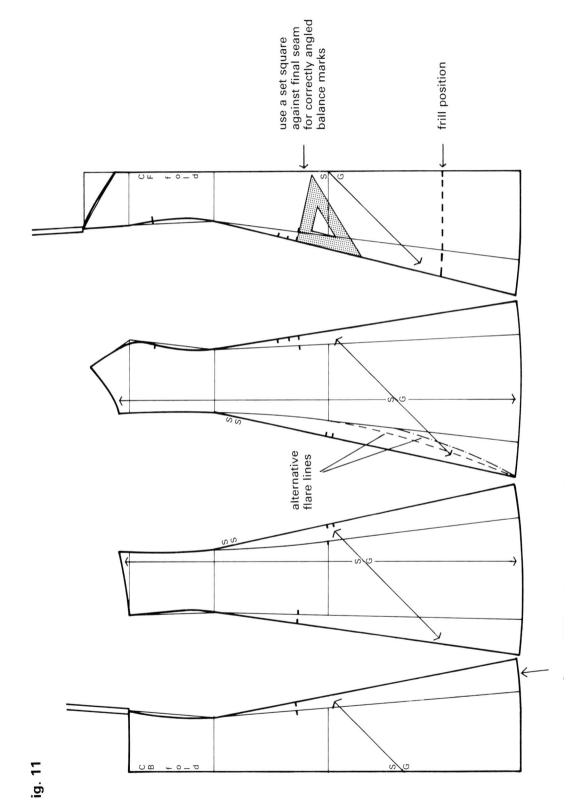

Fig. 11

use a set square
against final seam
for correctly angled
balance marks

frill position

alternative
flare lines

6 cm additional flare giving a total hem circumference of 2.25 m

STYLE 'B' – BRA-TOP, PULL-ON PETTICOAT (in stretch fabric)

The bra-top petticoat allows a close fit over the bust, a somewhat 'slinky' fit between bust and hip and is flared at the hem line. As a pull-on style, the waist size must be carefully considered so that it will go comfortably over the shoulders but since a stretch fabric is assumed, adherence to the minimum girth measurement (i.e. body bust measurement) is not as important as for non-stretch fabrics. In this example for a size 12, the pattern waist is reduced to approximately 76 cm after checking that 76 cm of the cloth will stretch to the minimum girth measurement of 88 cm for size 12.

CF and CB seams will help to achieve the slinky look without the need for waist darts. Choose the lace before planning the pattern.

Refer to Fig. 12

(1) Outline the Petticoat Block. Include the bust, waist and hip lines and the front waist dart only as far as a level midway between bust and waist lines. Omit the back dart.

(2) Measure waistline from CB to CF and from this subtract 76 cm. The remaining amount is removed equally from CB, side and CF seams. Connect waist points up to top edge and down to hem, passing through hip points. Smooth off waist points. Adjust and check hem line as in Fig. 8. Lower CF top edge to 1 cm above bust line or as required.

(3) To plan bra section: trace off bra area from the plan in Fig. 12, from new top edge to midway between bust and waist lines. Include the bust dart, 'waist dart' and SG line parallel to SG on skirt section.

Refer to Fig. 13(a)

(4) Firstly, plan the lace marker pattern on the traced off section. (A marker pattern is a size or shape guide for cutting trimming materials such as lace, leather, commercially embroidered or beaded fabrics, etc.) Cut through centre of 'waist dart' and fold out bust dart; pattern should remain flat. Draw position of the lace trim parallel to new V'd front edge. Place a balance mark towards underarm.

Refer to Fig. 13(b)

(5) Secondly, plan the undercup area. Unpin top of pattern and cut through bust dart up to the point. Place one 'waist dart' line on top of the other to see the undercup area minus its dart. Draw in the seam

Bra-top, pull-on petticoat – Style B

line following the underbreast curve. (On a size 12 medium cup, approximately 8 cm down from bust point – plus or minus 0.5 cm for other sizes.) Lift the line slightly towards side seam; place two balance marks to control gathers.

Refer to Fig. 13(c)

(6) Replace the bra top plan onto the main pattern *aligning the bust lines*; trace the underbust seamline through onto the main pattern, including the balance marks. (Best done with a tracing wheel.)

(7) Remove the dart from the skirt pattern at underbust level so that it will fit the bra top after gathering. There are two ways of doing this:
 (i) As in Fig. 13(c), fold out down to hip line and cut up from hem line; the hem will open approximately 2 cm, but the hip circumference will stay the same.
 (ii) As in Fig. 13(d), fold out from underbust point down to hem line; the hem circumference will remain the same, but the hip will become 1 cm smaller.

(8) **To complete pattern** trace off lace marker pattern including balance marks. Trace off lower cup area with the bust dart (or remains of it) transferred into underbust gathers (see Fig. 13(e)). Place differentiating balance marks on skirt seams.

For shoulder straps, see Petticoat Block, paragraph 7, on page 42.

Note Other uses: petticoat patterns are easily adapted for some nightdress and evening dress styles of a similar shape and fit.

Bra-top, pull-on petticoat — Style B

Fig. 12

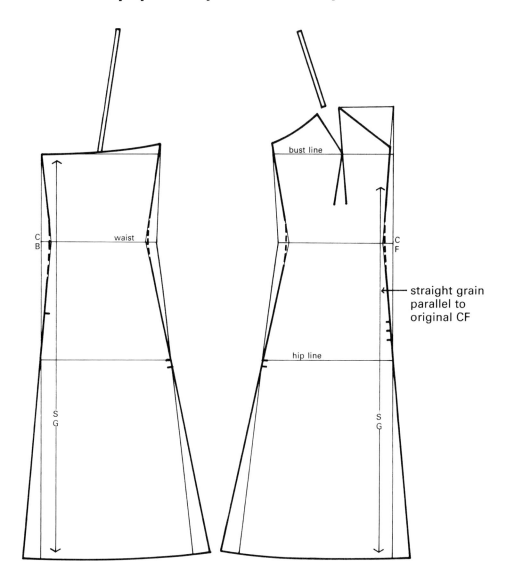

Fig. 13(a)

lace marker pattern

Fig. 13(b)

waist dart lines

fold out dart
down to pivot point
at hip line

pivot
point

hip line

open

Fig. 13(e)

gather

Fig. 13(c) .. or .. **Fig. 13(d)**

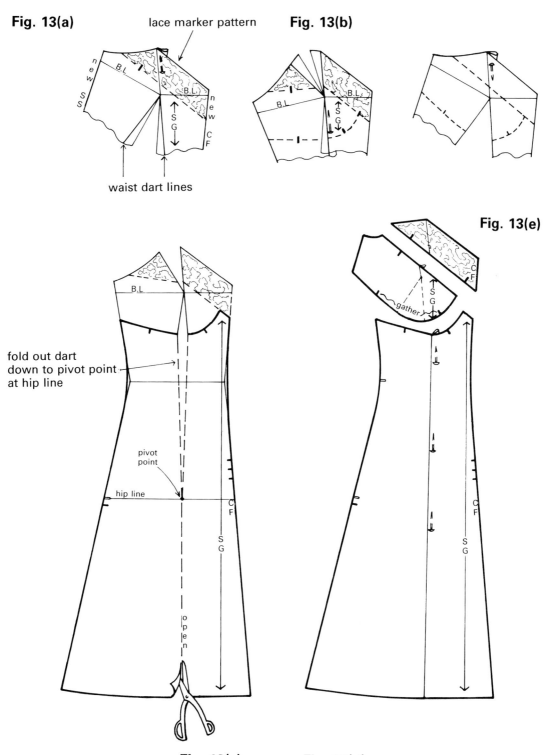

CAMISOLE TOP

A lightweight under bodice, the camisole was originally made in linen and worn to protect the corset from soiling in the days when washing was more of a chore than it is now. The modern camisole is more likely to be a wisp of a garment made from the lightest weight silk, cotton or lace and worn more to allure than as a laundry aid.

Camisoles are invariably cut from the Petticoat Block and are usually straight but may be fitted, with thin ribbon or self rouleau shoulder straps to hold the top in place. They can vary in length from midriff to hip and are often elasticated at the waist.

Camisole patterns make very effective sun-top styles when cut in plain or printed cottons.

STYLE 'A' – CAMISOLE WITH ELASTICATED WAIST
Refer to Fig. 14
(1) Outline the Petticoat Block down to hip line. Mark chest, bust and waist lines. Omit the back and front waist darts (used only for fitted styles).
(2) The amount of 'puff' (or blouson effect) above the elasticated waistline depends on the design requirement and the fabric. For a lightweight silky fabric 5 cm would not be excessive, but remember that *whatever is added on the flat pattern always appears halved when the garment is worn* – therefore estimate accordingly.
    To add in the amount either:
Cut through the pattern waistline and add 5 cm in between; or
Outline pattern to waistline, shift pattern 5 cm downwards and complete the outline to hip level.
(3) The side seam slits on this example are 10 cm long. Mark a balance point and round off the corners. Straighten the side seams between underarm and top of slit – it is easier to elasticate a straight waisted shape.
(4) For front lace panel: draw new neckline from bust dart to CF on bust line. From new CF neck point, measure down 12 cm and mark bottom of panel. Connect up to bust point and along CF side of bust dart, rounding off point at bust (dot-dash line). Place balance marks above bust point and near to CF.

Note The dotted line beyond CF shows that if a strip lace is used a 9–10 cm wide lace will be needed.

Style 'A' camisole can be trimmed with three small buttons and rouleau loops at the CF, narrow rouleau shoulder straps and a matching bound top edge (under the arm and round the back). Elasticate the waist with soft, narrow elastic sewn onto the wrong side along Style 'A' waistline – see Fig. 14.

Camisole Top – Style A

Camisole Top – Style A

Fig. 14

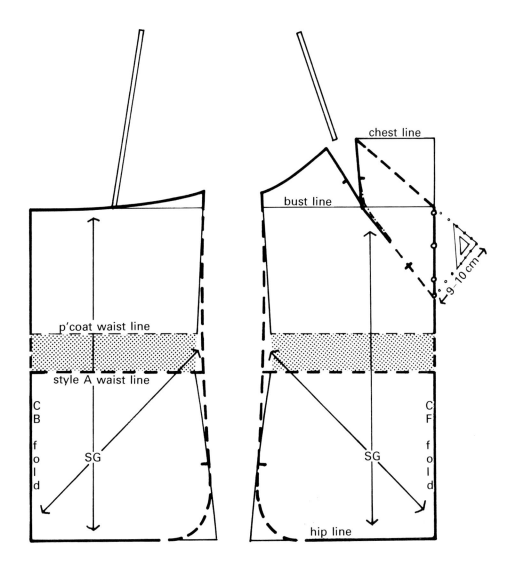

chest line

bust line

9–10 cm

p'coat waist line

style A waist line

CB fold

SG

CF fold

SG

hip line

CAMISOLE VARIATION – STYLE 'B'
Refer to Fig. 15
(1) Outline the Petticoat Block down to the hip line or to required length. Include the chest and bust lines.
(2) Use chest line for the straight front neckline. Measure down 17 cm for CF point, connect back to bust point and then round under the arm parallel to curved top edge. Place balance marks on either side of bust point.
(3) Use the Petticoat Block side seam to give a slightly fitted shape.
(4) Eliminate bust dart in lace panel; round off bust point on lower part of camisole.

Style 'B' can be trimmed with narrow rouleau straps and a matching bound underarm and back top edge. There is no need for an opening – the garment will pull on over the head. The lace, where it joins the lower part, can be appliquéd.

Fig. 15

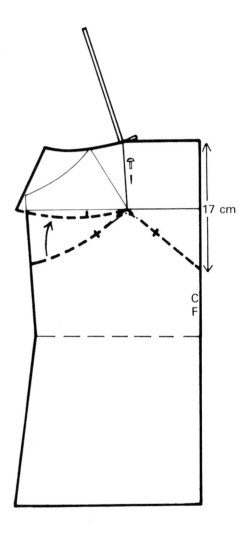

17 cm

C
F

Camisole Top – Style B

VEST OR SINGLET

Originally a vest was a close-fitting undergarment with long or short sleeves, or shoulder straps, extending from just below to well below the waist. It was cut in fabrics of an insulating nature and was worn specifically to keep out the cold.

Now, as with other categories of underwear, a change of fabric can extend its use to outerwear to serve as a simply shaped top to accompany skirts or suits, or as a 'cover-up' in beachwear.

Singlet is the name given to vests or T-shirts worn by men, but such limitations are now dismissed.

The greatest influence over a vest pattern is the fabric it will be cut in. When a stretch fabric or knit is called for, the pattern must be cut accordingly (see Chapter 5). For non-stretch fabrics there is a choice of suitable blocks depending on the design – the Dartless Bodice Block for sleeved and sleeveless styles; the Petticoat Block for more fitted, shoulder-strapped styles. Whichever block is used, the important points to remember are:

(a) The cut and shape should be as simple as possible – no darts or midbody seaming to show through to top clothes.
(b) Vests are usually cut without openings and therefore the waist size must not be reduced below the body bust measurement (minimum girth to pull over shoulders), unless cutting in stretch fabrics.

56

STYLE 'A' – SLEEVELESS VEST

Refer to Fig. 16

(1) Outline the Dartless Bodice Block, omitting the back and front waist darts. Continue CB and CF lines below the waist; mark the required length – here it is 20 cm below the waist, i.e. hip level. Square across.

(2) For side seams: square down from underarm points for straight seams and for a generous measurement over the hip.

   (For shaped side seams, use the Dartless Bodice Block side seam and shape gently over the hip – dotted line. If this shaping is insufficient, hollow out more but check that waist is not too small to pull over shoulders, i.e. waist should equal body bust measurement.)

(3) **For neck and armhole shaping**: decide on depth of new neckline at back and front, and shoulder width – here centrally positioned which helps it stay on the shoulders in wear. Re-shape neck and armholes with patterns pushed together, ensuring good curves when shoulders are joined.

Suitable fabrics: lightweight cottons and silks or equivalent synthetics, single cotton jersey.

Suggestions for finishing neck and armholes: bound edges, lace edged, overlocked and double top-stitched.

Sleeveless Vest – Style A

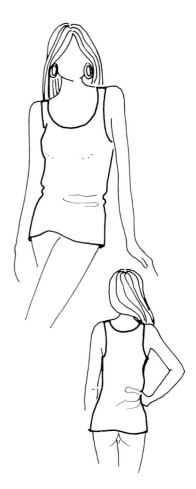

Sleeveless Vest — Style A

Fig. 16

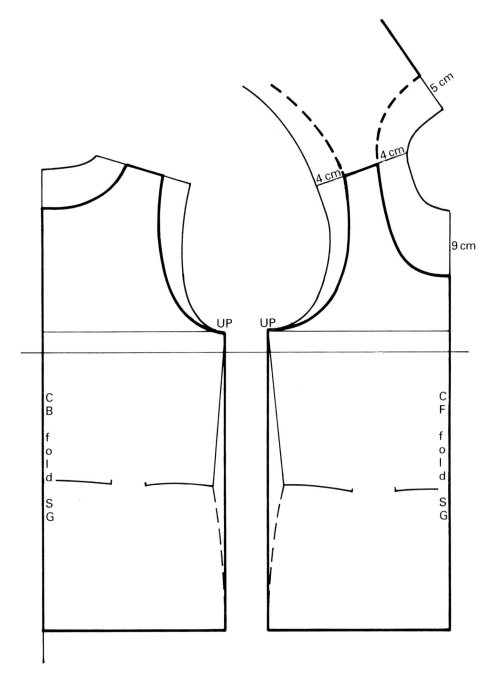

STYLE 'B' – SHOULDER STRAPPED VEST

Refer to Fig. 17

(1) Outline the Petticoat Block to hip length or as required. Omit the back and front waist darts.

(2) For front neck shaping and lace yoke: decide on CF depth of 'V' – here it is 2 cm above the bust line. Connect up to top of bust dart. Remove the bust dart from the lace yoke pattern – for method, see Petticoat Block, Fig. 9. After dart removal, draw the lower edge of yoke, 5 cm parallel to new neckline.

Refer to Fig. 18

(3) To complete the main front pattern, convert the remaining bust dart into easing, tucks or gathers placing balance marks on both main pattern and yoke, on either side of bust to control the fullness. Trim off points caused by dart.

(4) For shoulder straps: see Petticoat Block, paragraph 7, on page 42. Make the finished width quite narrow, e.g. 0.5 cm.

Note Both vest styles may be cut on the bias if required.

Shoulder Strapped Vest – Style B

Shoulder Strapped Vest — Style B

Fig. 17

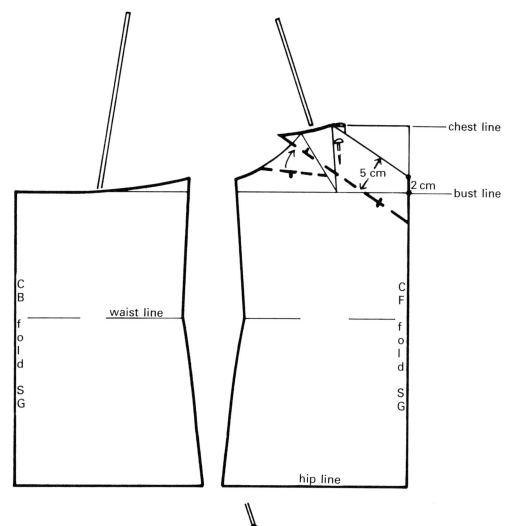

chest line

5 cm

2 cm — bust line

C
B
f
o
l
d

S
G

waist line

C
F
f
o
l
d

S
G

hip line

Fig. 18

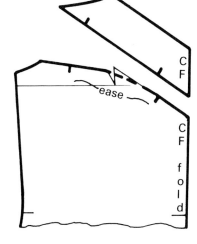

ease

C
F

C
F
f
o
l
d

BRA PATTERNS

In order to give sufficient support, the bra is one of the most fitted of the lingerie blocks. It may be cut from any close-fitting bodice block but the essential point is to remove all the ease at bust level and the surrounding areas, as the bra must fit exactly to perform its function well (see illustration in Fig. 19). Therefore, the actual body measurements, i.e. without the ease allowed for movement in top clothing, are used to obtain the correct degree of fit. In styles where stretch or elasticated fabrics form the whole or are incorporated into the design, the bra should be even smaller than the bust measurement.

The cup area is the most likely part of the bra to be re-designed. The Bra Block, although constructed with vertical cup shaping, is seldom used exactly in this way for bras. It is easier to design cup seams, gathers, etc. if the areas where they are required are not visually obstructed by darts. Therefore, as a vertical bra seam is the *least* likely, this is the most convenient position for the initial cup shaping on the Bra Block. However, vertical seaming can play a part in swimwear design. Horizontal or diagonal cup seams are more suitable for bra designs, providing better support and uplift and a more pleasing appearance underneath top clothing. Re-designing the cup seam is merely a matter of simple dart manipulation − drawing in the new seam and folding out the upper and lower cup darts; whichever direction the new seam takes, the only rule is that it should cross the bust point (or at least not stray too far from it). See examples of cup seam positions in Figs. 26(a), 26(b) and 29.

Most bras designed for everyday use have a separate rib section under the cups, usually elasticated for grip and comfort. The more shapely this section is, the more support it offers. Shoulder straps, too, should be at least partially if not wholly elasticated for more comfort and less restriction.

In industry, moulded seamless cups are produced using special heat setting equipment in conjunction with suitable fibres, e.g. polyamide (nylon) and synthetic elastomers. This process, not being available outside the lingerie industry, can be emulated by clever pattern cutting and a sympathetic choice of fabric. For example, transparent and/or flesh coloured lightweight fabrics used in conjunction with non-seamed cups can produce the equivalent of a 'no-bra-bra' which is virtually invisible and, in fact, the simplest cut in bra design. See Styles A and B.

Even more of a 'no-bra-bra' are the Posẽs (pronounced *pos-ease*), separate adhesive cups without straps, or indeed anything else. These are simply cone shapes, commercially produced rather like the moulded seamless cups mentioned above, but trimmed around the inside with adhesive edging. See illustration in Fig. 30.

When cutting bras of a more complex structure with several component parts which may be similar in shape, the manner in which the pieces are balance marked for sewing together needs careful thought (see Figs. 26(a)−29) − incorrect assembly can lead to some very odd results.

The Bra Block

The Basic Dress Bodice Block is the best choice for the preparation of a bra block. It is close fitting with the maximum amount of bust shaping (i.e. full-sized darts). To prepare the Bodice Block for bra adaptation, all the ease allowances must be removed (see Size Chart on page 6), reducing the base to body measurements in preparation for a perfect bra fit.

Fig. 19

On the left – the body contour clothed in the Basic Bodice Block with normal 'top clothes' ease shows the difference between body and bodice outline.
On the right – as the bra fits the body exactly, the same difference exists.

Refer to Fig. 20

(a) Outline the back Bodice Block (on page 13), lightly in the area of the side seam and waist dart. Include the bust line and continue this across the paper for correct positioning of the front bodice. (The bust line is most important as it is the main guide to drafting a pattern between two major control areas, namely shoulder and waist).

(b) Measure along bust line from the CB and mark the body bust measurement ÷ 2. This point becomes the bra CF, establishing the correct width of the pattern *without the former ease allowed for top clothing*. Place the CF of the Bodice Block on the bra CF ensuring that the block bust line sits on the line drawn from the CB and that CB and CF of blocks are parallel. The side seams will overlap by the amount of ease added when the block was constructed. Outline the front block lightly in the area of side seam, waist dart and bust dart. Include the chest line.

Refer to Fig. 21

(1) Draw the bra side seam halfway between the overlap. (This side seam position is more suitable for lightweight bras and bikini tops. For bras offering more support use the forward side seam — see paragraph 5 below.) The overlapped seam lines may now be erased to avoid confusion.

(2) Double the bust dart on armhole side only. Lengthen back waist dart 2.5 cm above bust line. Double back and front waist darts.

(3) **To shape top and lower edge of bra block** see tables below.

(4) Mark strap positions as shown in Fig. 21.

(5) A forward side seam is often used in bra design to exercise more control over the cup section. Mark its basic perpendicular position equidistant from bust point to CF. This forward side seam does its job more effectively if tilted approximately 1 cm towards the CF on the lower edge.

Refer to Fig. 22

(6) Trace off this basic bra block in one piece. Include the bust line, bra side seam and forward side seam, bust dart and front waist dart. Eliminate the back dart either by pivoting during tracing or by folding out after tracing.

(7) **To refine the top and lower edge of bra block**. After elimination of the back dart, a point will form on the top edge which is sometimes emphasised as the strap position. If not required for the design it may be smoothed off. An adjustment is definitely needed on the lower edge where the 'dent' is always filled in. Finally, the underarm area between bra side seam and bust dart is hollowed slightly (0.5 cm) for comfort.

CUP SIZING

Two measurements are required to establish cup size. The first and most important (surprisingly, perhaps) is the *rib cage* — taken around the body directly under the bust. This is the international measurement which appears on bra and foundation garment size labels. The second is the *bust* — taken around the body at nipple level. (The tape measure must not be allowed to dip at the back — keep it parallel to the ground). The difference between these two measurements

For top edge above bust line			
size 8	sizes 10 & 12	sizes 14 & 16	size 18
− 0.3 cm on each measurement	raise 1.5 cm at CB raise 3 cm at side seam raise 9 cm from bust point, marked on both sides of dart raise 2.5 cm at CF	+ 0.5 cm on each measurement	+ 1 cm on each measurement

For lower edge below bust line			
size 8	sizes 10 & 12	sizes 14 & 16	size 18
− 0.3 cm on each measurement	lower 2 cm at CB lower 4.5 cm at side seam lower 7.5 cm from bust point, marked on both sides of dart lower 2.5 cm at CF	+ 0.5 cm on each measurement	+ 1 cm on each measurement

Connect all these points to form bra block outline.

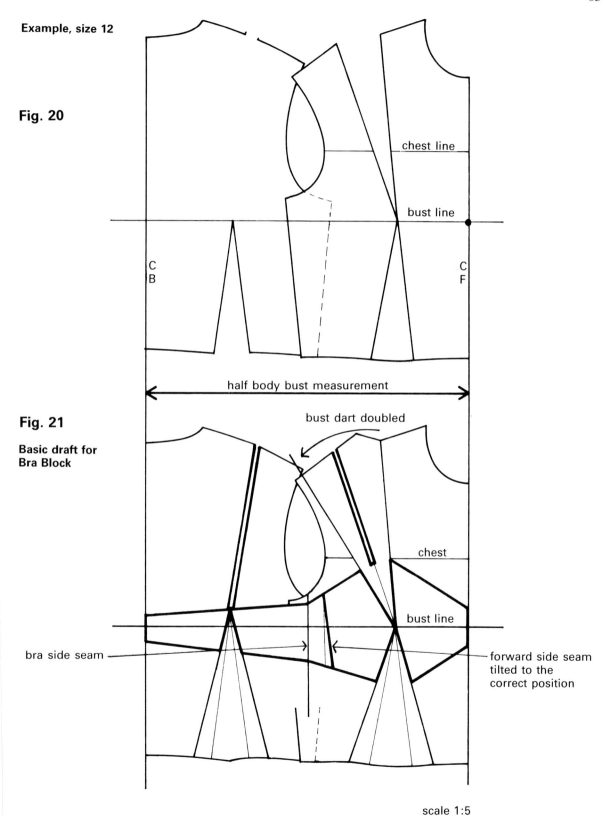

Example, size 12

Fig. 20

chest line

bust line

C
B

C
F

half body bust measurement

Fig. 21

**Basic draft for
Bra Block**

bust dart doubled

chest

bust line

bra side seam

forward side seam
tilted to the
correct position

scale 1:5

STYLE 'B' – SEAMLESS CUP BRA WITH
DÉCOLLETÉ NECKLINE

Refer to Fig. 25(a)

(1) Outline the Bra Block and include the side seam,
forward side seam and an indication of the back
dart position which will help when lengthening the
back strap. Transfer the top dart into the
underbust, making one large dart. (The bra may be
darted or gathered under the bust – see sketches.)

Refer to Fig. 25(b)

(2) Plunge the front neckline from the strap point to
maximum depth at the base of the CF. The
armhole side of the cup should reach to the bra side
seam, point (c).

(3) Whether the bra is darted, as in Fig. 25(c), or
gathered, it will be more comfortable if elasticated
around the underbust and lightly on the cup edges.
As the stretchiness of different elastics varies so
much, it is wise to try a length around the body to
determine the size.

(4) Whilst trying on the elastic mark the CF and point
(c), where the armhole side of cup will join elastic:
measure the pattern minus the dart (a−b, b−c) and
transfer this measurement to the elastic whilst still
around the body.

Note If no suitable decorative elastic is available an
attractive alternative is to make a narrow fabric casing
and fill it with ordinary corded elastic. If cut twice the
length necessary to fit the body, it will have an
attractive ruched effect when worn. See Fig. 25(d).

Seamless cup bra with décolleté neckline – Style B

Suitable fabrics:
lightweights such as crêpe de Chine,
cotton voile and lawn, lace and
equivalent weight synthetics.

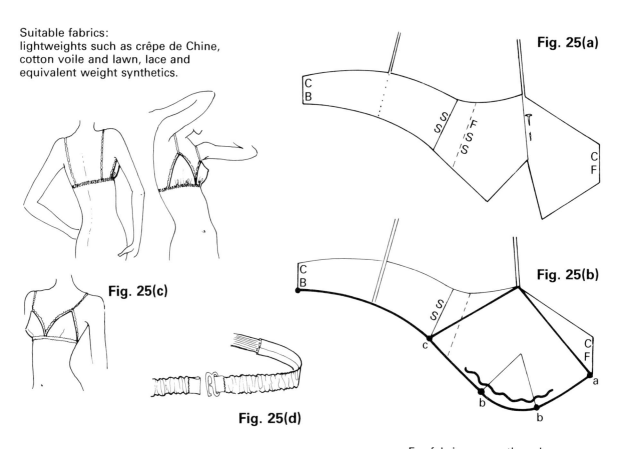

Fig. 25(a)

Fig. 25(b)

Fig. 25(c)

Fig. 25(d)

For fabrics see gathered
version but cut cups
double or use a medium
weight.

STYLE 'C' – SEPARATED, HALF CUP,
UNDERWIRED (may be worn strapless)
Refer to Fig. 26(a)
(1) Outline the Bra Block including the side seam,
forward side seam and the back strap position.
(2) Re-shape the cup to fit the breast outline: draw
lines 1 cm inside CF and 1 cm inside the forward
side seam. (The front strap position could align
with the latter.) Round off the lower corners 1 cm
at CF and 2 cm at the side. Mark point (a) at
junction of dart and cup shaping and point (b) at
junction of cup shaping and lower edge. The areas
rounded off will form extensions to the CF
separating section and the underarm region of the
bra back.
Refer to Fig. 26(b)
(3) Trace the upper and lower cup sections from the
basic draft in Fig. 26(a). Separate them on the
centre horizontal line and place balance marks for
re-joining. Fold out (or pivot) the darts during this
process, thereby transferring the cup shaping into
the horizontal seam. Round off the sharp bust
points caused by folding out darts (dotted lines).
(4) Trace the CF separating section from the basic
draft, squaring it at the top (neckline) edge and
rounding it at the lower edge.
Refer to Fig. 26(c)
(5) Replace the upper cup in position against the bra
back and re-shape the top of the cup, making it
shallower and gently rounded instead of pointed.
The re-shaping may need taking through to the bra
back for a well curved top edge.

Note The undercup seams require bias cut or shaped
casings filled with thin pre-formed underwires. See
page 248 for suppliers.

Separated, half cup bra, underwired – Style C
(may be worn strapless)

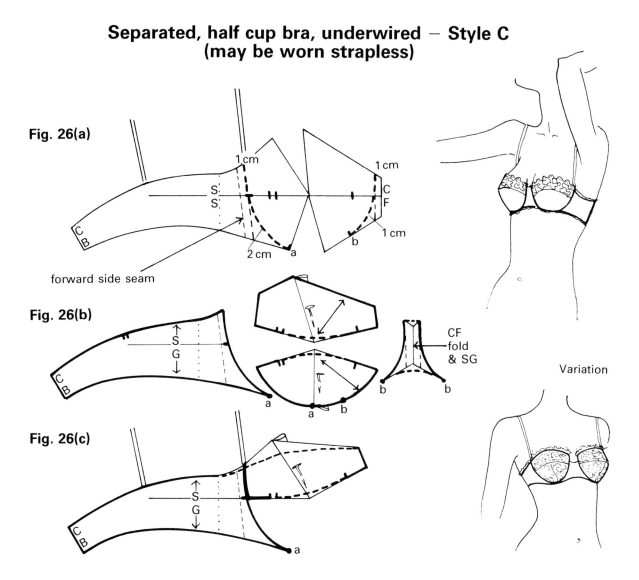

Fig. 26(a)

forward side seam

Fig. 26(b)

Fig. 26(c)

Variation

68

STYLE 'D' – SEPARATED, FULL CUP,
UNWIRED
Refer to Fig. 27(a)
Although similar in appearance to Style 'C' this softer,
unwired bra requires slight re-designing to replace the
security of underwiring. Shoulder straps are necessary,
together with re-shaping of the front neckline for the
attachment of these straps; the undercup area is made
more substantial for better grip.

Use the basic draft outlined in Fig. 26(a) and adjust
as follows:

(1) Make the CF portion (a minimum of) 1 cm deeper
under the cups and curve the (dot-dash) line
towards the unaltered side seam. This undercup
section may then be cut either:

(a) In one piece from CF to side seam; or
(b) Seamed halfway along (in line with the
underbust dart) allowing the side seam to be
eliminated. See Fig. 27(b).

(2) The neckline and front strap position should offer
more support. Return to the neckline shaping on
the basic draft and, using the bust dart position as a
guide, extend the neckline into a stump for the
strap. Scoop the line slightly towards the CF for a
more attractive line.

Note Elastication of the whole of the lower edge and
the top edge (from front strap to CB) will provide extra
comfort and security.

For more pattern ideas see Figs. 28 and 29.

Separated full cup, unwired – Style D

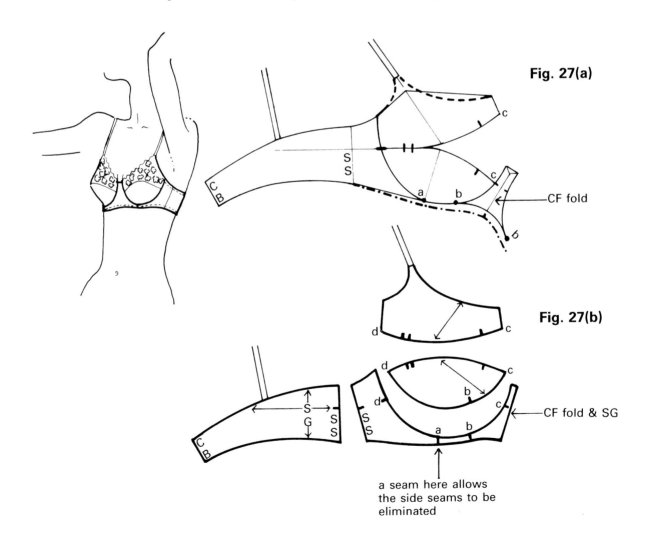

Fig. 27(a)

CF fold

Fig. 27(b)

CF fold & SG

a seam here allows
the side seams to be
eliminated

More pattern ideas

Fig. 28

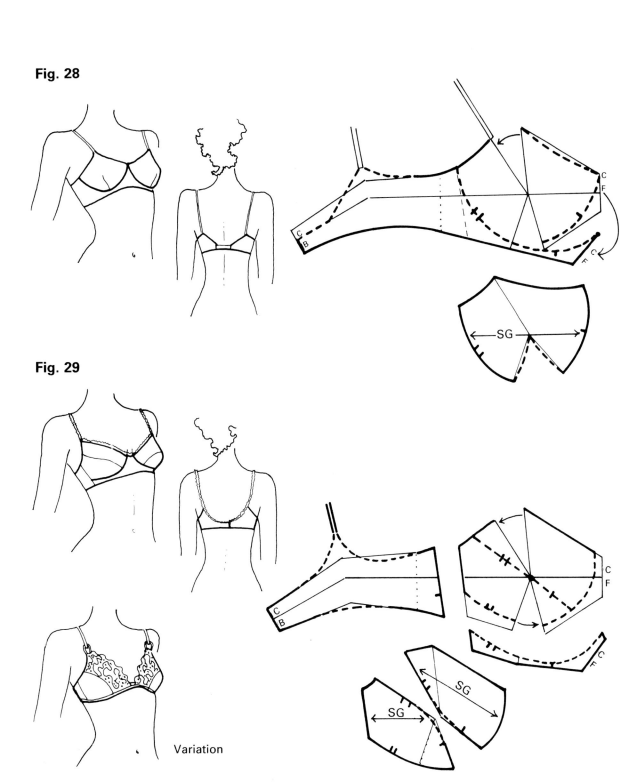

Fig. 29

Variation

STYLE 'E' – POSÉS
See illustration in Fig. 30
These are often made commercially using heat-setting equipment and heat-sensitive materials but the shapes can be produced via the Bra Block for sewing in more easily available materials. They can also be converted by the addition of straps into the simplest, tiniest bikini bra top, as in Fig. 31.

To make the pattern, refer to Fig. 32(a)
(1) Outline just the front of the Bra Block, including the two vertical darts, the bust line and bust point.
(2) Draw a circle around the bust point:
    radius for size 12 = 8 cm
    radii for other sizes plus or minus 0.5 cm

Refer to Fig. 32(b)
(3) Fold the upper dart into the lower, slashing the pattern through centre of lower dart to keep it flat. Secure the pattern in this position. This now larger dart will give a better outline to the cup if shaped like the breast. See dotted line.

(4) **Strap positions**
At CF on bust line (to hold cups together) –
    length = from cup edge to CF, doubled. Cut one.
At top edge on former dart line –
    length = 70 cm to tie on nape. Cut two.   ⎫ increase
At side on original bust dart level   ⎬ or
(dot-dash line) –   ⎪ decrease
    length = 55 cm to tie at CB. Cut two.   ⎭ 1.5 cm per size

Making-up Note   Cut out the cups in double fabric or one layer of fabric and one of lining. (A light to medium weight interlining can also be inserted if a firmer cup is required.) Make a casing around the edge to take thin, round boning or thick millinery wire. This, and the straps, will hold the cups where they are supposed to be.

Style E

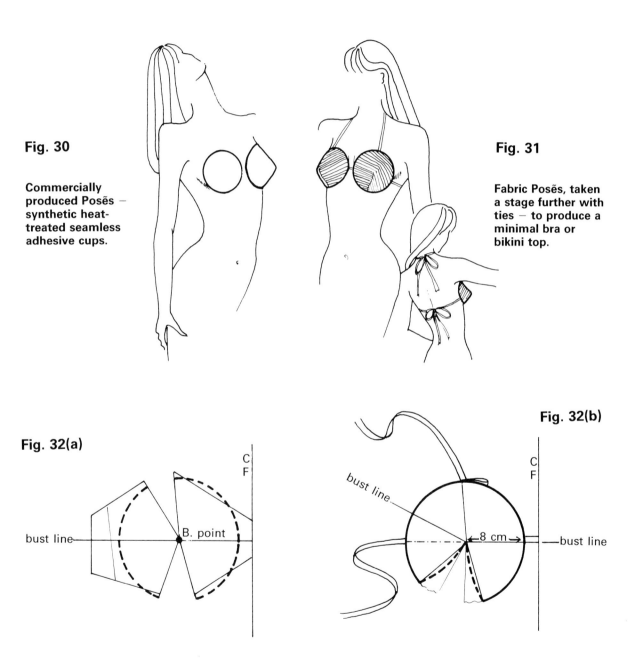

Fig. 30

Commercially
produced Posẽs —
synthetic heat-
treated seamless
adhesive cups.

Fig. 31

Fabric Posẽs, taken
a stage further with
ties — to produce a
minimal bra or
bikini top.

Fig. 32(a)

bust line

B. point

C
F

Fig. 32(b)

bust line

8 cm

bust line

C
F

CORSET

The fundamental requirement of a corset pattern is that it must fit the body exactly, even tightly, so that it may smooth or firm the curves. The degree of support and control depends, in addition to the cut, on the structure, use of material, stiffenings and bonings.

The One-Piece Dress Block will provide the best base, but to make it fit closely all the ease built in during construction for unrestrained movement in top clothes must be systematically removed. In the process the original darts are converted into seams which then serve as correct positioning for the boning.

For fabric suggestions, see notes at the end of this section.

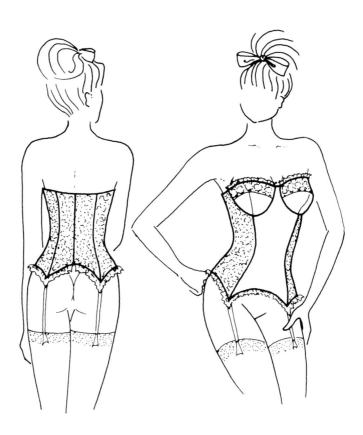

FROM DRESS BLOCK TO CORSET
Basic draft: refer to Fig. 33
(1) Outline the back and front One-Piece Dress Block on a level, down to the hip line. Include the bust, squared waist and top hip lines, and back and front waist darts. The bust dart must be doubled (on armhole side only) to begin the reduction of the chest circumference which will be continued later to provide a perfect fit.
(2) The chest circumference and rib cage measurements are crucial in obtaining a well-fitting corset. Their levels, both on body and pattern are located as follows:
Chest circumference − $\frac{2}{3}$rd upwards between bust and chest lines, square across to the bust dart, slope down to midway between UP and bust line and from there to CB.
Rib cage − Parallel to bust line at these distances: size 8 = 7.5 cm, sizes 10 & 12 = 8 cm, sizes 14 & 16 = 8.5 cm, size 18 = 9 cm
(3) Measure the One-Piece Dress Block on the levels listed below and compare with the actual body measurements from the size chart (page 6). (If you are cutting for personal measurements use the block nearest your size and substitute your own body measurements for the standard ones for that size.) To avoid making mistakes, chart the measurements as in the following example below for a size 12.

The differences between pattern and body measurements must be removed, carefully considering the body curves so as to achieve the smoothest possible skin-tight fit. Consult Fig. 33 to see how the amounts for removal are subdivided and applied to the appropriate areas with the body shape in mind.

Note   In this case 'grading down' is not the best way to reduce the pattern since it relies on standard proportional reductions to maintain the fit. The above reductions will change the fit, reducing it to the body size, by removing the varying amounts of ease at the different body levels.

(4) **For a guide to the 'petal' shaping** at lower edge of corset − draw curved lines above and below top hip line (located 10 cm above hip line) by amounts shown in circles.
(5) **Positioning and shaping of cup: refer to Fig. 34**
Firstly draw cup 'frame' − 1 cm inside forward side seam (to push breasts closer together), along rib cage level, 0.75 cm inside CF line − to provide a 1.5 cm wide separating section.
    Shape the top of the cup in a gentle curve as shown, sloping down to 2.5 cm above bust line. Round off the lower corners to suit the breast outline − see guiding measurements on diagonal lines from corners.
    Finally draw a seamline across the cup angled

	Pattern measurements of One-Piece Dress Block	Standard body measurement (or your own)	Difference (Ease) on whole pattern	Remove from half pattern
Bust	98 cm	88 cm	10 cm	5 cm
Waist	74	68	6	3
Top hip	92	88	4	2
Chest circumference	94*	82	12	6
Rib cage	87	75	12	6

* measured after doubling of bust dart.

74

Corset – Basic draft

Fig. 33

Example, size 12

scale 1:5

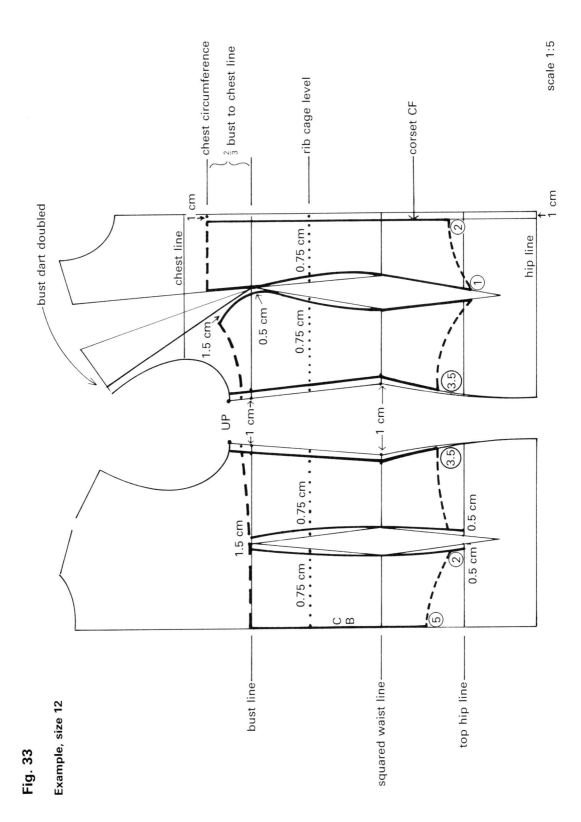

Fig. 34

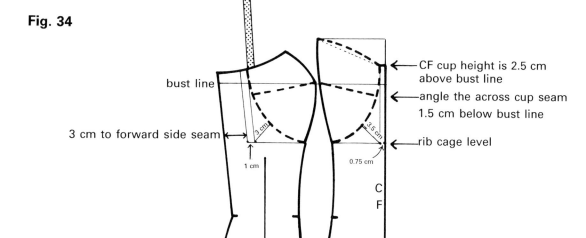

bust line

CF cup height is 2.5 cm above bust line

angle the across cup seam 1.5 cm below bust line

rib cage level

3 cm to forward side seam

3 cm

3.5 cm

1 cm

0.75 cm

C F

Fig. 35

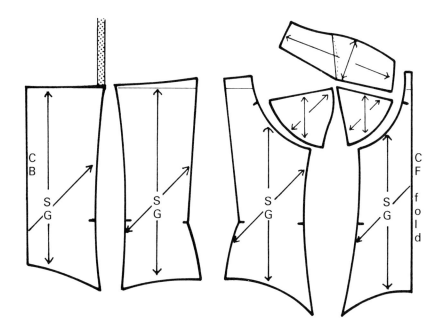

C B

S G

S G

S G

S G

C F fold

from 1.5 cm below bust line up to bust point(s).
Note positions of strap if required.

Refer to Fig. 35

(6) Trace all the panels separately from the plans — back corset from Fig. 33 and front from Fig. 34. Transfer balance marks for perfect re-assembly. The undercup is seamed in this example but may be cut in one piece by joining the seams at top and bottom of pattern but forfeiting their curvy shape. The two sections of the upper cup are invariably joined together, thereby eliminating an unsightly seam, especially when cut in lace or sheer fabrics.

(7) The direction of SG lines on corset patterns is so dependent on the type of fabric that a decision can only be made once the fabric has been chosen; the normal SG lines parallel with CB and CF serve as a basis for this decision.

(8) The top edge of the back corset may be lowered. In any case, round off the seam points while the tops of the pattern pieces are pushed together. See Fig. 36.

(9) **If suspenders are required** they should be attached to the panel seams which, for this purpose, are better positioned nearer the side seams where the suspenders will feel more comfortable. Re-direct the seam 2 cm towards the side, as shown in Fig. 37. It also helps if the back ones especially are elasticated and adjustable.

Notes To provide support the CB panels are often cut in power net — in which case they may be narrowed by an amount depending on its elasticity.

The vertical seams, excepting the CB, are cased and flat boned. The undercup seam is cased and boned with thin pre-formed underwires (see page 248 for suppliers).

The undercup section may be stiffened if required although this is not normally necessary for smaller sizes.

Closure is usually by hooks or lacing.

Fabric suggestions: the most commonly used fabric is lace (a unique fabric, being without a grainline) which may be stretch or non-stretch, used in conjunction with power net (Lycra spandex). Many other fabrics are suitable provided they meet the following requirements:

(a) washable
(b) strong (although not necessarily firm-woven)
(c) not too thick or bulky (seams will look unsightly)

The pattern should be cut with the maximum stretch (or bias, in the case of a non-stretch fabric) going around the body.

Other uses: corset patterns can become the basis for some styles of strapless evening dresses.

Fig. 36

place pattern pieces together at top and
smooth off points where seams join

or lower to below
bust line

C
B

bust
line

C
F

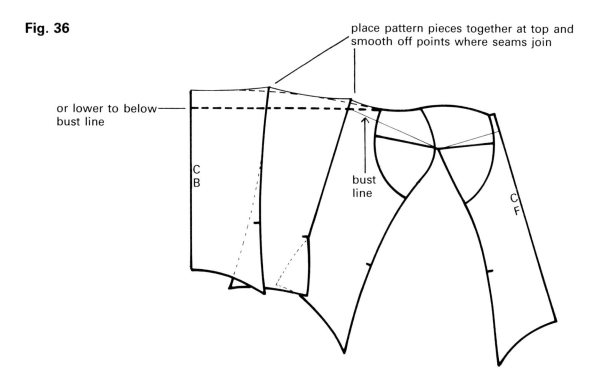

Fig. 37

Re-directing seams
for the attachment
of suspenders

C
B

S
G

side seam

ensure that new 'points'
are on the same level

WASPIE

The waspie – really a waist cincher – follows such similar lines to the corset that a pattern can easily be adapted from the basic draft on page 74.

The main difference is that a waspie has no cups, extending no higher than the rib cage level. The lower edge can be shaped like the corset to take suspenders, but is not usually quite so deep. The side and panel seams are boned for a streamlined appearance. Eyelets or grommets with lacing are most often used at the CF for the closure, although side or CB closures are possible without changing the shape of the pattern.

Refer to Fig. 38

(1) Outline the basic draft of the corset (Fig. 33 on page 00) from the rib cage level down to the hip line. Include the waist and top hip line.

(2) If attaching suspenders, redirect the back panel seam as shown in Fig. 37 (page 77). Curve the lower edge using amounts above and below top hip line (encircled) as a guide to height/shaping.

(3) The top edge may be shaped, e.g. into a shallow V at CB.

(4) For SG line, fabric and other information, see paragraphs 7, 8, and 9 and the final notes in the Corset instructions.

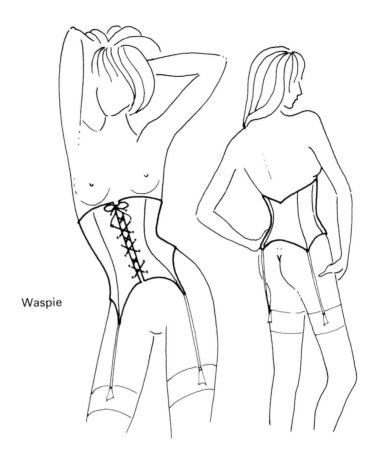

Waspie

Fig. 38

Example, size 12

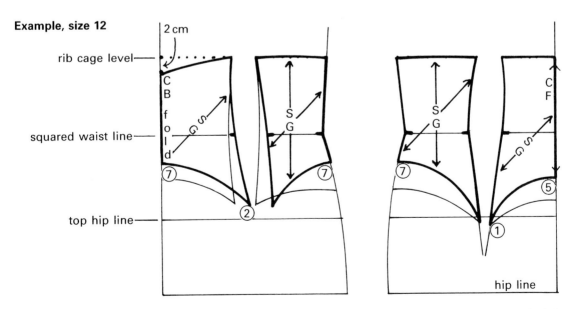

rib cage level

2 cm

squared waist line

top hip line

scale 1:5

BRIEFS, PANTIES AND KNICKERS

This selection of block shapes with their varying degrees of fit will supply the basis for most modern styles.

Briefs   Generally close fitting, without CF or CB seams and therefore requiring a separate crutch section. Can be cut waist-high or to hip bone level, and mostly in stretch fabrics.

Panties   A shorter version of a brief but hip length or lower. Usually has a high cut, elasticated leg.

Knickers   The general name for loose-fitting undergarments, usually with longer legs and a looser crutch fit than briefs or panties. The crutch section is cut in one with the main pattern (rather like a trouser pattern) and tends to hang loosely between the legs.

The blocks are easily constructed using the waist, hip and body rise measurements.

Note on elastic finished edges   Strip elastics, whether braided (corded) or woven, vary so much in their degree of stretch that it is impossible to give standard cutting lengths. The only sure way is to try on the elastic where it is required and cut it to fit. The measurement obtained can be re-used for different styles provided the same elastic is used.

The Waist Brief Block

The close-fitting brief is nearly always cut in stretch fabric for comfort − single cotton jersey or nylon (polyamide). If non-stretch fabrics are used, e.g. soft cottons or silks, cutting on the bias will allow fabrics to 'give' more. The waist and legs are elasticated.

An adequate crutch section in a brief should measure not less than 8 cm at its narrowest width and about 16 cm along its centre line. The crutch reinforcement piece is important because the garment is so fitted as to touch the body; it is therefore cut double, and if the main fabric is unabsorbent a soft cotton should be substituted for the inside layer.

Extra height is added at the CB waist to ease the fit over the bottom, even when using stretch fabrics. See Fig. 45 on page 87.

Refer to Fig. 39

$0-1$ = body hip measurement plus 5 cm ease allowance ÷ 2 (ease allowance may be decreased or increased to make a tighter or looser brief). Square down for CB and CF.

2 = Midway. Square down for side seam.

$1-3$ = body rise plus 4 cm ⎱ square inwards
$0-4$ = body rise plus 7 cm ⎰

$0-5$ = 2 cm (extra length over bottom − see Fig. 45 on page 87). Square a short line at 5 and curve across to front waistline.

$3-6$ ⎱ 4 cm centre crutch width (*8 cm on whole pattern*). Increase 0.5 cm (*1 cm*) on sizes
$4-7$ ⎰ 16 & 18.

$3-8$ = 6 cm ⎱ crutch reinforcement section.
$4-10$ = 10 cm ⎰ Square across.

$8-9$ = 5 cm (increase 0.5 cm on sizes 16 & 18). Drop 0.5 cm and curve line.

$10-11$ = 10 cm (increase 0.5 cm on sizes 16 & 18). Drop 1 cm and curve line.

$2-12$ = side seam length − 19 cm for size 12 (0.3 cm difference per size). Connect $6-9-12$ and $7-11-12$ with four straight guide lines.

For leg shaping
Divide each line in half.
Front: hollow 3 cm and 0.3 cm
Back: hollow 1 cm and 1 cm
Crutch sections: should have short right angles at 6 and 7; join front and back into one pattern piece which is then cut in double fabric − see Fig. 40.

VARIATIONS ON THE BASIC BRIEF BLOCK as drafted in Fig. 39
(1) For a wider brief:
Increase the ease allowance added over the body hip measurement. Conversely, decrease the allowance for a tighter fit; these adjustments make no difference to the shape of the brief, only to its size.
(2) For a bloomer type brief: refer to Fig. 41.
(a) Slash the pattern from leg to waist, avoiding the crutch seams, and add in the required amount evenly divided between the cut sections (in this case 5 cm between each).
(b) Add a little length at the side seams (2 cm) to give more 'bounce' to the style and gently curve a line back to the crutch area. Check that curves run well into crutch piece, which remains unchanged.
(c) Measure the whole of the widened leg and cut a frill to fit this measurement, either in self fabric or perhaps in lace. Elasticate the legs after attaching the frill.

Note Suitable fabrics for a wider cut brief or bloomers: soft but crisp cottons, especially broderie Anglais.

Waist Brief Block

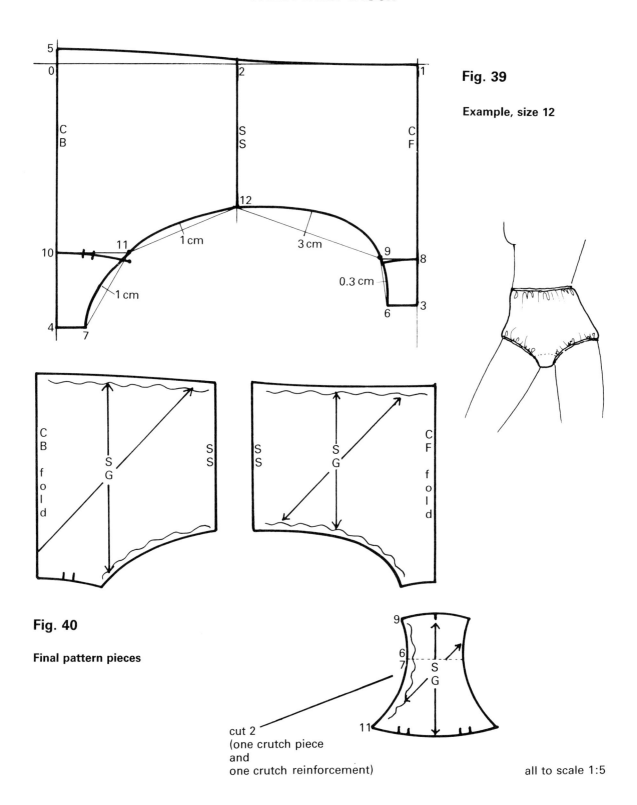

Fig. 39

Example, size 12

CB

SS

CF

5
0
2
1

11

10

1 cm

1 cm

3 cm

12

9

8

0.3 cm

6

3

4
7

CB fold

SS

SG

SS

CF fold

SG

Fig. 40

Final pattern pieces

cut 2
(one crutch piece
and
one crutch reinforcement)

9

6
7

SG

11

all to scale 1:5

Variation on the Waist Brief Block — a bloomer type brief

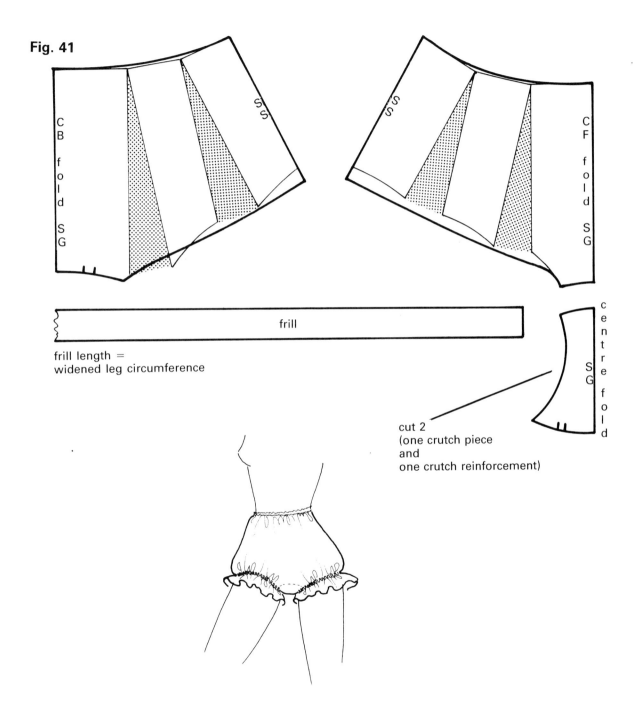

Fig. 41

frill

frill length =
widened leg circumference

cut 2
(one crutch piece
and
one crutch reinforcement)

Hip Brief Block

This shape falls somewhere between the Waist Brief Block and the Bikini Pantie Block — providing a briefer brief or a more substantial bikini pantie. Having become very popular it now accounts for a large part of brief and pantie sales.

Suitable fabrics could be drawn from those listed for the Waist Brief or the Bikini Pantie Block; the same CB height provision should be made to accommodate the bottom.

Its top edge sits on or just below the top hip level (hip bones). It is not quite so important to avoid a horizontal front crutch seam as with the bikini pantie; being more substantially sized it can withstand division by seams more successfully. The crutch section can therefore be treated similarly to that of the Waist Brief Block.

Top hip level and legs are elasticated.

Refer to Fig. 42

0−1 = body hip measurement plus 5 cm ease allowance ÷ 2 (ease allowance may be decreased or increased to make a tighter or looser bikini brief). Square down for CB and CF.

2 = Midway. Square down for side seam.

1−3 = body rise minus 6 cm ⎫

0−4 = body rise minus 3 cm ⎭ square inwards

0−5 = 2 cm (extra length over bottom − see Fig. 45 on page 47). Square a short line at 5 and curve across to front waistline.

3−6 ⎫

4−7 ⎭ = 3.5 cm centre crutch width (*7 cm on whole pattern*). Increased 0.5 cm (*1 cm*) on sizes 16 & 18.

3−8 = 6 cm ⎫ crutch reinforcement sections.

4−10 = 9 cm ⎭ Square across.

8−9 = 5 cm (increase 0.5 cm on sizes 16 & 18). Drop 0.5 cm and curve line.

10−11 = 9 cm (increase 0.5 cm on sizes 16 & 18). Drop 1 cm and curve line.

2−12 = Side seam length − 9 cm for size 12 (0.2 cm difference per size). Connect 6−9−12 and 7−11−12 with four straight guide lines.

For leg shaping:
Divide each line in half.
Front: hollow 2 cm and 0.3 cm
Back: hollow 1 cm and 0.6 cm
Crutch sections: should have short right angles at 6 and 7; join front and back into one pattern piece, which is then cut in double fabric, as in Fig. 40 of Waist Brief Block.

Note Other uses: the hip brief shape is often used for beachwear − see the bikini pattern in Chapter 4, page 170.

Apart from any style changes, only one technical detail needs changing to make this underwear pattern suitable for beachwear − detach the back crutch section, add it to the front brief and eliminate the front crutch seam (8−9).

Hip Brief Block

Fig. 42

Example, size 12

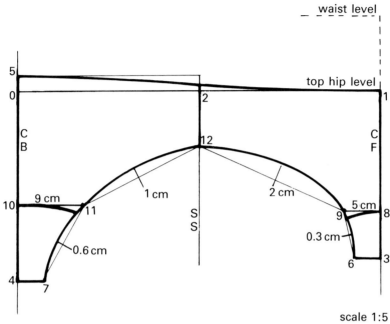

waist level

5
0
top hip level
2
1

C
B

12

C
F

1 cm

2 cm

10
9 cm
11

5 cm
9
8

S
S

0.3 cm

0.6 cm

6
3

4
7

scale 1:5

Bikini Pantie Block

This type of pantie, providing minimal coverage, used only to be found in beachwear. It is now also a popular choice in underwear, offered in stretch cottons, soft woven cottons and polyesters, lace, etc.

The garment is so tiny, especially the front, that a crutch seam across the lower part would look very unsightly. Therefore, after the initial drafting, the back crutch part is added to the front pantie, thereby eliminating the front and centre crutch seams. A separate reinforcement piece (important as garment touches body) is caught in with the back crutch seam but merely neatened and laid on the inside of the front pantie; it becomes more secure when caught in with the elasticated legs and is invisible in wear.

As with both Brief Blocks, extra back length is needed to accommodate the bottom. Also, notice that the front top edge is slightly lowered compared with the brief blocks; minimal panties look better if they dip slightly at the front.

The underwear version is usually elasticated at the top edge; the beachwear bikini is often tied to hold it in place. Both require elasticating at the legs.

Refer to Fig. 43

    0−1 = top hip body measurement ÷ 2 (no ease allowance necessary). Square down for CB and CF.
      2 = Midway for side seam position. (Although not used as such, it is a useful guide to length of elastic or ties.)
    1−3 = body rise minus 6 cm ⎫ Square inwards.
    0−4 = body rise minus 3 cm ⎭
    0−5 = 2 cm (extra length over bottom − see Fig. 45 on page 87). Square across.

    3−6 ⎫ 3.5 cm centre crutch width (*7 cm on whole*
        ⎬ = *pattern*). Increase 0.5 cm (*1 cm*) for size 16
    4−7 ⎭ & 18.
     3−8 = 6 cm ⎫ crutch reinforcement sections.
    4−10 = 9 cm ⎭ Square across.
     8−9 = 4.2 cm ⎫ increase 0.5 cm for sizes 16 & 18.
    10−11 = 8 cm ⎭
     1−12 = 2 cm drop for front height. Square across.
    12−13 = two-thirds of 1−2
     5−14 = two-thirds of 0−2 plus 4 cm
             Connect 13−9−6 and 14−11−7 with four straight guide lines.

For leg shaping:
Divide each line in half.
Front: hollow 1 cm and 0.2 cm.
Back: add 0.5 cm and hollow 1 cm.
Crutch sections: should have right angles at 6 and 7.

Refer to Fig. 44
To eliminate the centre and front crutch seams, detach and join the back crutch section to the front pantie. Finally, make a crutch reinforcement piece to be cut in a single layer of fabric.

Note 1   It is not necessary to curve the remaining back crutch seam on such tiny panties.
Note 2   As an example for size 12, elasticate each leg to 40 cm and the top edge to 73 cm (top hip measurement minus 15 cm), but check before cutting as the stretchiness of elastics vary.
Note 3   Other uses: this pattern may be used without changes for beachwear bikini bottoms − see the bikini pattern in Chapter 4, page 168.

Bikini Pantie Block

Fig. 43   **Example, size 12**

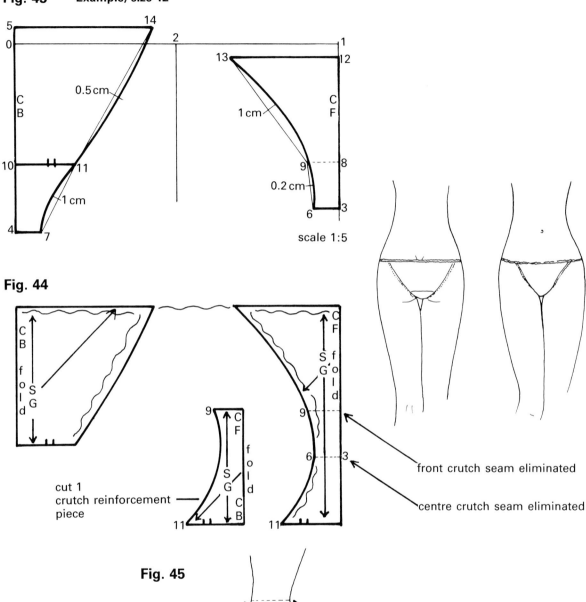

0.5 cm

1 cm

1 cm

0.2 cm

scale 1:5

Fig. 44

cut 1
crutch reinforcement
piece

front crutch seam eliminated

centre crutch seam eliminated

Fig. 45

front length

back length

centre crutch position

French Knicker Block

French knickers are known alternatively as a 'skirt' knicker because of the loose body fit and flared leg. They are usually associated with better quality lingerie, and often lace trimmed and cut in expensive fabrics, e.g. crêpe de Chine, silk satin or Swiss voile, which hang well, contributing to the 'skirty' appearance. Bias cutting often helps to achieve a similar effect when using less expensive fabrics such as cotton lawn, acetate and nylon or polyester. It is not necessary to use stretch fabrics.

The pattern resembles the top part of the trouser block in shape with the crutch part cut in one with the main pattern, not detached as in brief and pantie styles. However, it still needs some reinforcement in the form of a 'comfort gusset'.

As these garments are much looser than briefs or panties, the height added at the back waist needs only to be sufficient for the knicker to hang well.

The pattern may be cut on the straight grain for a bouncy appearance or on the bias for a more clinging look.

Refer to Fig. 46

$0-1$ = body hip plus 5 cm ease allowance ÷ 2 (ease allowance may be increased to make a looser knicker). Square down from both points.

2 = Midway. Square down for side seam.

$1-3$ = body rise plus 4 cm ⎫
$0-4$ = body rise plus 7 cm ⎭ Square outwards.

Draw secondary lines 2 cm above. Mark (f) and (b), inner front and back crutch points, 8.5 cm (for all sizes) out on these lines.

$0-5$ = 1 cm (extra length over bottom). Square a short line at 5 and curve across to front waistline.

$1-6$ = waist to hip length.

$6-7$ = $0-1$ plus 1.5 cm for extra width.

For crutch shaping:

Front: curve a line from 6 through a 4.5 cm diagonal

point to f (from diagonal line to (f) should be almost straight).

Back: curve a line from 7 through a 6.5 cm diagonal point to b (from diagonal line to (b) should be almost straight).

Square down from ends of curved crutch seams at points (f) and (b) for across crutch seam. Mark f1 and b1. Seam length should be no less than 3 cm, i.e. *6 cm total crutch width* for sizes 8−14 and 3.5 cm (*7 cm*) for sizes 16 & 18.

For leg shaping:

Connect side seam (at hip line) to f1 and b1 with straight guide lines. Curve leg shaping 1 cm up at centres and rule lines from centres to f1 and b1.

Refer to Fig. 47.

To complete patterns, place crutch seams together (b, b1 placed to f, f1) and check that the seam from 6−7 is well curved. Leave the blocks so placed to make 'comfort gusset' pattern.

For comfort gusset pattern:

Refer to Fig. 48

Make a half moon shape pattern extending approximately 1 cm beyond diagonal (dotted) lines for its length, straightened at the top for placing on the fold. The width should be slightly less than the knicker crutch width, to remain unseen. Cut one layer only in soft, absorbent cotton.

VARIATIONS ON THE FRENCH KNICKER BLOCK

The knicker block is suitable for side seam design details, e.g. short slits or Vs or the petalled effect shown in Fig. 49; or the side seams may be eliminated entirely and the knicker cut in one piece from centre front to centre back.

Note Other uses: French knicker patterns can be used to produce certain lightweight styles of shorts.

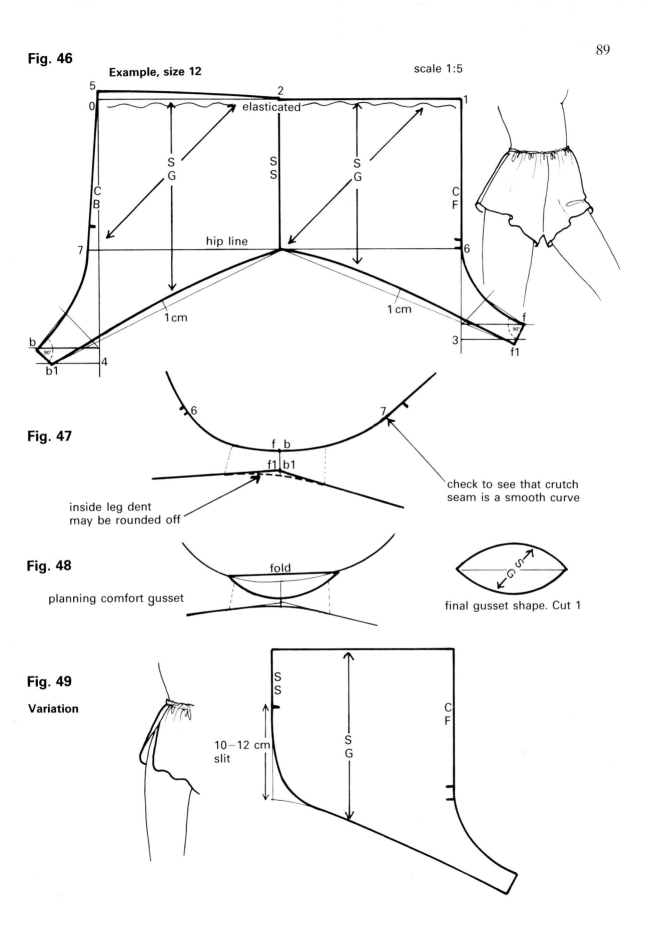

Fig. 46

Example, size 12   scale 1:5

elasticated

S G

S S

S G

C B

C F

hip line

7   6

1 cm   1 cm

b   f

90°   90°

b1   4   3   f1

Fig. 47

6   7

f b

f1 b1

check to see that crutch
seam is a smooth curve

inside leg dent
may be rounded off

Fig. 48

fold

planning comfort gusset

S G

final gusset shape. Cut 1

Fig. 49

Variation

S S

C F

10–12 cm
slit

S G

Cami-Knicker

Cami-knicker patterns are usually based on a combination of a petticoat top and a knicker pattern. The method of combining the patterns needs careful consideration to ensure the correct 'through body length'. All-in-one garments (either with or without a waist seam) can so easily be cut with excess length from neck to crutch — which would hang uncomfortably between the legs, or worse still, with insufficient length resulting in restricted movement.

Choice of style can do much to prevent these problems. Many manufacturers, who have to provide garments that will fit both the shorter and the taller woman, and who do not wish to over-complicate their sizing systems, favour styles with elasticated, blouson waists. This kind of style is both comfortable to wear and very flattering to most figure types, provided it is cut in a suitable fabric, i.e. soft, lightweight (crêpe de Chine, for example).

With today's stretch fabrics (or non-stretch cut on the bias) most styles are pull-on and the only necessary opening is on the crutch seam, which is closed with either a few tiny buttons or with lightweight snap fasteners. It helps to re-position the crutch seam slightly towards the front to make fastening easier.

Cami-knicker with elasticated, blouson waist

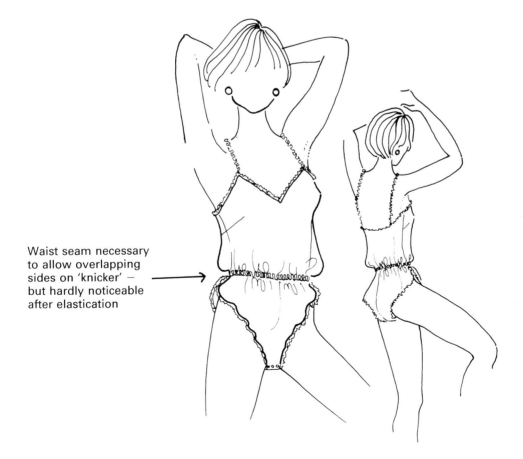

Waist seam necessary to allow overlapping sides on 'knicker' — but hardly noticeable after elastication

CAMI-KNICKER STYLE WITH ELASTICATED, BLOUSON WAIST

Preparation — Refer to Fig. 50

(1) Outline the Petticoat Block (see page 43) down to 8 cm below the dress waistline, omitting front and back waist darts. (The higher petticoat waistline is not suitable for cami-knicker styles.)

Dropping the pattern waist by 8 cm will provide a 4 cm blouson effect — remember that whatever is added to the flat pattern appears halved when worn.

(2) Measure along the new cami-knicker waistline from CB — petticoat side seam — CF. *It should not be less than half the body bust measurement, i.e. 44 cm for a size 12, if it is to pull on easily.* Any excess (which could make the style too bulky around the waist) may be removed equally on each side. Re-draw the lower part of the side seams to align with the top.

(3) Draw new position for bust dart well down into side seam (never place an underarm dart along the bust line — it looks very ugly in wear).

(4) Re-draw front neckline. Start with a straight line and then shape lightly.

Refer to Fig. 51

Outline the French Knicker Block (see page 89).

(5) **Back**

The CB and crutch area remain exactly the same. The side seam area (which will be overlapped at the waist instead of seamed through) must be re-shaped: Firstly, raise side waist point 2 cm. Then raise side leg length 9 cm. Re-draw waist, curving line as shown. Re-draw 'side seam' with a well-curved line from new side waist point to halfway along original hemline.

(6) **Front**

The design shows the front knicker cut without a CF seam, giving a more pleasing appearance when joined to a bodice and a less complicated fit in a crutch area that will be fastened. Therefore the front requires more alteration than the back: Measure the original CF length (from waist point (a) to crutch point (b)) with tape measure on its edge along the curved part. Continue the straight CF line well down below the original knicker leg. On this new CF line apply the original CF length measurement, so that a−b and a−b1 are equal lengths. Square across for the new crutch seam. Make its length equal with the back.

(7) **To re-shape front leg**

Connect side waist point to new crutch point, firstly with a straight line and then, after dividing into three parts, shape as shown.

Refer to Fig. 52

(8) Transfer the bust dart into the previously marked underarm position. Note the inner dot-dash line which is the actual sewing line, shortened back from bust point by 3 cm.

(9) Re-position the crutch seam towards the front to make fastening easier: remove 1.5 cm from the front and add it to the back. Allow an additional small underlap on the new back crutch seam to accommodate the buttons or snap fasteners. See also enlarged sketch.

(10) The crutch area will need reinforcing with a 'comfort gusset' as indicated by the dotted lines. See French Knicker Block for details (page 89).

Note 1 In this particular style the bodice part of the cami-knicker is best cut on the bias, for extra 'drapeability', but the knicker part may be cut on the straight grain.

Note 2 The waist edge of the cami-knicker bodice marks the position for the lower line of elastic casing.

Cami-knicker

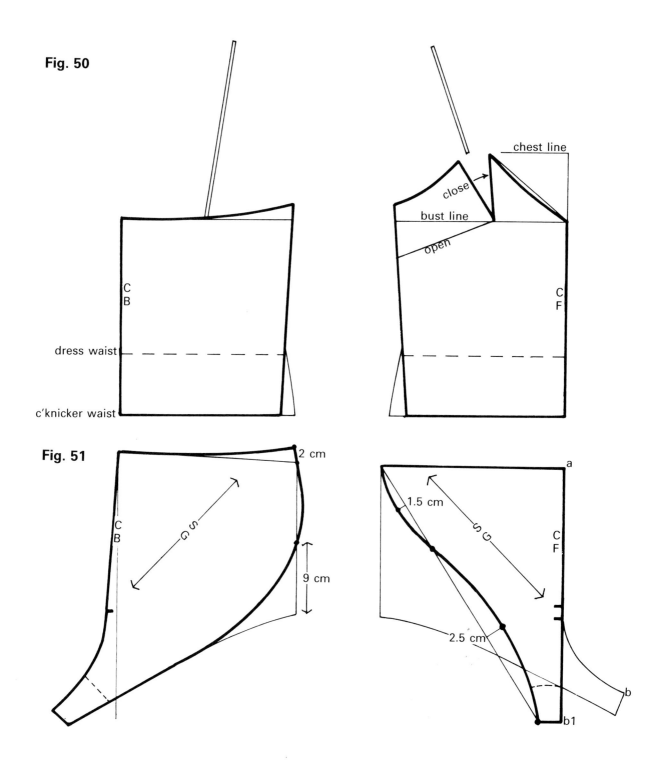

Fig. 50

chest line
close
bust line
open

C
B

C
F

dress waist

c'knicker waist

Fig. 51

2 cm

C
B

S G

9 cm

a

1.5 cm

S G

C
F

2.5 cm

b

b1

Cami-knicker

Fig. 52

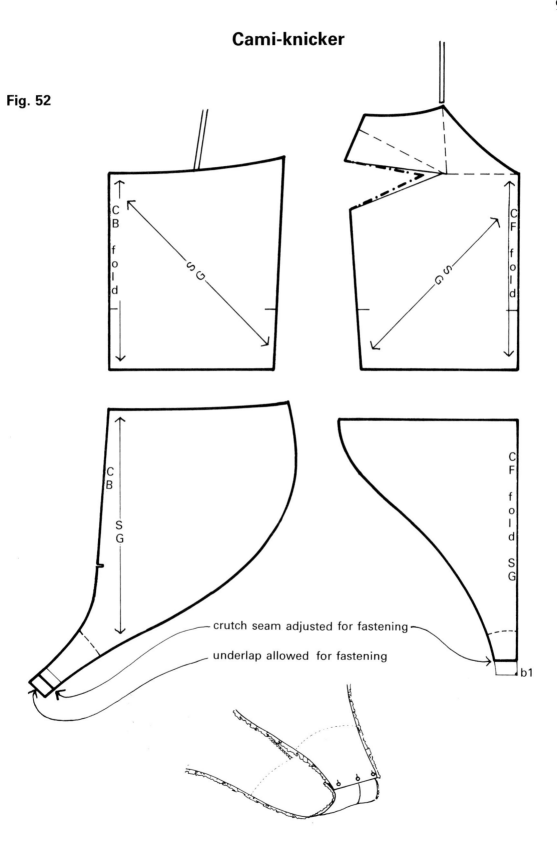

crutch seam adjusted for fastening

underlap allowed for fastening

CAMI-KNICKER VARIATION

Although it is usual to have an elasticated blouson waist in cami-knicker styles, there are occasions when a plainer look is required. The pattern pieces may be achieved in a similar way by using almost any petticoat design for the top half and any loose fitting knicker block for the bottom half. The only proviso is that the petticoat top should reach down to the natural (dress) waistline and the knicker should reach up to meet it, but with a small (1–2 cm) gap added in between for a comfortable fit. Once this rule of length has been observed, the garment may be cut with or without a waist seam as the design dictates.

Refer to Fig. 53

For a much simplified cami-knicker shape simply draw round any one-piece petticoat style in this book, marking the hipline clearly. Then superimpose the French Knicker Block, matching the hiplines, thus ensuring the correct through-body length. The hemline of the knicker may be left as is, or lengthened to give the appearance of a skirt.

Simplified cami-knicker

Simplified cami-knicker shape

Fig. 53

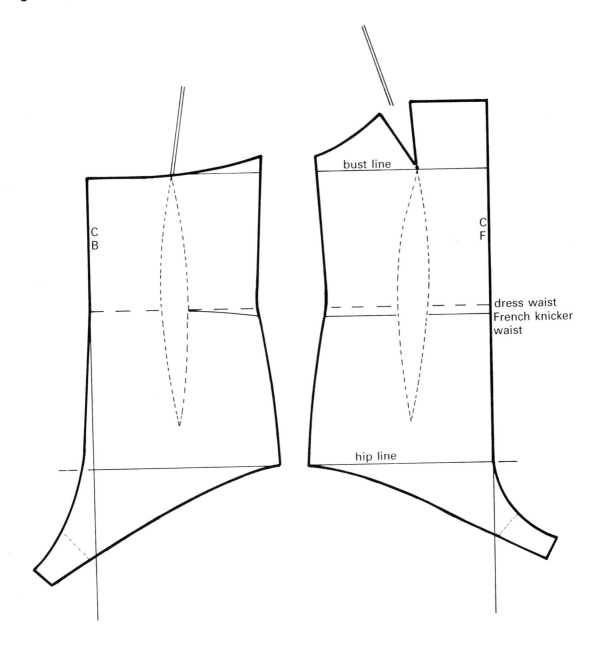

bust line

C
B

C
F

dress waist
French knicker
waist

hip line

3 LINGERIE — NIGHTWEAR

NIGHTDRESSES AND NIGHT SHIRTS

An important practical requirement of any nightwear is that it is comfortable, especially when the wearer is sleeping. Above all it must not restrict limb movement. This means appropriate styling, cutting generously and possibly using stretch fabrics.

The basis for any pattern depends on the individual design. So as to satisfy the need for unrestricted movement, choose blocks that are not too tight to start with. The One-Piece Dress Block and the Loose-Fitting Dartless Block lengthened according to need are both ideal bases for looser styles and those with sleeves. The Petticoat Block is an obvious choice for shoulder strapped nightdresses, but because it fits more closely it is wise to compare the chest measurement of the block against your idea of how the top should fit, before cutting the pattern.

When designing nightdresses or shirts with sleeves (particularly long ones) consider allowing extra width across the back, especially when using one of the more fitted blocks as a base. The Loose-Fitting Dartless Block already has sufficient room built in to allow the wearer to stretch without restriction.

The hem circumference also needs some thought − anything too tight will limit leg movement.

Nightdress

Full length shoulder strapped style cut from the Petticoat Block with a shaped band finishing the top, and a front cup section. Suitable fabrics: practically any lightweight cotton or silk or their synthetic equivalents. Choose fabrics with a good hang.

Basic Draft
Refer to Fig. 54
(1) Outline Petticoat Block lengthened as required (here CB waist to hem = 103 cm). Draw lower line of shaped band 4 cm down from top edge, dipping to a point at CF.
(2) Shape lower line of cup similarly to Bra Top Petticoat (page 51). Place balance marks on cup to control gathers into band and also on the back aligning with the strap position. Re-shape side seams slightly from undercup level.
(3) To introduce gathering:
As the back is *unshaped* where gathers will be, it is enough simply to widen it with a line drawn parallel to the original CB. Make sure the top is right-angled to fit into the straight band.

The front gathers emanate from the *shaped* undercup area and are therefore more successfully introduced by slashing and spreading the pattern. Firstly, decide where gathers will start from and place a balance mark on undercup seam, marking both cup *and* skirt patterns (in this case gathers start on the left side of the waist dart). Mark two slash lines between this point and the CF, cut and spread 10 cm altogether − the same as added to CB. All lines should be parallel.

Refer to Fig. 55
(4) Trace off the *top band*, folding out the top of the bust dart in the process. Remember to include the balance marks which will control the gathers.
(5) Trace off the *cup section*, transferring the lower dart into the upper, making one large dart, which will convert into gathers.
(6) Trace off the *skirt section*, including the balance marks for gathered areas.
(7) For shoulder strap length see instructions for Petticoat Block straps, note 7 on page 42. Make straps 2 cm finished width.

Make ties for back, 110 cm long and 2 cm finished width. Insert in side seam, aligned with lower cup seam.

Nightdress

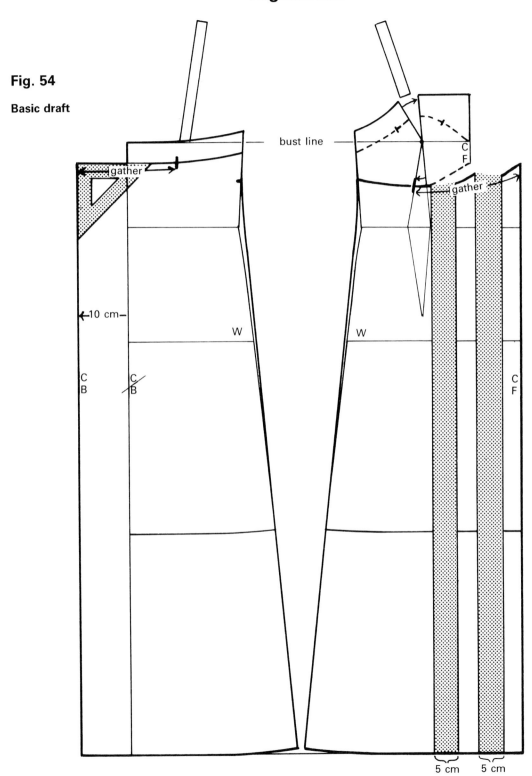

Fig. 54

Basic draft

Fig. 55

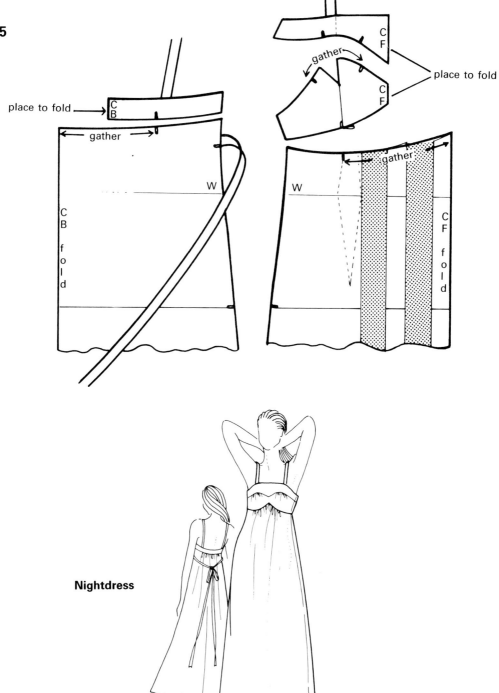

place to fold →

C
B

gather

W

C
B
f
o
l
d

C
F

place to fold

gather

C
F

W

gather

C
F
f
o
l
d

Nightdress

Nightshirt

A shortie, button-through nightshirt with a shoulder yoke and shirt sleeve. Suitable fabrics: light to medium weight cottons − reversible to cope with button and buttonhole bands and pocket top.

Refer to Fig. 56

(1) Outline the Loose-Fitting Dartless Block (page 30), lengthening as required − here nape to hem = 90 cm. Draw front yoke line 5 cm parallel to shoulder, back yoke line 5 cm wide at shoulder and at right angles to CB. (Back and front are joined at shoulder, making a one-piece yoke.)

(2) To introduce gathers at the back, first place a balance mark to define area of gathers, then redraw CB parallel to the block at the required distance to provide the extra material for gathering.

(3) **Mark pocket position** 15 cm wide × 17 cm long, well spaced between armhole and CF. Include a 2.5 cm turn-over line at the top. Round off lower edges of pocket. Shape the corners at hemline of nightshirt proportionately.

(4) **Make addition to CF for buttons and buttonholes.** Here a 4 cm wide button/buttonhole band has been allowed. Therefore addition from CF of block = 2 cm (to front edge) plus 4 cm (to fold back edge) plus a seam turning to tuck underneath before stitching in place. (See detail near hemline.)

(5) **Stand collar pattern**
Leaving a small space at CF, measure the rest of the neckline (lay patterns together to make this easier) and cut a collar to this measurement × 2.5 cm wide. Collar may be cut straight on such a simple type of garment.

Refer to Fig. 57

(6) **Sleeve and cuff patterns**
Choose the Extra Flat Headed Sleeve Block which will give the widest and most casual looking effect. Outline the block. No change to the general shape is necessary but slight curving of the wrist line is beneficial to shirt sleeves − raise 0.5 cm above

straight line on front, drop 1 cm below line on back. This allows a little extra length over the elbow to ease any strain on the fabric.

To work out cuff length, example size 12:

wrist	=	16 cm
ease	=	3
buttonstand	=	1.5
buttonhole stand	=	1.5
		22 cm

Cut pattern 22 cm long × 5 cm deep. Mark a fold line through centre (finished cuff depth − 2.5 cm). To allow sleeve opening: leave a 3.5 cm gap (c−a) on back sleeve, just left of SG line. This gap replaces the conventional slit opening and is the easiest way of providing an opening, forming a pleat when cuff is fastened.

To position cuff on sleeve: measure b−c on sleeve and transfer measurement to cuff, marking balance mark (b) that will match to underarm seam of sleeve.

Pocket and front edge details

Refer to Fig. 58

(7) Trace (lift off) pocket shape from its position on front of nightshirt. Allow a 2.5 cm height addition for the turn-over band, then a seam allowance all around. When making up, the turn-over band is pressed down onto the right side and top-stitched in place. This is a particularly quick and simple method of providing a banded effect, but note that a reversible (same both sides) fabric must be used as the construction method reveals the wrong side of the fabric.

The front edges of the nightshirt are dealt with in exactly the same way.

Note Other uses: shirts, beach shirts, dresses.

Nightshirt

Fig. 56

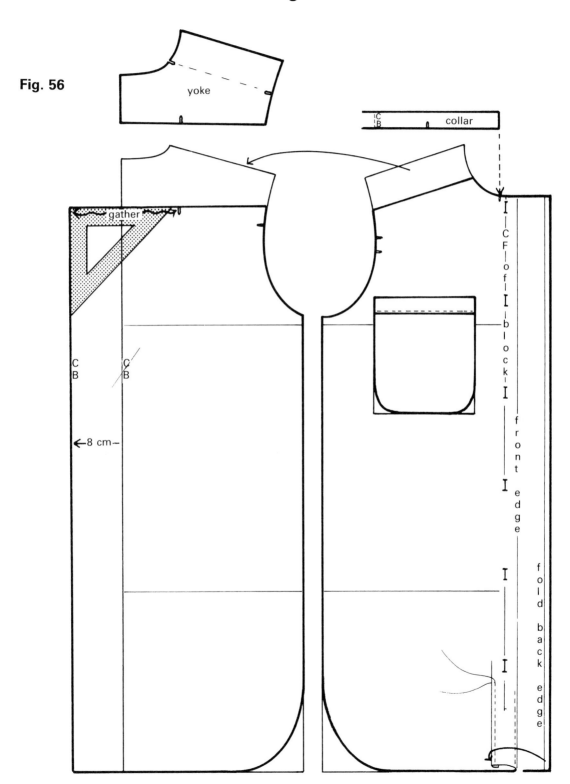

yoke

collar

C
B

gather

C
B

C
B

←8 cm–

C F of block front edge

fold back edge

Fig. 57

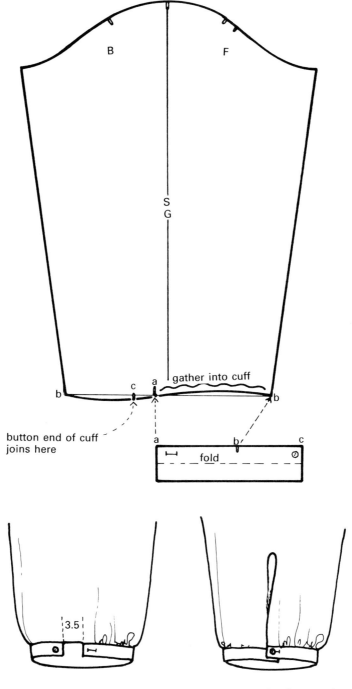

B   F

S
G

gather into cuff

b   c   a   b

button end of cuff
joins here

a   b   c

fold

3.5

sleeve opening of 3.5 cm
allows hand to pass
easily through

sleeve opening forms a pleat
when cuff is fastened

Fig. 58

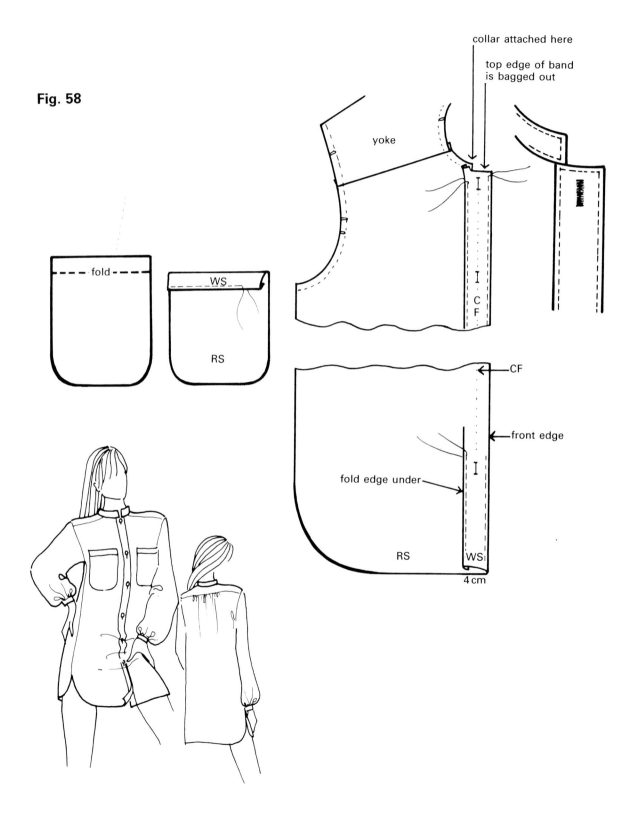

collar attached here

top edge of band
is bagged out

yoke

fold

WS

RS

I
C
F

CF

front edge

fold edge under

I

RS

WS

4 cm

PYJAMAS

Originally these were loose silk or cotton trousers, tied round the waist, worn by Muslim men and women. As adopted by Westerners, they are worn either for sleeping or for lounging in.

Fast, successful cutting of pyjamas relies much on the correct choice of block to start with. They are essentially roomy garments and are best cut from a loose, unfitted block. The Loose-Fitting Dartless Block suits this purpose admirably. Other closer-fitting blocks may be used but only in conjunction with stretch fabrics.

These pyjamas have a double breasted, easy fitting top, cut from the Loose Fitting Dartless Block. It has a CB inverted pleat (soft or pressed in) and rounded patch pockets.

The bottoms are cut from the Trouser Block but with modifications: the waist to crutch measurement (body rise) is lengthened and extra width is allowed through the pattern, both allowing plenty of room when bending. The waist is elasticated; the hem has a rounded slit detail at the ankle.

Pyjamas — easy fitting and double breasted

106

PYJAMA TOP
Refer to Fig. 59
(1) Outline the Loose-Fitting Dartless Block
    (page 30), lengthening if required – block comes to
    hip level. Enlarge neckline by lowering 1 cm at CB,
    1.5 cm at shoulder and 2 cm at CF. Draw new
    neckline curve starting with short right angles from

CB and CF. Continue the new neckline 10 cm
beyond CF and 2 cm down from squared line. From
this corner draw double breasted edge to cross CF
approximately 40 cm from neck. Curve well down
into hem line. Draw in button and buttonhole
positions.
(2) **Make addition to CB for inverted pleat.** Here,

Pyjama top

Fig. 59

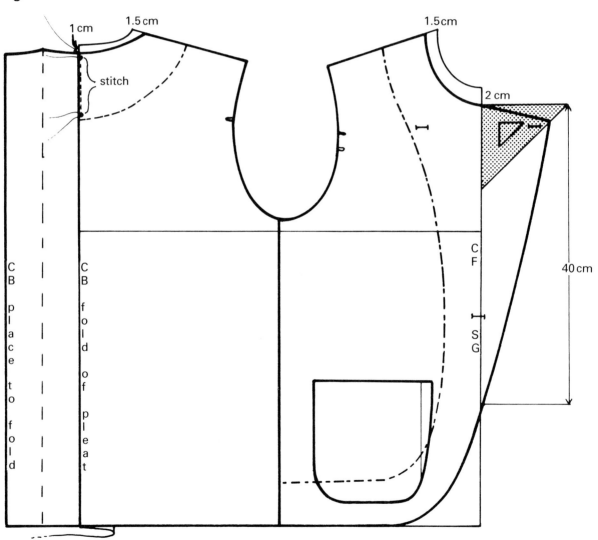

inner facing
edges

10 cm is added to the half pattern (20 cm total pleat). Mirror the back neck shaping, so that when pleat is in place it will run in line with neck edge.

(3) **Draw pocket shape**, well sited between curved front edge and side seam. Note the addition of 2 cm to top of front edge of pocket. This gives the optical illusion that the pocket is straight despite it being set against this curved edge.

(4) **Facings** need to be wide enough to ensure buttonholes are on double fabric (top inner buttonhole especially).

(5) In this example, the ordinary Loose-Fitting Dartless Sleeve Block has been used, but the Extra Flat Headed version could be substituted if an even looser, shirt-like sleeve is required. Whichever is used, shape the wrist lightly − raising 0.5 cm on front sleeve, dropping 0.5 cm on back. A narrow facing for the wrist may be necessary if fabric is not very pliable, otherwise a small hem allowance will be sufficient − turned up and top-stitched into place.

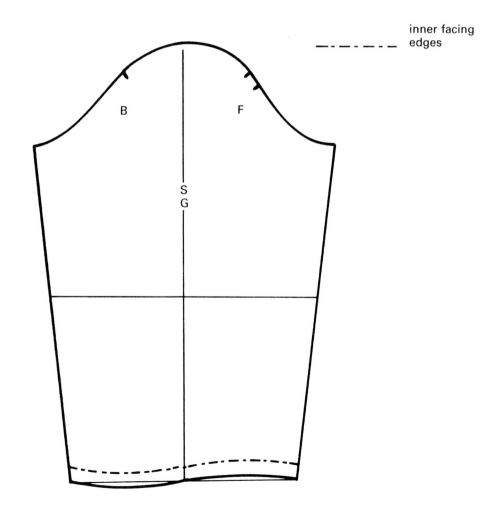

inner facing edges

PYJAMA BOTTOMS

Refer to Fig. 60 and design sketch

(1) Draw a line through the centre of your paper, in excess of the Trouser Block length. Place the front block with its outside leg along this line and pivot pattern out from side hem point to 5 cm away from line at hip line. Holding or weighting the block in this position, outline it up to the hip line only and mark the position of the original SG line at the hem and the waist.

(2) Remove block; connect this SG line, lengthening it well beyond the waist level. Measure 3 cm up from the hip line, replace hip line of block on this upper mark and, aligning the SG lines, finish outlining the block. Ignore the waist darts — these will

contribute to the fullness.

This has the effect of introducing 3 cm extra length from waist to crutch and 5 cm extra width at hip level, loosening the pattern for a pyjama fit.

(3) Repeat this whole procedure with the back Trouser Block, but before completing the outline of the hip to waist portion a further addition of 3 cm into the *CB length only* (pivoting from raised hip point) will provide even more room for comfortable bending.

(4) **Complete the pattern** by re-drawing the new CF and CB lines where additions have been made. Connect waistlines with a flowing curve. Finally, shorten the hem by 3 cm (length gained at hip) so as to maintain original waist to hem length.

Pyjama bottoms

Fig. 60

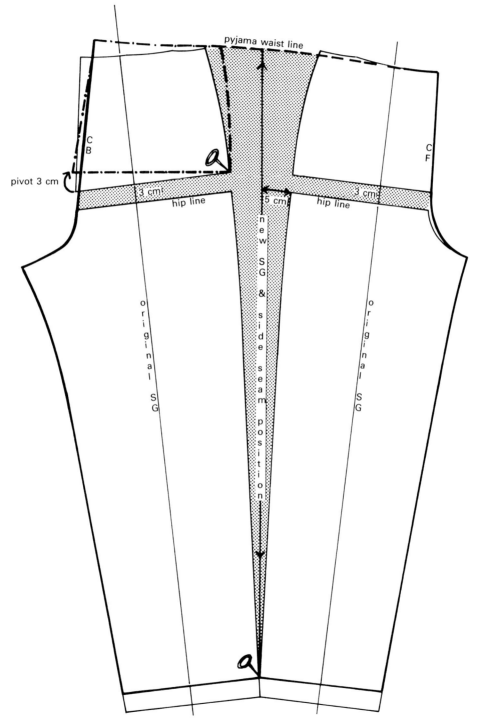

Refer to Fig. 61

(5) **To make height addition for elastic casing**
First determine the width of the elastic – example here is 2 cm wide – and the width of the 'frill' above the casing – 3 cm. Add these amounts in total above the new waistline, then double this amount to provide the back of the frill/casing.

(6) **To make ankle scallop**, measure 6 cm out and 10 cm up and connect with symmetrical curves.

(7) Add seam turnings to pattern. Make a narrow facing for trouser hem (dot-dash line) which will be held in place by 1 cm wide top-stitching.

Note The pattern works well with back and front cut in one piece as the diagrams show, but in the case of fabric width restrictions use the new side seam position as a dividing line.

Other uses: pyjama top patterns can adapt to light-weight jacket styles; pyjama bottom patterns will also produce lightweight day or evening pants.

Fig. 61

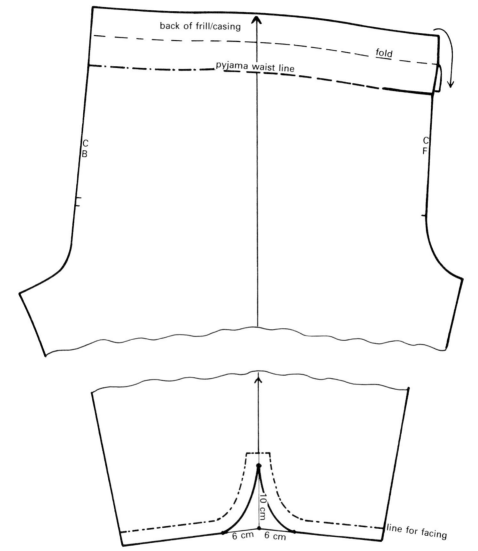

SLEEP-SUIT

A two-piece sleeping suit, the top of which can be worn tucked in or loose outside. It has a scooped neckline and a kimono-type cap sleeve detailed to match the suit bottom. The Dartless Bodice is the block closest in fit and shape, although a little extra width around the bust will provide a more comfortable sleeping garment.

The bottoms are a wrap-around style — not only at the waist but also through the legs! Being generously cut in all directions they are supremely comfortable.

Both garments are finished with a lace edging. Suitable fabrics: almost any lightweight soft fabric, e.g. cotton lawn, cotton voile, batiste.

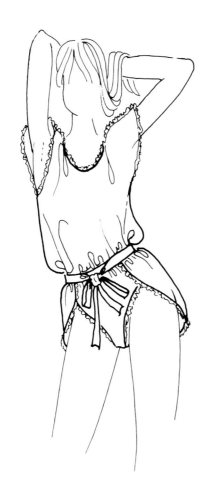

Sleep-suit

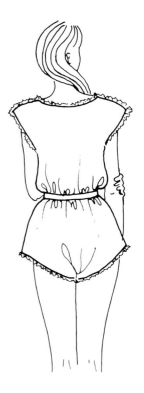

SLEEP-SUIT TOP
Refer to Fig. 62
(1) Outline the Dartless Bodice Block to the waist.
Lengthen as required – here 15 cm is added
beyond CB waistline and squared across to CF.
(2) Decide how loose the garment is designed to be
around the bust. The Dartless Block has 10 cm ease
over the bust. The example shown here has 16 cm.
Adjust side seams equally, squaring from bust line
through adjusted points down to hem line.
(3) Raise ends of block shoulders by 1.5 cm, re-
drawing new shoulder seams well beyond armhole.
Decide on length of shoulder/sleeve (here 24 cm
from original neck point) and mark corners. Lower
armhole 1 cm below bustline and connect this to

new shoulder corner, forming edge of sleeve.
Round off corners *after* re-shaping neckline so that
you can judge the relationship of the curves to each
other.
Re-shaping neckline:
(4) **To scoop neckline** measure 8 cm along shoulders.
Re-draw neckline down to 6 cm below block neck
in front and 4 cm at the back. Check the flow of the
curve with shoulders placed together.

Now curve shoulder ends, and hem corners to
match. Place a balance mark for height of slit and
another at base of armhole.

No facings are necessary – edges finished with
lace (or frill).

Sleep-suit top

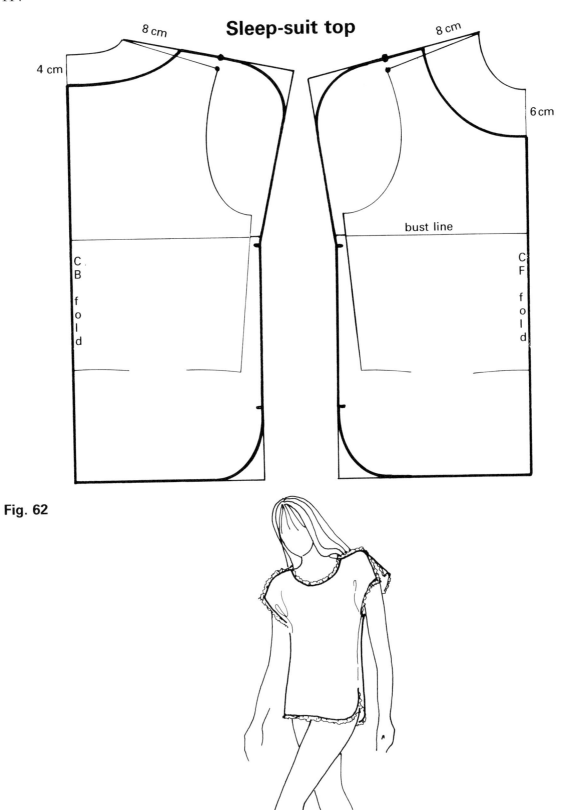

8 cm

8 cm

4 cm

6 cm

bust line

C
B
f
o
l
d

C
F
f
o
l
d

Fig. 62

SLEEP-SUIT BOTTOMS
Refer to Fig. 63

$0-1$ = body hip measurement plus 5 cm ease ÷ 2.
  2 = midway point for front side seam.
$1-3$ = body rise plus 9 cm.
$0-4$ = body rise plus 12 cm.
$0-5$ = 1 cm added for length over bottom. Curve line
      across to beyond point 2.
$\left.\begin{matrix} 3-6 \\ 4-7 \end{matrix}\right\}$ = 8 cm, half crutch width.
$2-8$ = 6 cm overlap on back side seam.

Connect $7-8$ with a straight guide line and divide line in three. Further divide the crutch end in half. For back leg shaping refer to Fig. 63. Connect $2-6$ with a straight guide line and proceed as for back.

To fit the waistband – example size 12:
Front waist $(1-2)$ is gathered to 17 cm, total 34 cm (increasing 2 cm per size).
Back waist $(5-8)$ is gathered to 22 cm, total 44 cm (increasing 2 cm per size).

Sleep-suit bottoms

Fig. 63

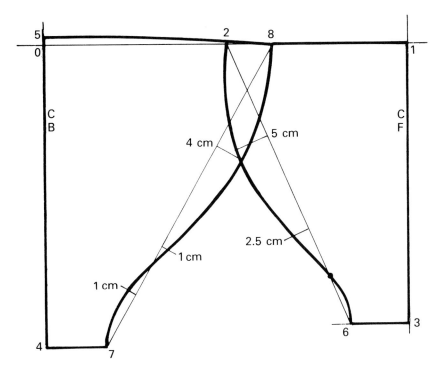

116

Refer to Fig. 64

For front waistband: cut one pattern 34 cm long × twice the required depth.

For back waistband/ties: cut one pattern 150 cm long (44 cm plus two tie ends each of 53 cm). Depth as for front.

Note 1 The crutch seam may be eliminated and front and back cut in one, as in Fig. 64(a).

Note 2 Cut on the bias or straight grain; the garment will hang better if cut on the bias.

Note 3 As the style is so loose the height addition at CB waist is less than usual. (For comparison see the briefs and panties blocks, on pages 81–89).

Note 4 Leg edges could be finished in the following ways:

(a) Overlocked and edgestitched − the least expensive.

(b) Bound with self or contrast fabric − moderately expensive.

(c) Frill or lace edged (as in this example) − the most expensive.

Note 5 Closure of the waistband (before tying) could be with snap fasteners *or* buttons and buttonholes. Whichever is chosen, the use of a double fastening on each side allows an adjustable waist size. See Fig. 64(b) and Fig. 64(c).

Note 6 Other uses: the sleepsuit top pattern will produce a lightweight blouse/top pattern ... and the sleepsuit bottoms could make an interesting pair of beach shorts.

Sleep-suit bottoms

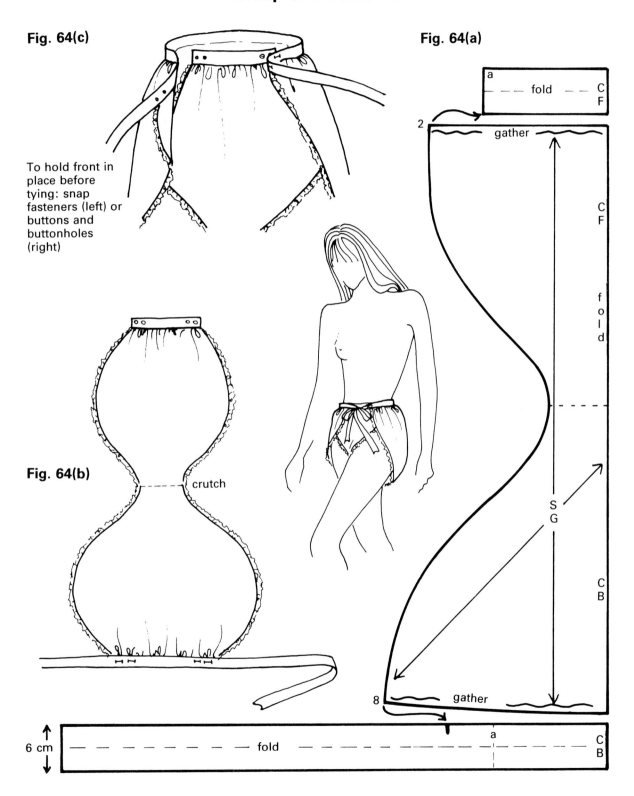

Fig. 64(c)

To hold front in place before tying: snap fasteners (left) or buttons and buttonholes (right)

Fig. 64(b)

crutch

6 cm

fold

Fig. 64(a)

a

fold — C F

2

gather

C F

f o l d

S G

C B

8

gather

a

C B

DRESSING-GOWNS AND HOUSECOATS, BATHROBES AND NEGLIGÉES

These are all styled from generous sized blocks to make the garments more comfortable by not inhibiting free movement even when worn over a nightdress or pyjamas. The main differences between them arise not from any striking difference in styling but from the fabrics, most suited to their different uses, that they are cut in, e.g. wool, man-made pile fabrics, quilted cotton/polyesters, towelling and sheer fabrics such as voile.

The Loose-Fitting Dartless Block is very suitable for most of the styles that follow except the negligée which, having narrower shoulders, is best cut from the ordinary Dartless Block.

Note Dressing gowns are often cut collarless so that pyjama collars can be worn outside without a clash of styles. This has further merits with co-ordinating nightwear ranges.

Fig. 65
Body pattern

Dressing-gown

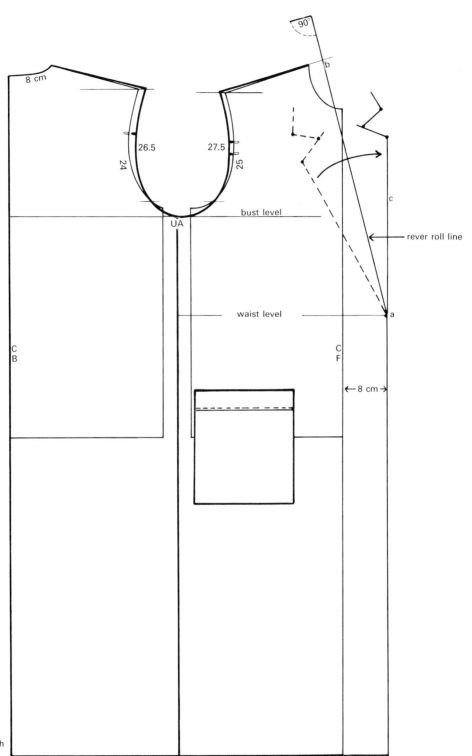

90°

b

8 cm

26.5   27.5

24   25

bust level

UA

c

rever roll line

waist level   a

C
B

C
F

← 8 cm →

CB length
120 cm

Dressing-gown

BODY PATTERN

Refer to Fig. 65

(1) Outline the Loose-Fitting Dartless Block, lengthening as required (in this example nape−hem = 120 cm).

To further enlarge for a generously cut dressing-gown add:

2.5 cm to each side seam
1 cm to each shoulder length
1 cm to X back and chest width, at levels halfway around the armholes.

Lower the underarm to bust level, re-shaping armhole to touch original at 2.5 cm above bust level. Measure new back and front armholes in readiness for sleeve adjustment.

SLEEVE

Refer to Fig. 66

(2) Outline the Extra Flat Headed Sleeve Block (on page 32) including points 1, 2, 3 and 4. Lengthen line 3−4. Apply the new back armhole measurement plus 0.5 cm ease, along the curve between 1 and 3 extending as necessary to 3a. Re-draw the new back sleeve head curve against the edge of the block sleeve head whilst positioned midway 1 and 3a (rather as one might do when grading). See Fig. 67. Repeat with the front sleeve.

(3) **Refer to Fig. 68**

The sleeve head is now the correct size for the new enlarged armhole. Complete it by transferring balance marks from armhole, measuring up from U/A points.

Dressing-gown sleeves are best kept fairly narrow at the wrist for practical reasons (so they don't dip in the marmalade!), therefore remove equal amounts from each side and draw a straight seam line up to 3a and 4a.

Because the sleeve is now shapelier, the wrist will appear more level if curved. Raise 1 cm at the centre and curve the front wrist as in Fig. 68 − the back wrist may remain straight but angled. Check the smoothness of the line by forming the pattern into a roll, bringing the new underarm seams together, so that you can see the sleeve hem as it will appear when the sleeve is sewn together.

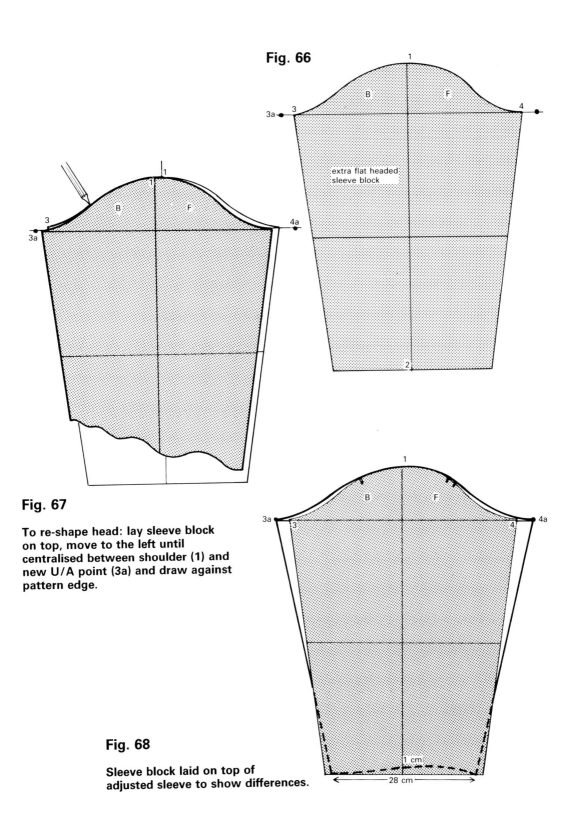

Fig. 66

extra flat headed
sleeve block

Fig. 67

To re-shape head: lay sleeve block
on top, move to the left until
centralised between shoulder (1) and
new U/A point (3a) and draw against
pattern edge.

Fig. 68

Sleeve block laid on top of
adjusted sleeve to show differences.

COLLAR

Refer to Fig. 65

(4a) Add wrap to CF and decide on depth of rever.

(4b) Add amount of collar stand beyond shoulder/neck point (in this case 2.5 cm). Rule the rever rolling line between a and b and continue beyond b equal to half the back neck measurement. Square to the left.

(4c) Draw in rever shape and front collar where they will lie in wear. Transfer to other side of rever roll line for pattern outline.

Refer to Fig. 69

(4d) Divert rever roll line to point d, located 5 cm along squared line, i.e. double the collar stand allowance (if you wish the collar to lay flatter on the shoulders, increase the diversion still further). Square on line b−d for CB of collar.

(4e) Apply amount of collar stand to the left. Square down toward shoulder and blend line well into the neck curve, missing the CF neck point if necessary to run into a good line with the rever. (See this piece trimmed off in Fig. 70.)

(4f) Apply amount of collar fall to the right (fall = twice the stand allowance). Square from CB and curve line well into front of collar.

Refer to Fig. 70

(4g) Trace off the collar to separate it from the front bodice (including the balance mark at breakpoint). Do not be tempted to separate the patterns by cutting as it is all too easy to lose the shoulder/neckpoint corner of the dressing-gown front (marked x on Fig. 69), necessarily overlapped during the course of collar construction. This would result in a front shoulder seam too short for the back!

Finally, check size of collar against size of neckline and place a balance mark at the shoulder.

123

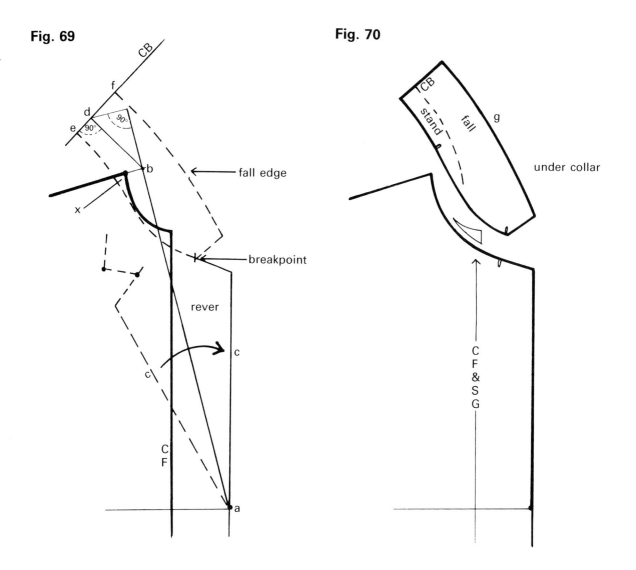

Fig. 69

CB

f

d

e 90° 90°

b

x

fall edge

breakpoint

rever

c

c'

c'

C
F

a

Fig. 70

CB

stand

fall

g

under collar

C
F
&
S
G

Refer to Fig. 71

(5a) Complete by cutting a top collar pattern a little larger than the under collar.

(5b) Make back and front facings to finish the neck and front edge. (Front facing may be grown-on if fabric width allows, i.e. cut in one with the front dressing-gown pattern and folded on the edge.)

(5c) Make a belt pattern three times the waist measurement ...

(5d) ... and a pocket pattern as planned in Fig. 65. Add a turn-over at the top to be stitched down on the *right side* if fabric has no discernible right and wrong side, or onto the *wrong side* if it has.

Fig. 71(a)

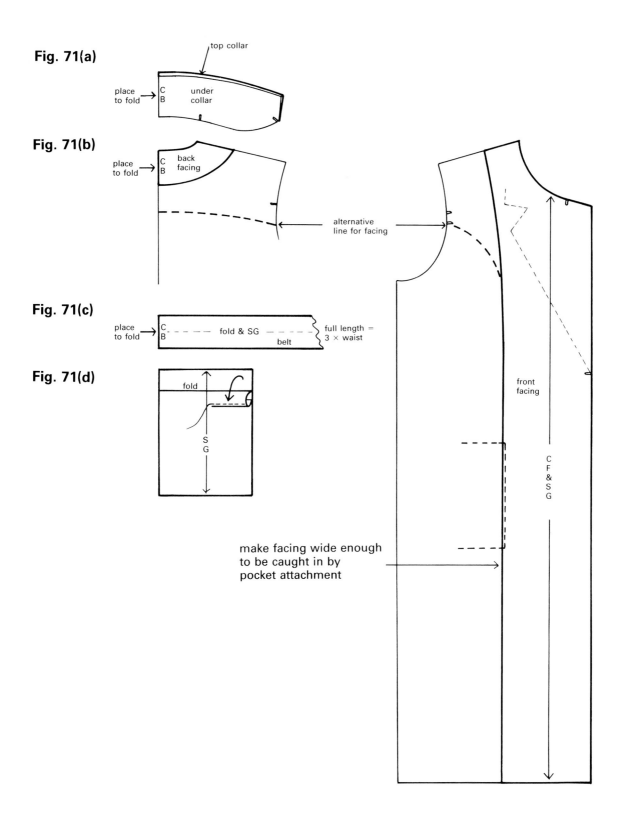

top collar

place to fold → C B   under collar

Fig. 71(b)

place to fold → C B   back facing

alternative line for facing

Fig. 71(c)

place to fold → C B   — — fold & SG — — belt   full length = 3 × waist

Fig. 71(d)

fold

S G

front facing

C F & S G

make facing wide enough to be caught in by pocket attachment

Bathrobe

This style has simple T-shaped kimono sleeves and a generously wrapped front, ideal for lounging at home or on the beach, where the hood is a particularly useful addition.

Suitable fabrics: terry towelling, brushed cotton or other absorbent materials.

Bathrobe

Firstly, adapt the Loose Fitting Dartless Block to a simple kimono shape
Refer to Fig. 72

(1) Outline the blocks, placing shoulders together but with a 2 cm gap between shoulder/armhole points.
(2) Fit the Extra Flat Headed Sleeve Block into the armhole cavity with the underarm points touching the side seams and equidistant from the bodice underarm points.
(3) To further enlarge for a generously cut bathrobe, add 2.5 cm to the underarm seams of sleeve and bodice.
(4) Connect a straight (dotted) line between shoulder/neckpoint and centre wrist point. This becomes the kimono shoulder seam and dividing line. Trace patterns from draft separately.

Fig. 72
Positioning of bodice and sleeve blocks for a kimono style

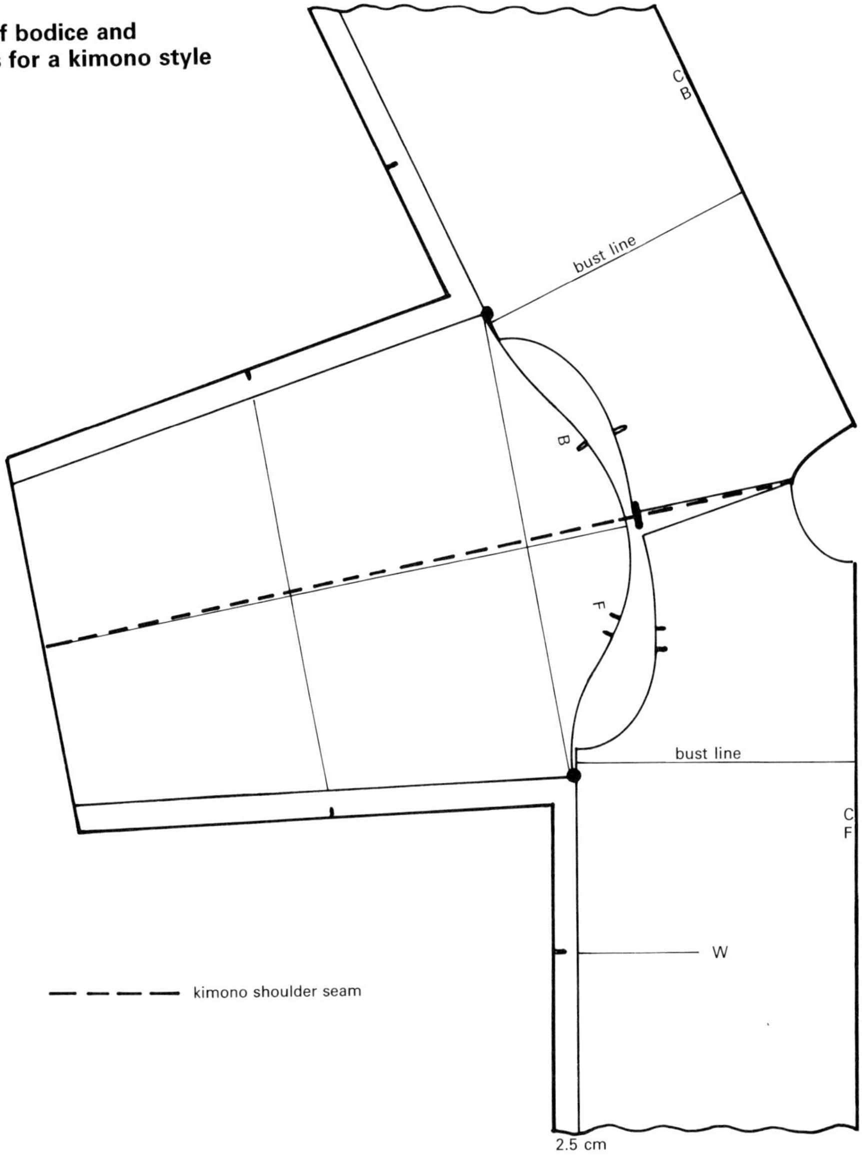

128

(5) **Equalizing back and front kimono slants**
Refer to Fig. 73
On such a simple kimono shape it is customary for the sleeve and body underarm seams to be identical in angle and in length. The best way to check this is by laying the traced-off front pattern on top of the back, matching the shoulder/neck points – there will be a parallel gap between CF and CB. Note that the back sleeve angle is 'tighter' than the front. To equalize them, slash the back from the underarm point almost up to the shoulder point and open until the sleeve seams

run in line with the front as in Fig. 74.

(6) **To complete the back kimono pattern**, fill in:
   (a) the gap between shoulder and underarm
   (b) the gap between back and front side seam
   (c) the dent on back shoulder/sleeve seam.

The extra width gained across the back is beneficial to the loose bathrobe style which follows. The front pattern needs no adjustment at this stage, but serves as a guide to the back.
   The blocks are now ready for styling.

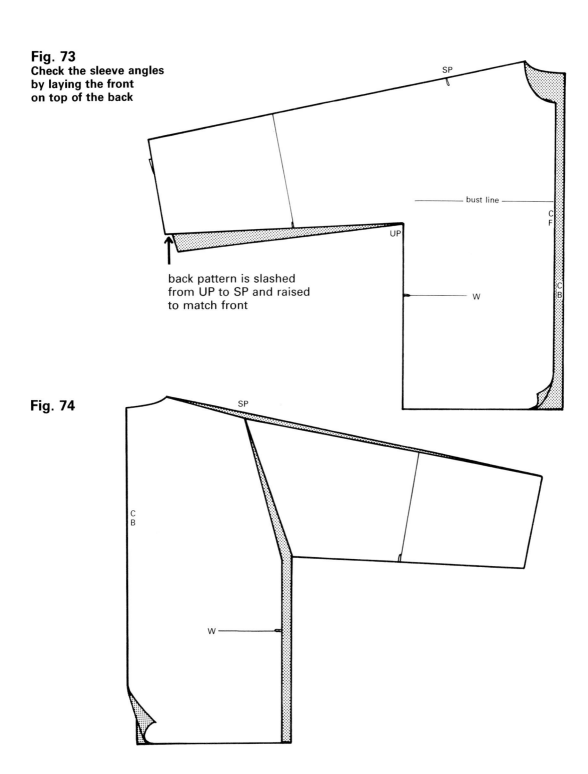

Fig. 73
Check the sleeve angles by laying the front on top of the back

back pattern is slashed from UP to SP and raised to match front

Fig. 74

Refer to Fig. 75

(7) Lengthen as required – the nape to hem length as in design sketch = 120 cm. Add a 12 cm wrap allowance beyond and parallel to CF.

Round off underarm corners measuring out 6.5 cm along midway angles. Curve the lines from elbow to waist.

(8) **The hood pattern** is cut in one with the front bathrobe but separated at the back and shaped. The neckline must be enlarged to take the hood successfully.

Mark new neckpoints (a) 2 cm from block neckline along shoulders. Re-draw the back neckline from (a) to a new CB neckpoint 1 cm lower than block.

(9) **For front hood**: continue the CF line up to hood height (b), measured 43 cm from base of front neck. Continue the wrap line also to this height. Square lightly across. Mark point (c).

c–d = 1 cm. Connect d–b, continuing line.
b–e = 5.5 cm

For seam adjoining back hood: draw a line parallel to CF from (a) and curve from 20 cm above into (e).

(10) **For back hood**: measure the new back neckline curve (CB–a). Apply this measurement between (f) and (g) on a line squared from the extended CB. Square up from (g).

g–a = 1.5 cm. (a) on hood will match (a) on back neckline.
f–h = 37 cm. Square across.
h–i = 14 cm

For seam adjoining front hood: square down from i–j, then curve line down to (a). Place a balance mark for matching seams approximately 6 cm up from (a) on back and front hood.
For CB rounded seam:

h–k = 5 cm
CB line–l = 2 cm. Curve line through points i–k–l–f.

(11) Refining the fit of the hood:
Round off the corner between front hood and shoulder seam (dotted line).
Transfer this shaping onto back hood and shoulder.

(12) **Note**   When the hood is cut following these instructions it frames the face quite loosely. If you would prefer a closer fit (maybe when using stretch fabrics) fold out a 4 cm wide 'dart' on front hood (dot-dash lines), smoothing the hood edge afterwards to fill in the dent. This of course alters the angle of the hood in relation to the front pattern (beware when using striped fabric!). Whichever hood you choose, the CF line serves as the straight grain.

The hood edge (and sleeve hems) may be rolled over.

(13) Complete the pattern with a belt and pocket:
Belt pattern length = waist measurement × 3, which will provide a generous length.
Finished width = 2.5 cm, therefore pattern width = 5 cm.
Add seam allowances all around pattern.
Belt loop positions: centre of belt loop is 5 cm down from waist level.

(14) **Welt pocket**
Refer to Fig. 75
For the height position measure 13 cm from waist level, and tilt line for the required pocket angle. The welt should not be overlapped by the front edge when worn; therefore its distance from the CF should be no less than the wrap width. Note that the shape of the pocket bag is rounded towards the CF, i.e. hand-shaped, and therefore more comfortable to use than a squarer, symmetric shape.

Fig. 75

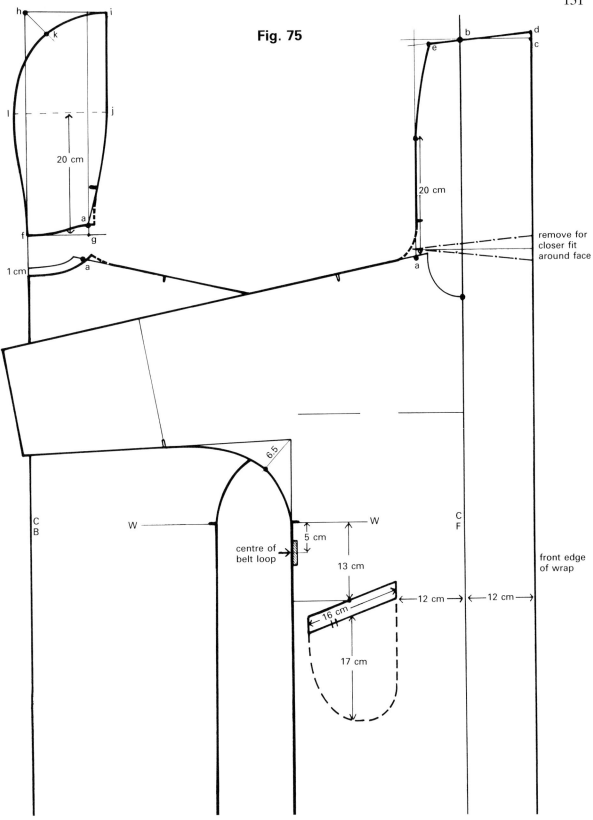

20 cm

20 cm

l ⋯ j

h   i

k

a

f   g

1 cm

a

a

remove for
closer fit
around face

6.5

C
B

W ⟶   ⟵ W

centre of
belt loop

5 cm

13 cm

16 cm

17 cm

C
F

front edge
of wrap

⟵ 12 cm ⟶ ⟵ 12 cm ⟶

b   d
e   c

Refer to Fig. 76

(14a) Trace welt from plan in Fig. 75 and cut on the fold for back of welt.
Place balance marks towards one end.

(14b) Trace inner pocket bag that will lie against garment from the plan, adding balance marks to match the welt.

(14c) Cut another pocket bag pattern with 2 cm extra height to cover the gap caused by the welt and pocket seam turnings.

Note   Fabric width: kimono sleeved styles require very wide fabrics if the back pattern is placed to the fold. If your chosen fabric is not wide enough there are two alternatives:

(a)   Introduce a centre back seam.

(b)   Keep the centre back on the fold and place a seam separating the sleeve from the body, as shown in Fig. 77. In this case the lower part of front and back sleeve may then be joined together; use the former seam line as the straight grain.

Fig. 76

Welt pocket pattern

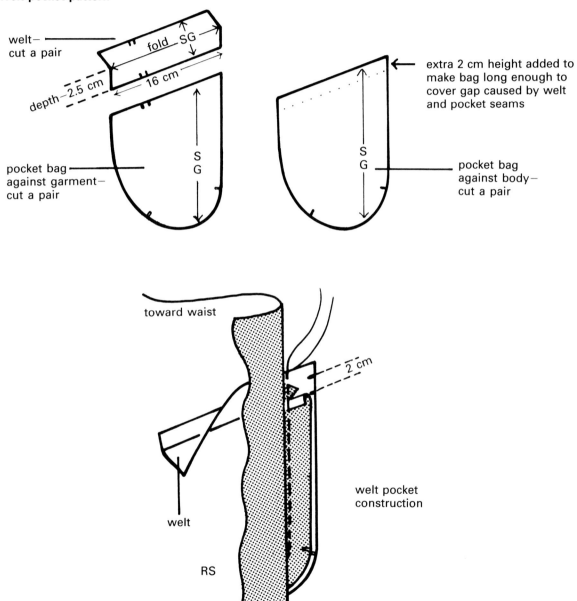

welt —
cut a pair

fold SG

16 cm

depth — 2.5 cm

pocket bag
against garment —
cut a pair

S
G

extra 2 cm height added to
make bag long enough to
cover gap caused by welt
and pocket seams

pocket bag
against body —
cut a pair

S
G

toward waist

2 cm

welt

welt pocket
construction

RS

134

Fig. 77

**Separation of sleeve from
body for narrow width fabrics**

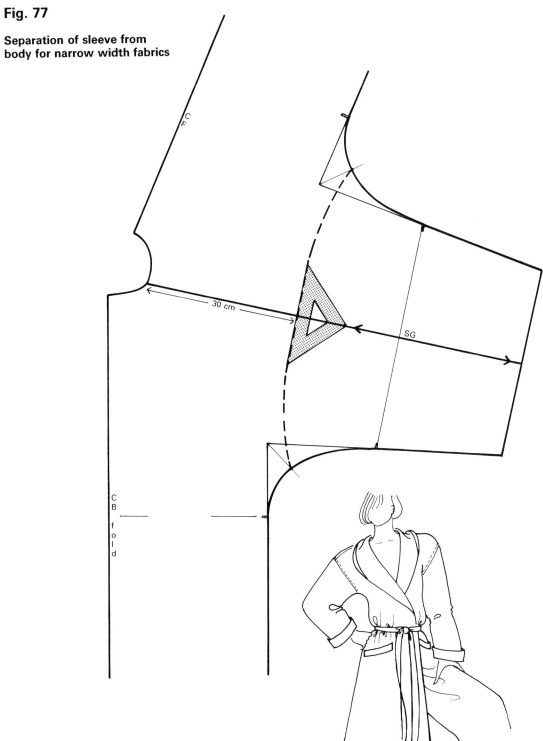

CF

30 cm

SG

C
B
f
o
l
d

Negligées

These are essentially soft, feminine, wrapped garments which may be worn over (co-ordinated) nightdresses. They are invariably cut in transparent or translucent fabrics, with a decided air of glamour.

This particular style, with a set-in sleeve gathered onto the shoulder, is best cut from the Dartless Bodice Block which has narrower shoulders than the Loose Dartless Block as used for the dressing-gown and bathrobe.

The basic draft
Refer to Fig. 78
(1) Outline the Dartless Bodice Block with at least 30 cm space between UPs. The waistline is unnecessary – merely indicate its level. Lengthen as required – here CB nape to hem = 110 cm (120 cm when frill is attached later). Square across for provisional hemline; square down from UP's for provisional side seams.

(2) Add initial flare to side seams – 15 cm from each provisional side seam at hem level. Curve the hemline as directed in Fig. 8, on page 44 of Petticoat Block section.
Refer to Fig. 79

(3) **To successfully increase the flare further**, slash from hem to centre shoulder on each pattern and spread 15 cm. (Such large amounts of flare are best added *around* the body rather than in total at the side seams.) Fill the dent in back and front shoulder seams (caused by slashing and spreading) by connecting each end with a straight line. Place the new shoulders together so that neckline and armhole may be altered in good flowing lines.

(4) **Neckline**
Lower the back neckline 1 cm. Scoop the front neckline into a low, curvy V shape (note straight guide line between shoulder and bustline). It should cross CF on or near the bust line. For the front wrap extend 7 cm at waist level (for double button fastening) and 10 cm at hip, which is 20 cm below the waist, curving around to the new side seam in a good line.

(5) **Armhole**
When designing sleeves with full, gathered heads it is not advisable to set them into the normal armhole as this can promote a somewhat droopy shouldered appearance. These sleeves look better if their position is exaggerated, according to the design – either lifted up on the shoulder for a square look or set well down below the shoulder bone for a definite dropped shouldered look.

In this example where a square look is required, remove 2 cm from the shoulder length and re-shape the armhole accordingly. Remember that whatever length is taken from the shoulder should be added to the sleeve head height so that overall length is not lost.

(6) **Blouson, waist casing and buttonhole positions**
Refer to Fig. 80
The blouson effect is required around most of the waistline but not on the front wrap edge, where it would cause a gaping neckline. Cut the patterns along the now curved waistline, dividing the back in two but leaving the front joined at the wrap edge. Spread by the amount of blouson required, e.g. 8 cm (remember: whatever is added on the flat pattern appears halved in wear). Re-draw the side seams from UP to hem; the front wrap edge will need re-curving.

The bottom of the waist casing sits on the lower slashed line. Make the casing deep enough to accommodate the width of the elastic.

The buttonholes are planned through the middle of the casing and either side of CF/SG line (continued in line with the upper part of pattern). It is a good idea to extend the casing up to the front edge, even though elastic will stop just short of inner buttonhole position, so that buttonholes are made on double cloth for added strength.

(7) **Elastic casing pattern**
Refer to Fig. 81
Place the back and front patterns together at side seam and trace the shape of the elastic casing. Mark clearly where elastic will stop.

(8) **Sleeve**
Outline the sleeve block belonging to the Dartless Bodice Block. The wrist dart will not be needed. Firstly add to the sleeve head the 2 cm removed from the negligée shoulder. Then decide exactly where the head fullness is required by measuring down from the negligée shoulder seam (see dots on armhole on Fig. 80). Locate these points on the sleeve head and draw vertical lines ready for cutting and introducing fullness.

(9) **Sleeve width**
Before arranging cut sleeve pieces, draw a vertical line – which will act as the new sleeve centre/SG – and a right angled horizontal line – the new underarm line. Spread the sleeve sections evenly as shown. In this example 18 cm extra width has been allowed. Re-draw the sleeve head in a good rounded shape well above the original to provide the puffed head (4 cm at centre line), running smoothly into the unchanged underarm areas. Transfer the balance marks across, on a horizontal level, from the original block.

(10) **Sleeve length**
To provide the blouson effect above the wrist frill, simply add 5 cm in length below the block wrist line. Measure up from the new sleeve hem for the depth of frill (10 cm) and mark the position of the elastic casing parallel to the hem. Make a pattern for the casing.

(11) **The frill pattern**
Frills fall best when cut on the lengthwise grain (warp). The crosswise grain (weft) can be used but the frill will appear more bouncy and the pattern will have to be pieced.

The frill could be the same depth all the way round (10 cm) or as here, narrowed on either side of the waist level for a less cluttered look.

For generous gathering make the frill twice the length of the edge it will attach to. It is preferable to make a complete frill pattern – rather than a half pattern placed to the fold, which is not so easily placed correctly on the fabric when cutting out.

Fig. 78

Basic draft for negligée

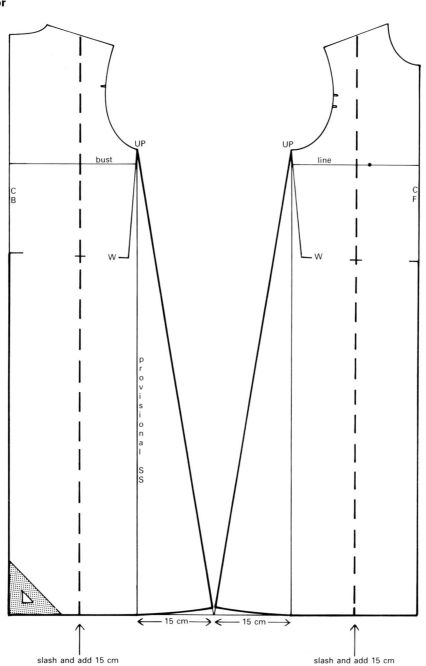

138

Fig. 79

**Adding more flare
to negligée**

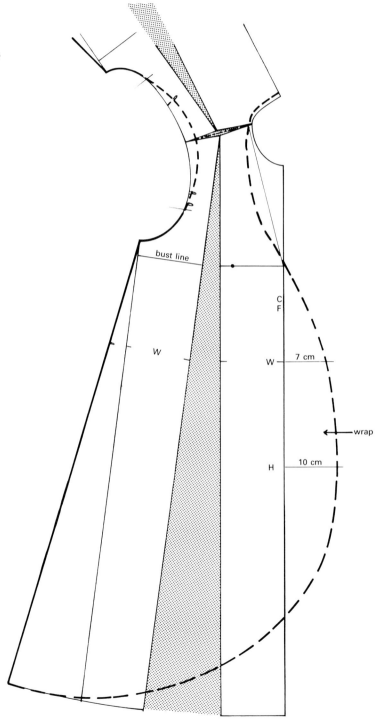

bust line

C
F

W — 7 cm

← wrap

H — 10 cm

W

Fig. 80

**Elastic casing and
'blouson' allowance**

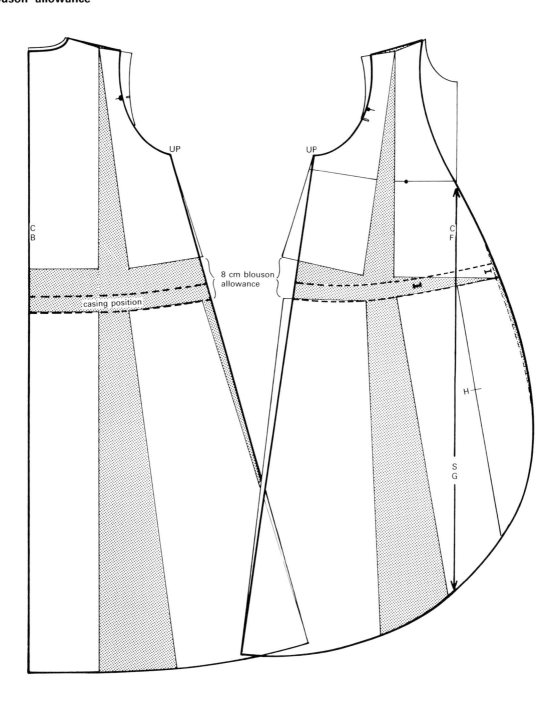

140

Fig. 81

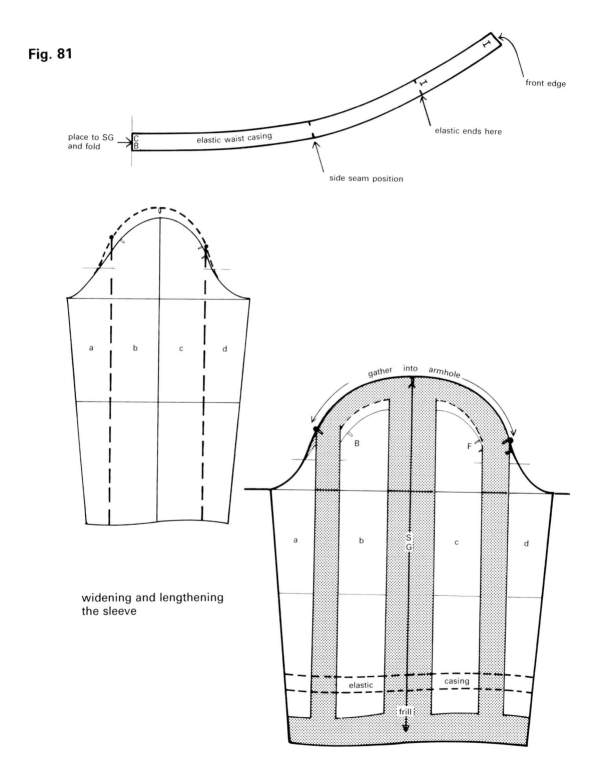

place to SG and fold

C
B

elastic waist casing

side seam position

elastic ends here

front edge

a b c d

widening and lengthening the sleeve

gather into armhole

B

F

a b

S G

c d

elastic casing

frill

BED-JACKET

Bed-jackets were more popular in the days before central heating but some people still like to wear them, not necessarily for warmth but more often to make themselves feel glamorous when they are unwell and confined to bed.

They are cut quite simply − with the interesting features in the upper half and often with a pretty sleeve design. The back is intentionally kept plain as any fullness would only get crushed and design details would not be seen anyway. The fastenings can be the simplest type − ties look prettier than buttons.

Suitable fabrics: almost any that are not heavy or stiff, or that crease readily, e.g. soft quilted or unquilted satin, cotton/polyester prints. Also, make full use of trimmings − strip lace, ribbons, frills, embroidery, etc.

Refer to Fig. 82

(1) Outline the back and front Dartless Bodice Block including the bust line. Lengthen to approximately 10 cm below waist and straighten side seams.

(2) **Draw yoke line** about 12 cm below CF neck, angled up to armhole as required. To introduce gathers — draw two vertical lines spaced over bust and entering yoke seams as shown. Cut and spread the sections parallel to each other and add the required amount in between each section (here 5 cm). Re-draw top seam, where it will gather into yoke, with a good curve. Place balance marks to control gathering.

(3) On such a style, with gathering at bust level, there is no need for a wrap-over on the CF; just mark tie positions.

For frill — measure complete CF edge plus neckline from CF to CB. Double this measurement to provide generous gathering. Double again for the complete pattern length. Suggestion for frill depth — 2.5 cm. To avoid the process of finishing the frill edge, cut the pattern on the fold, i.e. 5 cm deep altogether. Read further comments on frills in Negligée section, page 136.

(4) **Sleeve**

Refer to Fig. 83

Prepare the Dartless Bodice Sleeve Block similarly to the bodice — straighten the underarm seams by squaring from the underarm line. Add 3−5 cm in length to allow sleeve to puff just above elasticated wrist. Draw two vertical lines centrally through sleeve. Wrist dart can be ignored for this style.

(5) Cut on lines from the head down to, but not through, the wrist. Spread for gathering (here 5 cm at top of head in each section). Re-draw the head, lifting slightly at centre for a well-curved line. The wrist curve will also need adjusting. Finish wrist hem with lightweight elastication.

Bed-jacket

Fig. 82

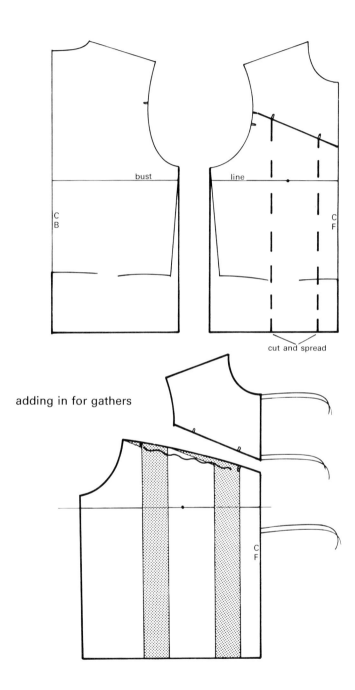

bust line

C B

C F

cut and spread

adding in for gathers

C F

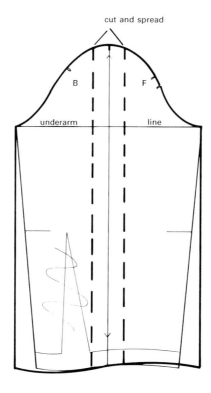

Fig. 83

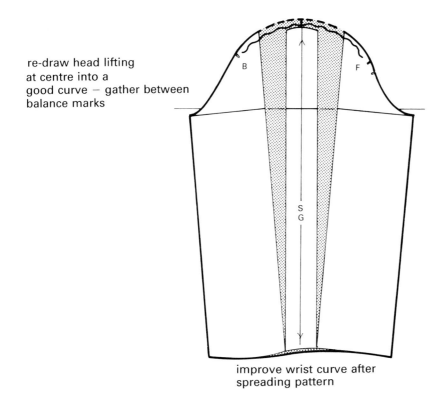

re-draw head lifting
at centre into a
good curve − gather between
balance marks

improve wrist curve after
spreading pattern

KIMONO

Originally kimonos were long, loose Japanese robes with wide sleeves, and were held together with a wide sash or obi – up to 30 cm wide and 4 metres long. Nowadays, at least in Europe, they are worn as rather elegant dressing-gowns or wraps and are also included in many leisurewear ranges.

They are cut on the simplest of lines, the pattern pieces being almost rectangular. The main interest is in the sleeves, which have the most effect on the overall appearance. They are usually very wide, sometimes even wing-like, as shown here in the main example. There is a traditional and ingeniously simple way of providing concealed pockets, as illustrated in Fig. 86. A gap is left when sewing both the side and sleeve seams. This gives access to the sleeve bottom which forms a pocket and at the same time allows freer arm movement.

Because kimonos have the minimum of seams they are wonderful vehicles for huge, spreading textile designs, these being most often placed on the back of the garment where they are uninterrupted by collars, openings, etc.

Suitable fabrics: silk or rayon or their synthetic equivalents and cotton (not too lightweight). Kimonos are often lined in a way which makes them reversible, e.g. one side in plain fabric, the other in a brightly coloured flamboyant print. Piped seams add interest. Traditional kimonos often have padded or quilted hemlines, helping them to hang well.

Basic Draft
Refer to Fig. 84

(1) Towards right-hand side of paper draw a vertical line for CB and CF. Towards the top draw a right-angled line for shoulder and sleeve.

Place the back of the Dartless Bodice Block in the corner and trace the outline. This acts as a guide to the neckline size, shoulder/sleeve length and waist level. Measure CB length; from nape − ankle = 140 cm.

(2) Transfer the shoulder point of the block onto the horizontal line and, placing the head of the Dartless Bodice Sleeve Block to this point, mark the elbow line as a guide to sleeve length.

(3) **Pattern width** $= \frac{1}{4}$ body hip measurement plus 8 cm ease. This amount of ease provides a fairly close-fitting kimono:

e.g. Size 12 $-\frac{1}{4}$ body hip $= 23.5$ cm
$\frac{1}{4}$ ease $\qquad\qquad\quad$ 8
$\overline{\qquad\qquad}$
31.5 cm
$\overline{\qquad\qquad}$

quadrupled for whole pattern $= 126$ cm

Increase the ease for a looser-fitting kimono. Draw a line parallel to CF and CB for side and sleeve seam. For armhole depth measure down $\frac{2}{3}$rds distance from shoulder to waist and mark U/A point.

(4) **Sleeve**
In this style the top sleeve length is 11 cm below elbow line. Square down for wrist opening and width of sleeve, which can vary from the minimum at U/A level to very wide at about $\frac{4}{5}$ths nape to ankle length. They may be shaped as required but are traditionally rounded on the *outer* corner and squared on the *inner*.

(5) **Wrap, Neckline and Collar**
For front wrap, add 12 cm width beyond CF starting at a level 30 cm below waist. This may be rounded at the hemline if required.

For back neck, widen block neckline by 1 cm.

For front neck/collar, connect a line from widened neckpoint to starting point of wrap. Square across 9 cm for end of collar, which may be straight or rounded. Continue the line beyond the shoulder for the back collar, measuring widened back neck curve for the length. Square across for CB of collar; width = 6 cm. Connect to lower front collar.

Refer to Fig. 85

(6) Trace the front and back kimono patterns separately from the basic draft, followed by the sleeve and collar.

Sash Finished width = 8 cm. Pattern measurements = 16 cm × 2 metres long. When making up kimono leave a gap between collar and neckline (from waist level down) to pull sash through, thereby avoiding crushing the collar. Sash may be tied at front or back.

(7) **Concealed pocket** If choosing the medium width sleeve you have the opportunity of making the end of the sleeve work as a pocket by seaming not only along the bottom but also a little way up towards the U/A point (see Fig. 85), leaving a gap for access as illustrated in Fig. 86. It would not be practical to do this with the widest width of sleeve.

Fig. 84

Kimono basic draft

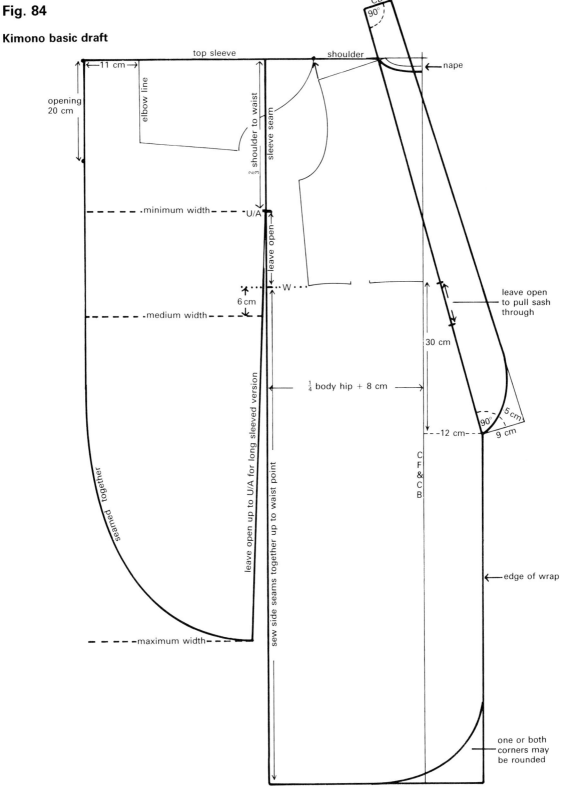

top sleeve

shoulder

nape

CB

90°

←11 cm→

opening
20 cm

elbow line

sleeve seam

$\frac{2}{3}$ shoulder to waist

minimum width — U/A

leave open

6 cm

W

medium width

leave open
to pull sash
through

30 cm

$\frac{1}{4}$ body hip + 8 cm

90° 5 cm

9 cm

–12 cm–

C
F
&
C
B

leave open up to U/A for long sleeved version

sew side seams together up to waist point

seamed together

maximum width

edge of wrap

one or both
corners may
be rounded

Fig. 85

Kimono — finished back and front

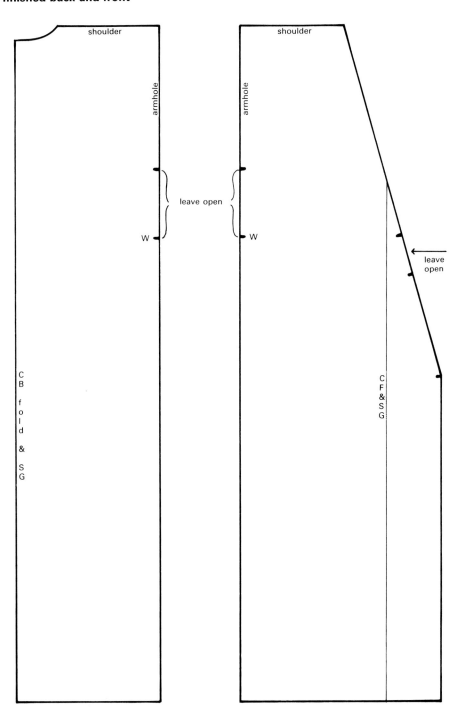

149

Fig. 85

Kimono — finished sleeve, collar and belt

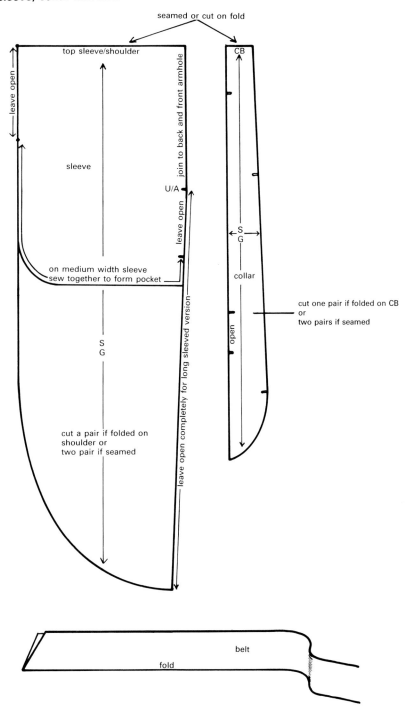

Fig. 86

U/A

W

pocket

gap left in underarm
sleeve seam for access
to pocket

PART 2 FURTHER DEVELOPMENTS

4 BEACH AND LEISUREWEAR

ONE-PIECE SWIMSUITS

Successful swimsuit cutting depends on a combination of factors which need careful consideration during the design and pattern-making processes.

(1) Choice of fabric and its suitability for the design: Stretch or non-stretch? The designs and patterns for each are necessarily quite different. See comments below and list of swimwear fabrics on page 155.

(2) Appropriate choice of blocks as a base from which to start:
As swimsuits nearly always fit the body closely, choose blocks that do the same. In the following instructions for two swimsuit blocks — one for slightly stretch and non-stretch fabrics, the other for stretch fabrics only — the same base has been used to make it easy to compare the two.

(3) Body trunk length, correctly measured and applied to the flat pattern: the lengthwise fit of a swimsuit is just as important as the fit around the body, especially as it is more difficult to alter once the garment is cut.

The following will help with specific problems and may be applied to all swimwear:

(1) Test the pattern by cutting a toile (a trial garment cut in similar but less expensive fabric than that chosen for the eventual garment in order to test the pattern and solve any problems before going into mass production — in many design rooms this is a matter of course and very good business practice). This is particularly important for stretch swimsuits. In this case use inexpensive jersey, and for styles in non-stretch fabrics substitute calico.

(2) Getting the crutch width right is vital — discomfort will result if cut either too wide or too narrow. Before you complete the pattern check it against a pantie that has been worn and found comfortable.

(3) The best types of seams to use:
Superlocked (narrow plain seams, pressed together, double stitched and overlocked). Nearest domestic equivalent is called 'overedge-stitch seam'.
Flat fell seams.

(4) Possible fastenings: hooks and eyes, the S hook, buttons, large (plastic) press-studs, grommets (jumbo eyelets) and lacing, self-ties and zips.
Use only woven nylon elastic — it stays elastic when wet.

(5) Pale coloured fabrics, especially if thin and fine, are inclined to be transparent when wet. If this is seen as a problem, the areas can be cut in double fabric or lined.

Swimwear Fabrics

Most specialist swimwear fabrics are composed wholly or mainly of synthetic fibres which offer several distinct advantages over natural fabrics:

(1) They are less absorbent, do not sag with the weight of water, dry more quickly and have wet strength.
(2) Those containing Lycra or Spanzelle offer a degree of control as well as being stretchy. More often than not the stretch is two-directional (weft *and* warp) which is essential for one-piece swimsuits.
(3) Single stretch (usually weft) should be reserved for two-piece swimsuits and bikinis, cut with the stretch going around the body.
(4) They are able to withstand exposure to sunlight, sea water and chlorinated water and are resistant to many chemicals and also to perspiration.

Stretch fabrics suitable for all swimwear	Non-stretch woven fabrics suitable for bikinis, two-piece swimsuits and one-piece swimsuits when stretch is not important
Lycra Spanzelle stretch towelling cotton jersey ciré (surface treated for a seal-like appearance) (1) Pattern pieces should be placed on whichever straight grain will produce the maximum stretch around the body. (2) Any interfacings, linings etc., must stretch also (or be cut on bias).	seersucker cotton piqué denim gingham crinkle crêpe sharkskin voile Woven fabrics can be cut on the bias for more pliability.

Basic Swimsuit Block

with built-up shoulders

Refer to Fig. 87

(1) Outline the back and front One-Piece Dress block to well below hip level. Make sure the CB and CF are parallel and that blocks are on the same horizontal level. Include the back, chest, bust, squared waist and hip lines. Include the waist darts and indicate the bust dart with a dotted line, from bust point to chest level only.

(2) Measuring down the CB from the squared waistline, apply the body rise. Square across to CF on this level. For the crutch section (the equivalent area to the curved seam on trousers and shorts) measure down one quarter of the body rise measurement, plus 1 cm extra on back only. Square across for crutch seams on these levels and mark crutch width at 3 cm (increase 0.5 cm on sizes 16 & 18).

(3) **For side seam adjustment** The ease allowed on the dress block at bust, waist and hip is not required for swimsuits − even when cut in non-stretch fabrics. Remove this from the side seams − more from the back than from the front (for no other reason than to simplify measuring.)

	back	front
at bustline	2 cm	1.5 cm
at waistline	2 cm	1.5 cm
3.5 cm above hipline	1.5 cm	1 cm

Use the dress block side seams to help you draw the new side seams.

(4) **For leg shaping**
Standard leg height − 3.5 cm above hipline.

	from CB	from CF
width at body rise	$\frac{1}{4}$ body hip ÷ 2	$\frac{1}{4}$ body hip ÷ 4 − 0.5 cm

Connect crutch − body rise − leg height with straight guide lines. Divide each line in half and hollow out leg shapes as in Fig. 87. Keep the body contours in mind when drawing the curves. The back seat area of the block should be wide enough to give good coverage whilst the front is quite cut away.

As usual, good continuous curves are ensured if you place the lower part of the back side seam against the front to see if leg shaping needs adjustment. This also applies to the crutch seams. See Fig. 88(a).

(5) **Inner crutch re-inforcement piece**
Mark curved lines 1 cm above the back and front

body rise levels. Cut this pattern in one piece without a crutch seam, as in Fig. 87. Fabric suggestion: soft absorbent cotton.

(6) **Built-up shoulder straps and neckline**
This softly shaped swimsuit has no need of a bust dart − the method of drafting the shoulder straps is very simple and in normal cases provides the necessary degree of fit around the neckline and armholes. The only exceptions are:

(a) when a more moulded shape is required for the chosen design.
(b) when dealing with personal fittings for very prominent busts − i.e. out of proportion with the rest of the figure.

In these cases refer to Note 2 at the end of this section.

Square a line across sheet 1 cm down from nape of neck. Draw a second, parallel line 2.5 cm below, just in the central area.
For back strap:

$$a-b = \tfrac{2}{3}\text{rds} \times \text{back width}$$
$$b-c = \tfrac{1}{3}\text{rd} \times \text{back width}$$

Curve neckline and armhole down to bust line with lightly drawn lines (may need adjusting later).
For front strap:
Repeat a−b−c exactly, then curve armhole similarly to back but draw front neckline higher − 7 cm above bust line.

Basic swimsuit with built-up shoulders

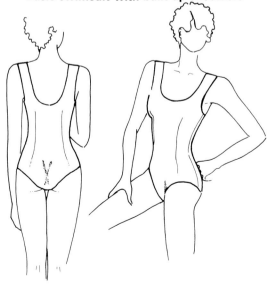

157

Basic Swimsuit Block — with built-up shoulders

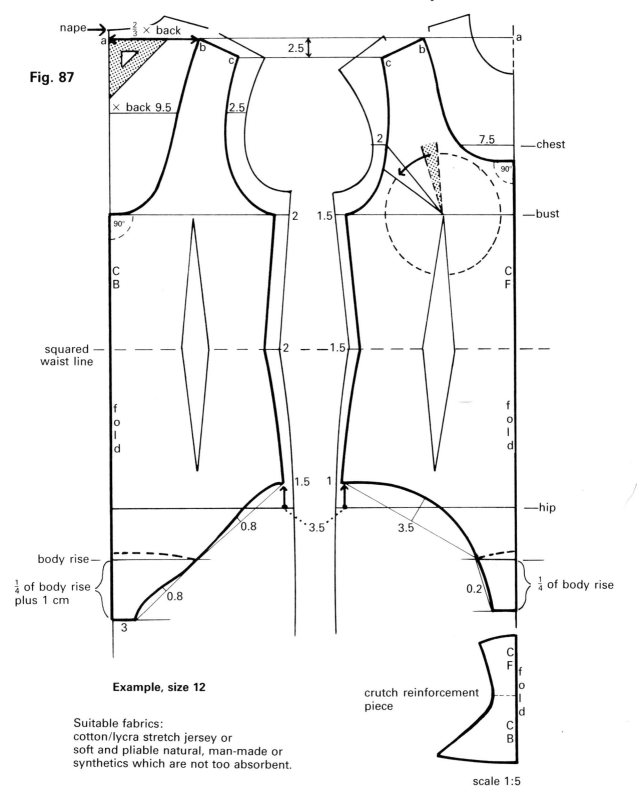

Fig. 87

nape

$\frac{2}{3}$ × back

2.5

× back 9.5

2.5

2.5

chest

bust

7.5

90°

90°

2

2

1.5

C B

C F

squared waist line

2

1.5

f o l d

f o l d

1.5

1

0.8

3.5

3.5

hip

body rise

$\frac{1}{4}$ of body rise plus 1 cm

$\frac{1}{4}$ of body rise

0.8

0.2

3

Example, size 12

Suitable fabrics:
cotton/lycra stretch jersey or
soft and pliable natural, man-made or
synthetics which are not too absorbent.

crutch reinforcement piece

C F f o l d

C B

scale 1:5

158

Fig. 88(a)

push back and front
swimsuit blocks together
at side and crutch seams
to check that leg is
well shaped

Fig. 88(b)

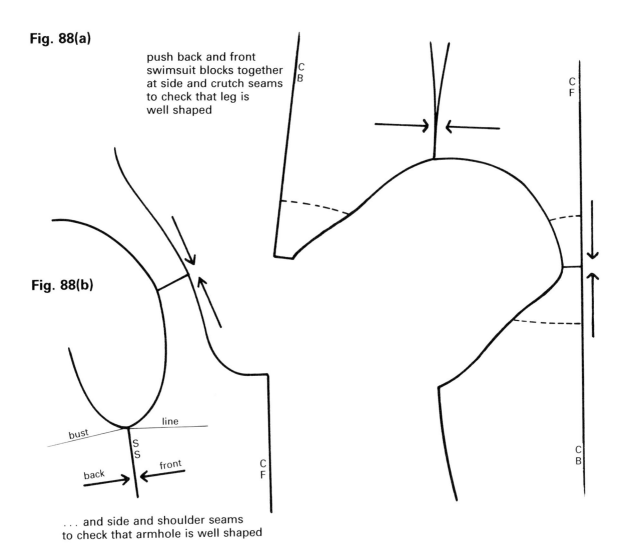

... and side and shoulder seams
to check that armhole is well shaped

Refer to Fig. 88(b)
To check good continuity of neck and armhole curves, place blocks together at shoulders and then at underarms. Adjust if necessary.

Note 1 The direction of straight grain lines on swimwear patterns depends on the type of fabric chosen for the style. As a general guide:

• For firmly woven non-stretch fabrics – place at 45° to CF and CB (bias cutting).
• For pliable, woven non-stretch, e.g. cotton crepe – parallel to CF and CB.
• For stretch fabrics and knits, where the greatest stretch can occur either in the weft or in the warp – determine the direction of greatest stretch and place the straight grain lines so that pattern may be cut with maximum stretch *around* the body.

Note 2   When a bust dart is required:
Refer to Fig. 87
The indicated bust dart (dotted lines) must be transferred into the armhole before it can be used.

Easiest method of transfer is to place transparent paper over, trace dart lines through and pivot (swing) from the bust point into the armhole. Use the (tracing) wheel to transfer through onto block.

The front armhole curve will then certainly need adjusting – fold out dart and take a midway curve. See Fig. 89.

Once the bust dart has been transferred into a usable position it may then be further manipulated into other positions or introduced into any seam passing close to the bust point.

Note 3 In the majority of swimsuit styles, the crutch section is detached from the back swimsuit pattern and added to the front. This eliminates an uncomfortable seam from the narrowest part of the crutch and strengthens the seat area where it is re-sited.

Note 4
Position for pre-formed cups Draw a circle around the bust point – radius for size 12 = 8 cm. Plus or minus 0.5 cm for other sizes.

Fig. 89

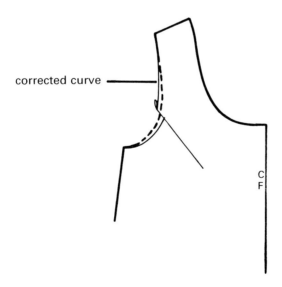

corrected curve

Variation on the Basic Swimsuit Block

WING SEAM STYLE
Refer to Fig. 90
(1) Outline Swimsuit Block (page 00) and include bust, waist and hip lines and all darts, lightly drawn.
Front swimsuit
(2) The two front darts are used as a basis for the Wing seam (a version of the Princess line, but with seams starting from the armholes instead of from the shoulders). Draw the seam lines, rounding them so that they resemble the body shape, and place balance marks above and below bust point for correct control of seam when sewing. The side seams are similarly re-drawn. The armhole will need re-shaping – place armhole ends of Wing seam together matching the balance marks and adjust the curve.
Back swimsuit
(3) The back Wing seam, although based on the dart, benefits from re-direction at the top – so that the seam may enter the armhole low down and then at

the bottom, so that there is a finely balanced division between the panels to flatter the figure. All mid-seam placements such as Wing seams and Princess line seams depend on a good visual balance between centre and side panels.
(4) **High cut leg shaping**
Raise leg 5 cm at side seam and re-shape down to crutch seam. It is not advisable to alter the crutch seam – already at minimum width.
(5) Before tracing the panels separately from the planned pattern, draw in SG lines on side panels, parallel to CB and CF.
Complete pattern with seam and small turn-over allowances at neck, armholes and legs – to be neatened and edge or top-stitched into place.

Fabric note Choose a minimum or moderate stretch fabric (see Stretch Gauge on page 244) or a very pliable non-stretch (woven) fabric.

Variation on the Basic Swimsuit Block – Wing seam style

Fig. 90

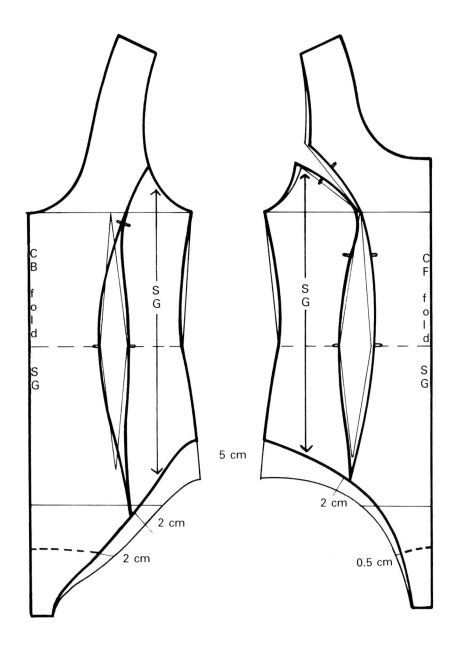

Suitable fabrics: as for the Basic Swimsuit Block

162

Styles based on Swimsuit Block with built-up shoulders

Styles based on Strapless Swimsuit

Variation on the Basic Swimsuit Block − Strapless style

(for use only with stretch fabric)

This may be adapted from either the One-Piece Swimsuit block − page 157 − or the One-Piece Dress Block, whichever is available. The result is a very fitted body shape without the need for waist darts. The side and CB seams cope well with the fitting but only in conjunction with moderate or maximum stretch fabric − see Stretch Gauge (page 244). The top of the swimsuit fits snugly around the chest, mainly due to the use of a doubled bust dart converted into gathers radiating from the side seam. Depending on the size/shape of the breasts and the effect required the need may arise for pre-formed bra cups attached to a full or part lining and therefore remaining undetected from the right side of the swimsuit.

Refer to Fig. 91
Adaptation from Basic Swimsuit Block (dotted lines)

(1) Outline the back and front Basic Swimsuit Block. Include the chest, bust, squared waist and hip lines. *The bust dart* is necessary for this style – draw it in the initial position (see Note 2 of Basic Swimsuit Block on page 159) which is the shaded area in Fig. 87 and then double its volume to tighten the top of the swimsuit into a snug fit.

(2) **For further side seam adjustment**
Noting the measurements at bust and waist levels, re-draw the inner side seams with the body contours in mind. (Substitute figures between blocks when adapting from the One-Piece Dress Block.) No adjustment is needed to the lowest part of the side seam. The CB requires similar shaping to complete the fitting.

(3) **Shaping top of swimsuit**
Front:
Here the chest line is used as a basis for the top edge but it may be lowered and shaped if required. Carefully fold out doubled dart to bust point and continue drawing the top edge down towards the bust line, merging with the Swimsuit Block armhole.
Back:
Placing the strapless side seams together, continue shaping the top on the back swimsuit, dropping 2.5 cm below bustline at CB.

(4) **Converting bust dart into gathers**
Firstly, decide position of gathers – usually a few centimetres down from the top edge and extending about 5 cm down the side seam, although this may be lower for a larger or lower bust.

Place balance marks to define position of gathers. Draw two lines well within these balance marks, aimed at the bust point. Refer to Fig. 92. Cut on lines almost to the point and fold out bust dart. The area between the balance marks will spread open, forming the area of gathers. Secure or re-make pattern in this position.

(5) Complete pattern with a SG line parallel to CB and seams and turn-over allowances as in paragraph 5, Wing seam style swimsuit (page 160).

Note 1 If thin straps are required they are best positioned between 9 and 14 cm from CB and CF.

Note 2 Position for pre-formed bra cups is indicated on the Basic Swimsuit Block. For size 12 radius = 8 cm from bust point, plus or minus 0.5 cm for other sizes.

Note 3 This strapless fitted swimsuit may serve as a basic strapless block for adaptation to other styles. However, it must be stressed that this basic pattern can only be used for stretch fabrics. Since stretch fabrics vary so much in their elasticity it is unwise to complete the making up process without trying on a sample garment to test the fit. Any adjustments may then be made before completing an individual garment or going into mass production. The degree of stretch required for the pattern to work properly can best be shown by attaching to the pattern a swatch of the fabric to be used.

165

Strapless Swimsuit – for use only with stretch fabrics

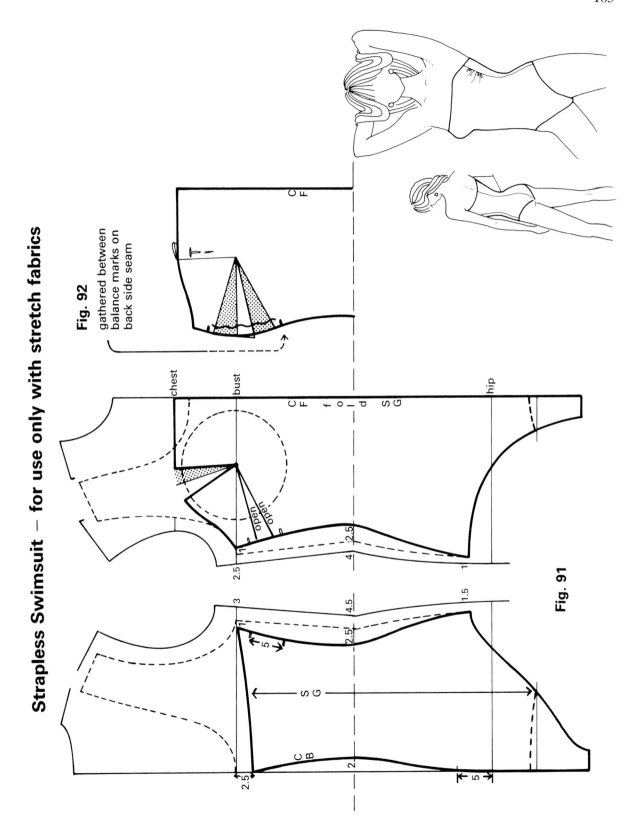

Fig. 92

gathered between balance marks on back side seam

chest

bust

C
F
f
o
d
S
G

hip

2.5

4

2.5

open

1

Fig. 91

3

4.5

5

2.5

S
G

1.5

2.5

C
B

2

5

BIKINIS

Bikini tops and bottoms are so closely related to bras and briefs that the blocks made for these may be used as a base.

Refer to the following bra and brief styles in the Lingerie Section, the patterns of which may be used with or without changes to produce bikini styles.

Bras:	Briefs:
Style A, page 65	Hip Brief Block, page 85
Style B, page 66	Bikini Pantie Block, page 87
Style C, page 67	
Style E, page 71	

There are, however, differences in styling – bikini tops do not usually need to offer support and are certainly not meant to be inconspicuous – therefore many of the constraints applied to bra designing can be waived. Indeed, bikini tops are often much simpler in style and shape, more eye-catching through use of boldy coloured plain and printed fabrics, and more interesting with gathers, pleats and tucks replacing some seams. Bikini bottoms on the other hand are often more complicated in style than everyday briefs. Because they are on show decorative effects such as complex cutting, novelty fabrics and trimmings are used to make bikini bottoms look as little like briefs and panties as possible.

Similar design details applied to tops and bottoms will unite the two garments into one outfit.

There are very few fabric restrictions for bikinis – those that soak up lots of water are to be avoided but almost anything else may be used providing it will withstand exposure to sunlight, sea and chlorinated water. As with other swimwear stretch fabric is a good choice if suited to the design, but two-way stretch is not so necessary as for one piece swimwear.

STYLE A – DRAW-STRING BIKINI SUITABLE FOR WOVEN FABRIC
Bikini top – Refer to Fig. 93

(1) Trace Bra Block from basic draft (Fig. 21 on page 63). Shorten both ends of forward side seam by 1.5 cm re-shaping underarm area to narrow the back. Disregard small back dart – this will contribute to ruching.

(2) Place differentiating balance marks at top and bottom of forward side seam (as this seam slants, the cups and back sections must be correctly joined when sewing).

(3) Slash cup pattern on bust line, from CF and from side seam, up to but not right through the bust point. Fold out top and bottom darts, spreading pattern to provide gathers. Curve seam lines over gaps.

(4) Make CF covering strip for gathers. Length = 4 cm × 1 cm + seam allowances. Make shoulder strap pattern. Length = 80 cm including bow × 2 cm (to finish 1 cm wide) + seam allowances.

Make back pattern $1\frac{1}{2}$–2 times longer – split through centre, spread apart and fill the gap. This is cut in double fabric and filled with elastic to give ruched effect.

Note Hook fastening at CB or CF as preferred. Short lengths of flat boning cut to fit and inserted in CF and side seams will give a more streamlined appearance.

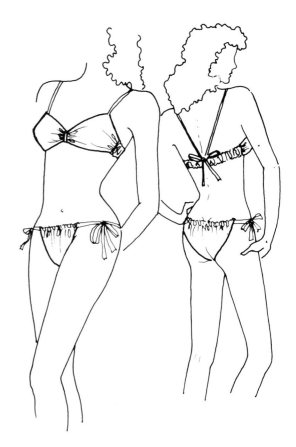

Draw-string Bikini – Style A

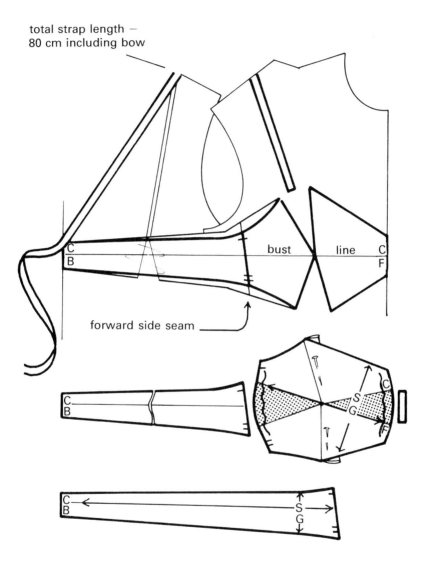

Fig. 93

total strap length –
80 cm including bow

bust   line

forward side seam

Bikini bottom – Refer to Fig. 94

(5) Trace Bikini Pantie Block (Fig. 44, page 87) and
add a casing for tie, 1.5 cm wide. Angle the ends
for folding over.

(6) Make hip tie pattern. Length = half hip
measurement + 2 bow allowances, each 35 cm (i.e.
for size 12: 47 cm + 35 cm + 35 cm = 117 cm).
Therefore length = 117 cm × 2 cm + seam
allowances. Elasticate leg after sewing back crutch
seam and attaching lining. See Fig. 95.

Note Straight grain lines usually serve to position the
pattern correctly on the fabric in order that the garment
hangs well. Bikinis, usually tiny and clinging, do not
benefit from the 'hang' of the fabric and therefore the
lines are otherwise employed – to position correctly for
fabric effects, e.g. stripes, checks, optimum elasticity in
stretch fabrics, etc.

168

Fig. 94

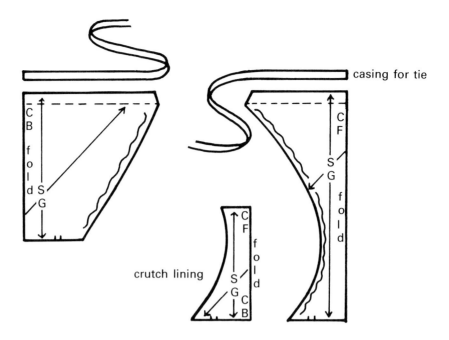

casing for tie

crutch lining

Fig. 95

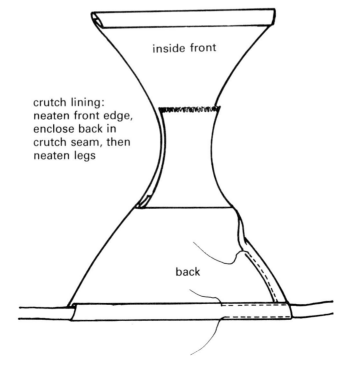

inside front

crutch lining:
neaten front edge,
enclose back in
crutch seam, then
neaten legs

back

Variations on Style A bikini bottoms

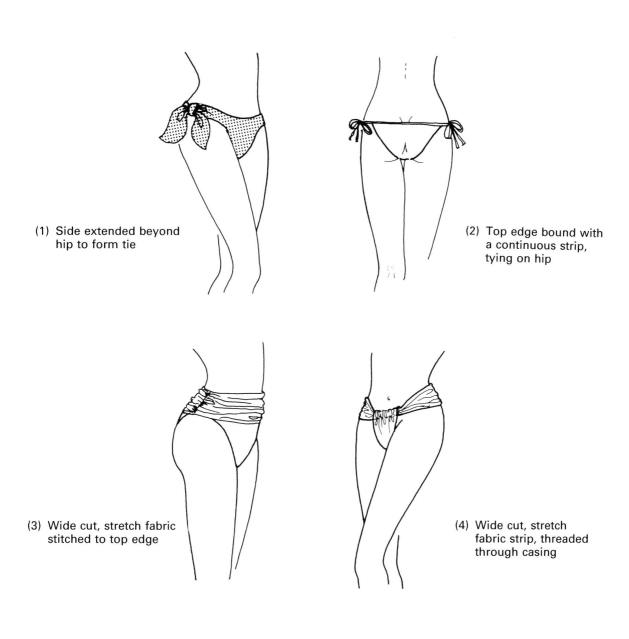

(1) Side extended beyond hip to form tie

(2) Top edge bound with a continuous strip, tying on hip

(3) Wide cut, stretch fabric stitched to top edge

(4) Wide cut, stretch fabric strip, threaded through casing

STYLE B – WITH CROSS-OVER BANDING,
SUITABLE FOR STRETCH FABRIC

Bikini top – Refer to Fig. 96

(1) Outline the Bra Block (Fig. 22, page 64). Leave room on right-hand side to trace right bra cup (when cutting for asymmetric styles, a whole pattern is necessary). Include the bust line, forward side seam and all the improvements made to the top and bottom edges.

(2) Lower top edge at CF until length = 4 cm. This allows just enough room for the band to cross over. Fold out top bust dart temporarily and from lowered CF point re-draw top edge curving line up to dart, then lowering 1 cm at underarm and along the back. Erase the original top edge to avoid confusion.

(3) Folding paper on CF line, trace through the re-shaped cup section so that, when unfolded, you will have the whole cup area ready to plan the asymmetric design.

Refer to Fig. 97

(4) Two of the bust darts – upper left and lower right – are obstructing the designing of the cross-over band lines. Fold these out, transferring into the opposite darts and slashing through their centres to keep pattern flat.

(5) Draw in the lines of the band. Place balance marks either side of centre to show limits of gathering, plus a double mark for correct assembly. (Left and right cup pieces look very similar when cut in fabric and it is only too easy to muddle them without good markings.) Draw dot-dash lines where gathers are required, inside balance marks.

(6) **Refer to Fig. 98**

Notice positions of SG lines – across pattern pieces – to place for maximum effect from stretch fabric. Trace each cup from below and above crossover band, transferring darts into cut dot-dash lines for gathers. Secure pattern in this position. Draw curved seamlines in gathered areas, trimming points from cut sections.

(7) **Refer to Fig. 99**

The back may be banded continuing on from the front but minus the gathers – or left plain if preferred. Hook fastening at CB. Boning side seams will improve appearance.

Bikini Bottom – Refer to Fig. 100

(8) Outline the back and front Hip Brief Block (Fig. 42, page 85) on a level, leaving room on either

side to double patterns over. Include the waist level marking, crutch seams, front and back crutch lining levels – curve the back level 1 cm downwards towards leg.

(9) This block, originally devised for woven fabric, must be reduced in width to remove the ease allowance, to make it suitable for slightly stretch fabric. Fold out a 1.5 cm parallel strip on back and front. Curve the side seams 1 cm inwards at top hip level – for a snug fit without the need for elastic.

(10) Folding paper on CB/CF, trace the reduced pattern through as for bikini top and utilise bikini top instructions 5–7 to complete the pattern. See Fig. 101 for the finished pattern shapes.

Note The side seam may be eliminated on the band by joining the two patterns into one piece.

Bikini with cross-over banding – Style B suitable for stretch fabrics

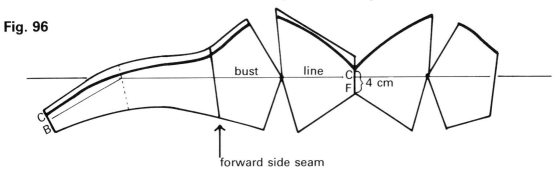

Fig. 96

bust line

C F

4 cm

C
B

forward side seam

Fig. 97

bust line

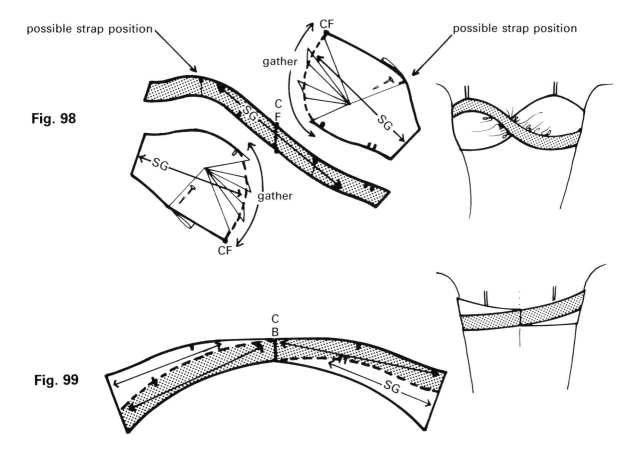

possible strap position

possible strap position

CF

gather

C
F

SG

SG

Fig. 98

SG

gather

CF

C
B

SG

Fig. 99

Strapless Bodice

For a strapless bodice that will stay up without support, *all* the normal ease included during the construction of the ordinary Bodice Block must be removed. This reduces the pattern to a skin-tight, self-supporting shape which works well without the need for boning or cupping, particularly on tiny young figures. However, for a more formal look, e.g. on evening dresses, to sharpen the appearance and smooth the fit, especially on larger sizes, boning and or cupping is advisable.

Choose suitable fabrics − firmly woven cottons or stretch fabrics for beach wear or silks and satins etc., lined or unlined, for evening wear. When a draped style is intended (evening wear) a more flimsy material would suit the purpose, mounted on a plain lining base to help hold the drapes in place.

Choose the closest fitting block as a basis, i.e. the Bodice Block on page 13. The object is to remove any surplus material (ease) until the bodice fits like a second skin. Begin by measuring the block on the important levels, i.e.
- Bust
- Waist
- Chest circumference
- Rib cage

Make a note of these measurements and compare them with the actual body measurements (either from the size chart on page 6 or own measurements for personal fittings). The differences between them are the amounts to be removed in various stages.

Make a table to work out differences between pattern and body measurements, ready to use when adapting pattern to new shape:

Example − size 12	Bodice Block	Body	Difference (ease)	...on half pattern
Bust	98 cm	88 cm	10 cm	5 cm
Waist	72	68	4	2
Chest circumference	98	82	16	8
Rib cage	86	75	11	5.5

Refer to Fig. 102

(1) Outline the back and front Bodice Block including the darts, chest, underarm and bust lines. Remove a *quarter* of the difference between whole pattern bust and whole body bust from each side seam. (If working from the size chart this amount is 2.5 cm.) Repeat this procedure at the waist level, although the amount removed will be much smaller as less ease is required *at the waist than at bust level*. (If using size chart, amount is 1 cm.)

(2) Double the bust dart on *armhole side only* − thus ensuring that the top fits the body snugly and any Princess line seaming is correctly positioned.

Refer to Fig. 103

(3) Place patterns together on new side seams. It is easier to measure and re-style the top of the strapless bodice if the pattern is kept flat, therefore cut through the centre of the underbust dart and fold out doubled bust dart.

(4) Draw the top edge from the chest line at CF, curving it below the U/A point and down into the bust line near the CB. Measure this line from CB to CF and compare with the body chest circumference measurement. If there is still an excess of pattern over body measurement, remove it from each side of the top of the back waist dart. Rule lines from here down to waist points, which are already correct. Fold one line over onto the other and re-curve the top edge if necessary.

Refer to Fig. 104

(5) With the top edge now correctly curved and fitted, unpin the pattern releasing the top bust dart and fold out the underbust and back darts. To tighten the fit under the bust, first locate the rib cage line: measure 8 cm down from the bust point. On this level mark a curved line parallel to the waist. Measure this line and compare with the body rib cage measurement. Any excess should be removed equally from each side of the underbust dart. Shape the lines to correspond with the body contour, rounding off the point on the bust. These fitting lines may now be treated as a seam as in sketch 1, page 176. This basic pattern can be adapted to provide many different designs. For some other ideas see sketches 2−5, page 176 and the halter neck variation on page 177.

Note In theory the term 'strapless' is generally understood to mean garments that are self-supporting, but in practice they are not necessarily without straps − these often being added solely for decoration.

In the case of shoe-string/rouleau or other narrow straps, these may be attached almost anywhere along the top edge depending on the design and effect required − the area that one must avoid is 6 cm or so either side of the side seam (see Fig. 103). If placed *inside* these marks, the straps will cut into the flesh when moving the arms.

Strapless bodice

Fig. 102

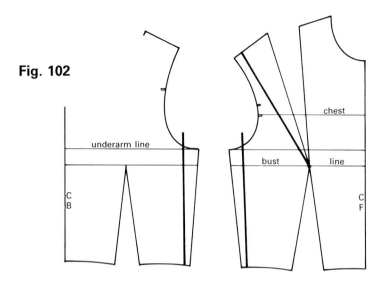

Fig. 103

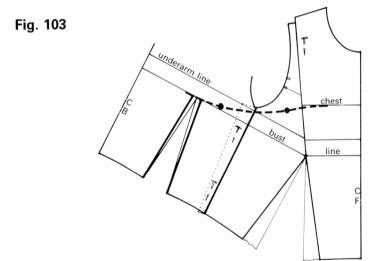

Fig. 104

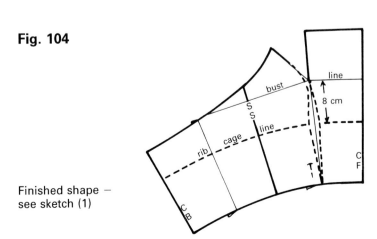

Finished shape —
see sketch (1)

Strapless Bodices

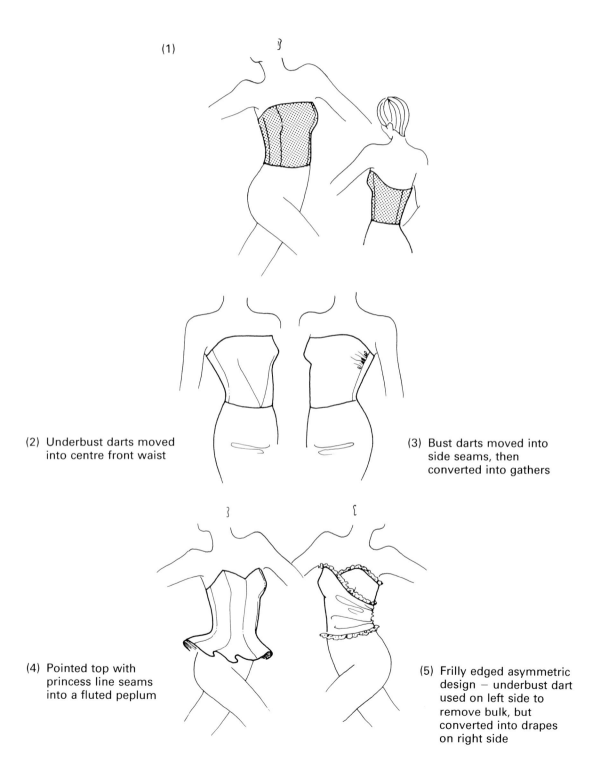

(1)

(2) Underbust darts moved into centre front waist

(3) Bust darts moved into side seams, then converted into gathers

(4) Pointed top with princess line seams into a fluted peplum

(5) Frilly edged asymmetric design – underbust dart used on left side to remove bulk, but converted into drapes on right side

FOR A HALTER NECK STYLE SEE FIG. 105 and instructions below
Having arrived at the end of stage (4) and Fig. 103 on pages 174 and 175 apply the halter neck strap as follows:

Refer to Fig. 105
(1) Place the back Bodice Block to the front with shoulders touching up to darts. Outline the back neckline and CB. These two lines serve as a basis for the halter strap, which should be situated centrally on the nape bone to feel comfortable in wear.
(2) Extend the back neckline 2 cm upwards at CB. Mark this point (a). Curve a new neckline from (a) through the upper third of the front neckline down to chestline, 9 cm from CF.

(3) Strap width (a−b) = 4−4.5 cm. Keep lines parallel around neck and right-angled to CB. Continue line parallel to new front neckline and join into the underarm area with a good curve.

Halter neck bands may be fastened in several ways:

- Button and buttonhole
- Hook and eye
- Extended to tie in a bow
- With a buckle

If the strap is neatened with a facing, this should be cut in one with the bodice facing.

Variation on the Strapless Bodice − Halter neck style

Fig. 105

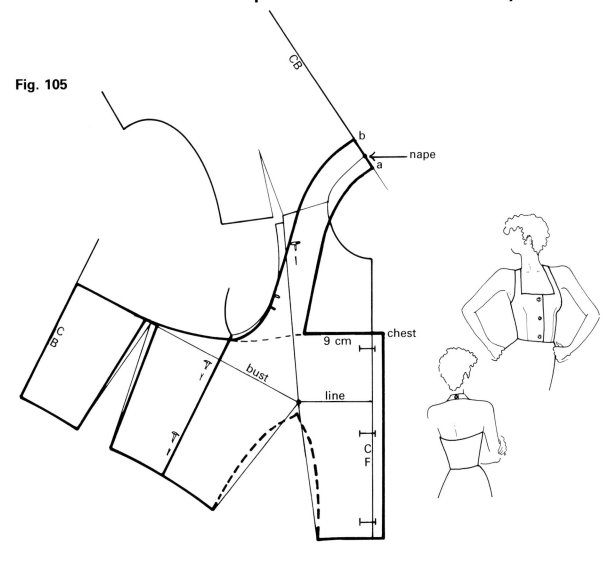

SHORTS

Shorts fall into four categories:

- **Skirt type** – loose legged, flared or full cut – adapted from the skirt block.
- **Tailored**, neat fitting, medium length – (this category would include styles with small front pleats). } adapted from the trouser block
- **Tight and short**.
- **Close fitting**, almost knee length, e.g. Bermudas – can be cut from the trouser block as is, being the only type benefitting from the special fitting arrangement on the back inside leg.

Much time and effort is saved if each category has its own block. According to the type required, there are considerable horizontal and vertical differences in the basic fit, and if the wrong block is used the pattern cutting process is prolonged and the resulting garment may not have quite the right look. It's almost like using the wrong tool for the job!

Skirt-Shorts Block

Refer to Fig. 106

(1) Outline the back and front Straight Skirt Block (page 11) with hip lines on a level and CB and CF parallel. Include the darts and indicate straight grain lines on CB and CF. Mark the body rise measurement plus 2 cm on the CF, measuring from waist.
Example for size 12: 28 + 2 = 30 cm. Square across for crutch line.

(2) **For back crutch** point measure out from CB and along crutch line $\frac{1}{10}$th of the total skirt block hip (including ease) *plus* 2 cm.
e.g. size 12: (99 ÷ 10) + 2 = (11.9) 12 cm.
For front crutch point repeat procedure but $\frac{1}{10}$th *minus* 2 cm.
e.g. size 12: (99 ÷ 10) − 2 = (7.9 cm) 8 cm.

(3) From crutch points square down 7 cm for leg length – square across for hemline. Curve crutch seams as shown in Fig. 106.

(4) For a slightly flared look – cut on lines drawn parallel to CB and CF, from hemline up to the base of the darts nearest side seams.
On the back shorts eliminate one dart completely – which automatically flares the hem.
On the front shorts reduce the dart to 2 cm which allows a little less flare than on back shorts.
(Allowing extra flare on the back is flattering to the figure.)

(5) As only one back dart remains, move it to a position between the two original darts as shown in Fig. 106 for a more balanced appearance.

The shape of the Skirt-Shorts Block

Skirt-Shorts Block

Fig. 106

Example, size 12

move remaining dart
over toward side seam

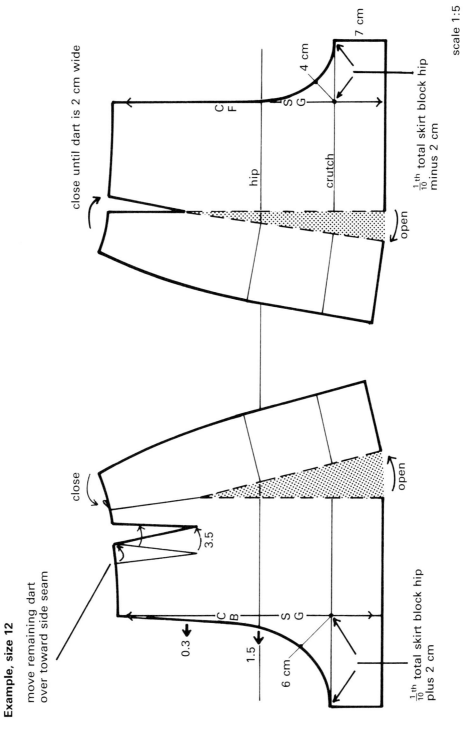

close until dart is 2 cm wide

close

open

hip

crutch

C
F

S
G

4 cm

7 cm

$\frac{1}{10}$th total skirt block hip
minus 2 cm

scale 1:5

0.3

3.5

1.5

6 cm

C
B

S
G

open

$\frac{1}{10}$th total skirt block hip
plus 2 cm

179

Tailored (neat fitting) Shorts Block

Refer to Fig. 107

(1) Outline the Trouser Block (page 23) to the knee line and include hip, crutch and SG lines.

(2) To alter the back crutch height and inside leg shape, making the back trouser suitable for shorts adaptations:

    (a) Place front inside leg against back, matching exactly at knee points and as closely as is possible at the crutch seam.

    (b) Raise back crutch to the height of the front, re-shaping the curve up to the hipline.

    (c) Make the back inside leg seam less concave (*suitable for trouser styling but* not *for the majority of shorts*) by adding 0.5 cm midway between crutch and knee and connecting back to these points with a good curve. See dotted line.

The block is now ready for styling.

**The shape of the
Tailored Shorts Block**

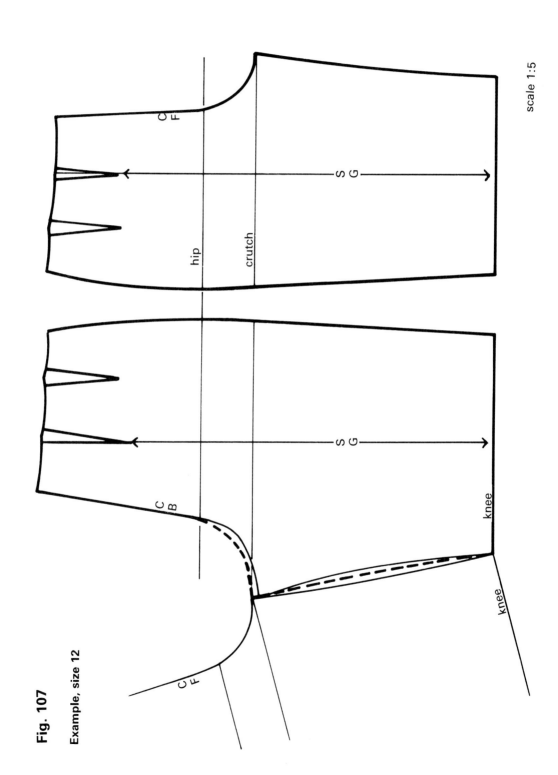

Tailored Shorts Block

Fig. 107

Example, size 12

scale 1:5

181

Short Shorts Block

Refer to Fig. 108
(1) Follow all the instructions for the Tailored Shorts Block, or simply outline the ready-made block to well below crutch level.
(2) For hem line, curve from crutch level at side seam to a point 4 cm down inside leg.

(3) For a closer fit around the upper thigh, remove two 2 cm wide 'darts' radiating from the hip line at CB and CF. Adjust the hem curve if necessary.

The block is now ready for styling.

**The shape of the
Short Shorts Block**

Short Shorts Block

Fig. 108

Example, size 12

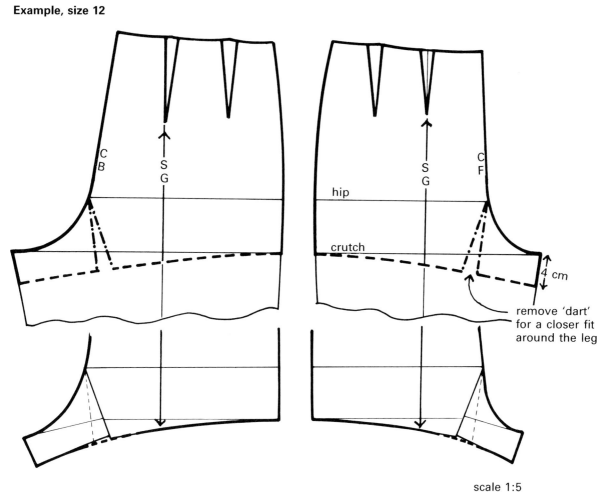

hip

crutch

4 cm

remove 'dart'
for a closer fit
around the leg

scale 1:5

Adaptations From The Short Blocks

STYLE A – ADAPTED FROM THE SKIRT-SHORTS BLOCK

Has a fairly full gathered waist, fastens at the back with a zip and waistband button and includes in-seam pockets.

Refer to Fig. 109

(1) Outline the Skirt-Shorts Block (Fig. 106) including hip line. Disregard darts – they will contribute to the waist gathering. Taking the front as an example, divide into three sections, cutting and spreading on the lines. Add more into the hemline than into the waist to accentuate the skirty appearance.

(2) **For the in-seam pocket**, first draw a rough outline on the skirt pattern to ensure the correct position; start about 10 cm down from the waistline and make the width 10–12 cm at hip level; the opening in the seam should be 15 cm for the hand to pass through easily. Mirror this shape beyond the side seam. The pocket bag may also be cut separately and joined to the side, prior to sewing the side seam. Note that the position of this adjoining seam is well inside the pocket, out of view. Therefore the side seam would require an extension.

This whole procedure is repeated for the back pattern.

(3) **For the waistband** – make the finished width fairly wide for this style – about 5 cm:

width of pattern = 5 cm × 2 = 10 cm

length of pattern = waist size + 1–2 cm for easy fit
+ button and buttonhole wrap.

**Style A –
Full-skirted shorts**

Style A – Skirt shorts

Fig. 109

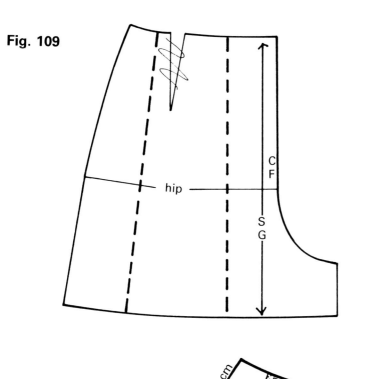

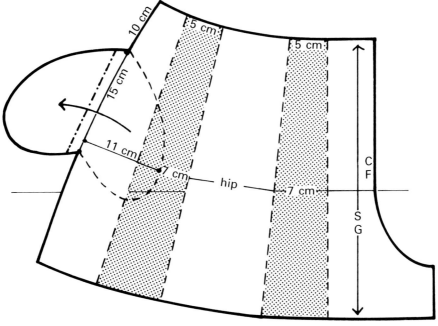

186

STYLE B – ADAPTED FROM THE TAILORED
SHORTS BLOCK
Has pleats from the front waist, fly front fastening, hip
pockets and turn-ups.

Refer to Fig. 110

(1) Outline front Tailored Shorts Block down to 5 cm
above knee level. Cut on straight grain line down
to, but not through, hemline and add 3 cm extra
into the waistline for a good size pleat – 4 cm
altogether including the small amount of dart on
either side of the line. Note new SG position.

The dart nearest side seam remains the same size
but is pleated instead of sewn as a dart.

(2) To simplify the back waist fitting, transfer the dart
nearest CB into the back seam *and* into the side
seam – half and half.

Move the remaining dart 2 cm over towards the
CB for a more balanced position.

(3) Add 3 cm flare to each side seam at hem level – up
to hip line. Add 1 cm flare to each inside leg seam
at hem level – up to crutch points. As these seams
are slightly curved, and should remain so, use the

inside leg edge of the front block to draw against,
simply pivoting out 1 cm at hem levels.

(4) **For turn-ups** – add 2 × 3 cm beyond the finished
length and then the usual hem allowance.

(5) **For hip pocket**
Draw a straight line 3 cm in from and 14 cm down
from front side waist point. Refer to Fig. 111. Plan
pocket bag on shorts pattern – 25 cm long and
14 cm at its widest point. Trace two pocket patterns
from this plan – the top pocket which faces out the
shorts pocket edge (x–y) and the under pocket
which lies next to the body and forms the side hip
part of the shorts pattern, once the 'corner' is
trimmed away.

(6) **Grown-on fly facing** Firstly, draw the line of fly
stitching on left of CF, curving into a point 21 cm
below waist (to accommodate a 20 cm zip). Mirror
this to the right of CF, adding 2 cm for the edge of
facing.

(7) Complete the pattern with a waistband as on Style
A but not as wide – 3 cm finished width.

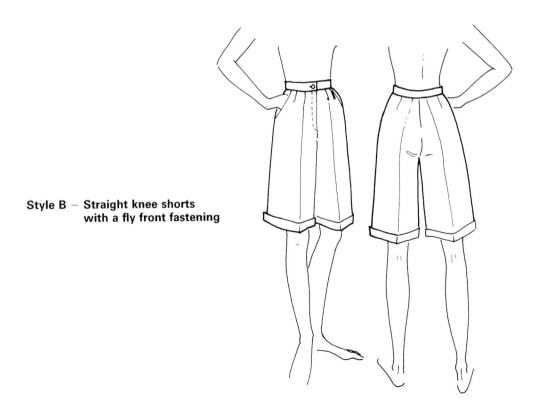

**Style B – Straight knee shorts
with a fly front fastening**

Style B – Straight knee shorts

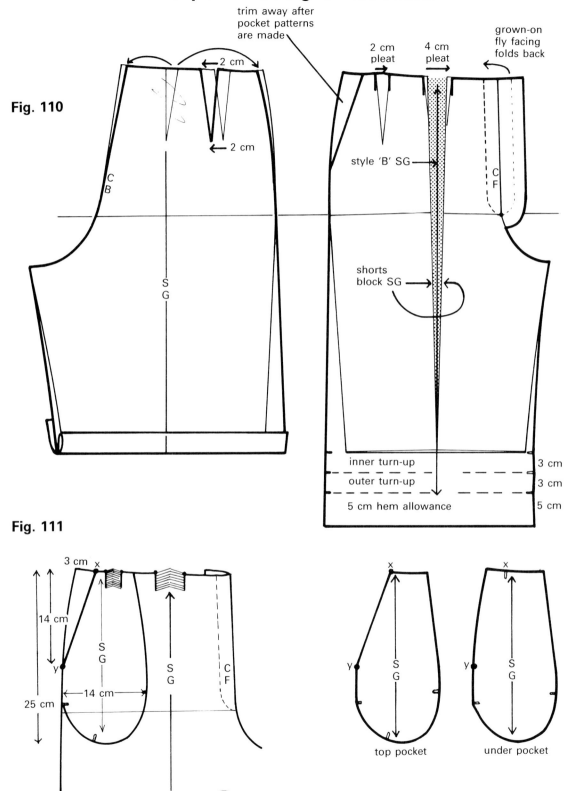

Fig. 110

trim away after
pocket patterns
are made

2 cm pleat

4 cm pleat

grown-on
fly facing
folds back

← 2 cm

← 2 cm

C B

S G

style 'B' SG

shorts block SG →

C F

inner turn-up — 3 cm
outer turn-up — 3 cm
5 cm hem allowance — 5 cm

Fig. 111

3 cm x

14 cm

S G

S G

C F

y

14 cm

25 cm

x

y

S G

top pocket

x

y

S G

under pocket

PLAYSUIT

A playsuit is a combination of bodice and shorts, frequently designed in one piece from neck to hem. It is most convenient if a block exists, ready combined and with the problems of neck to crutch length already solved, leaving the pattern cutter free to concentrate on the design in hand.

Although almost any bodice and trouser pattern may form the basis of a **One Piece Body Block**, one of the most useful combinations is that of the Dartless Bodice Block and the Tailored Shorts Block, both being of average fit and therefore adaptable to close or loose-fitting styles. Whichever blocks you choose, it is important that the waistlines are clearly indicated on each so that a correct join may be made.

The vital measurement determining the success of a one-piece body block is that of the full trunk length, i.e. from the nape, down in between legs and on up to CF neck point. This measurement must be taken fairly closely on the body (or it may be derived from the size chart on page 6) and to it is added an amount of ease to allow for bending and stretching.

Example, using size 12 measurements extracted from the chart on page 6 and measured from the Dartless Bodice Block*:

$$\begin{array}{rl}
\text{Nape}-\text{waist} = & 41 \text{ cm} \\
\text{CB}-\text{CF waist, through legs} = & 66 \text{ cm} \\
\text{CF waist}-\text{neck point} = & \underline{36.5 \text{ cm}^*} \\
\text{Body trunk measurement} = & 143.5 \text{ cm} \\
\\
\text{Plus general ease allowance,} & \\
\text{suitable for a playsuit} = & \underline{11 \text{ cm}^{**}} \\
\text{Pattern trunk measurement} = & 154.5 \text{ cm}
\end{array}$$

(** The ease allowance must be halved and added equally into back and front patterns.)

This total measurement is then used to check the pattern trunk length before completing and cutting in fabric, as one-piece body patterns are notoriously difficult to adjust afterwards.

The amount of ease allowed can vary but for general purposes may be assessed at 11 cm, although anything from 9−13 cm is considered standard depending on:

- Intended use.
- Closeness of fit of the current fashion.
- Leg length of garment − if above knee, less ease may be needed.
- Fabric − firm woven or stretch.

Special note In the case of a two-way stretch knit − which contains its own ease − it is possible to join block waists directly without allowing any extra in between, assuming that this suits the style requirements.

When placing the blocks together take care to ensure that they are perfectly aligned. Mistakes arising at this stage of preparation will result in a later inexplicably poor fit aggravated by a lack of waist seam to help with correction.

Playsuit

ONE-PIECE BODY BLOCK
Refer to Fig. 113

(1) Position the back and front Tailored Shorts Block towards the bottom of a long sheet of paper. Leave some space between outside leg seams. Mark the positions of the straight grain lines underneath block and lengthen to the top of the sheet. Make sure they are parallel.

(2) Outline the lower part of blocks up to hip line only, aligning the SG lines with those on the sheet of paper. Mark in crutchline.

(3) The ease allowance (for comfort when bending or stretching) should be added equally on back and front by moving blocks up towards top of sheet by 5.5 cm from hip line; finish outlining the top area of the block. Make sure the SGs are aligned when completing the outline.

(4) Mark in waist darts lightly − these will probably not be used in their present position when styling from the block but are useful reference when a fitted style is required.

(5) Square a line through side waist points from SG lines. This is the basic waist line. Place the side waist points of the matching size Dartless Bodice Block up to this line with CB and CF lines of bodice parallel with the SG lines on paper. The CB and CF points should be aligned, which means there will be horizontal gaps between side waist points. There will also be a small vertical gap between CF waist points of bodice and shorts if they have been correctly placed.

(6) The 'steps' at side waists need smoothing off. Take a midway point between each and curve up to U/A points and down to top hip level. To complete the block outlines, join up the gaps caused by the length increases just below hip lines.

One-Piece Body Block

Fig. 113

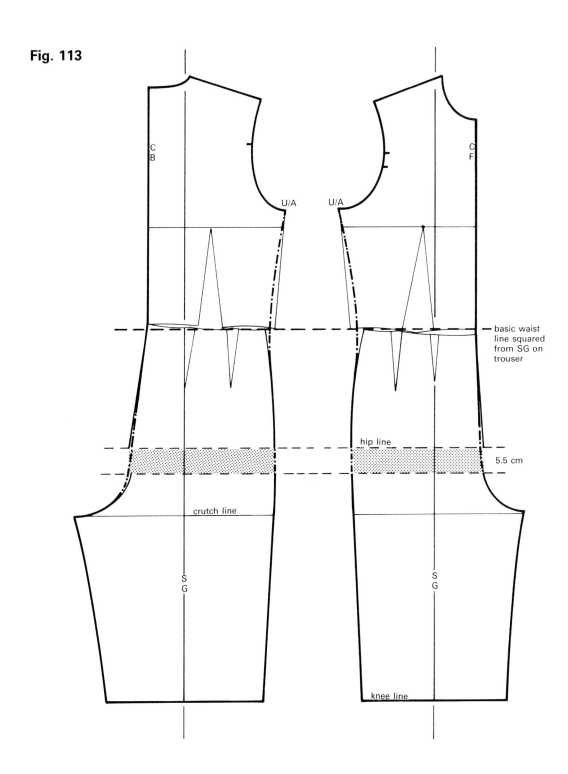

PLAYSUIT
Refer to Fig. 114

(1) Outline the One Piece Body Block from knee to basic waist line. Ignore the darts — they will contribute to gathered effect. Mark in the crutch and hip lines. Make sure that there are SG lines marked on the sheet of paper underneath the block and lengthened well beyond the shoulder seam. These lines will help you keep the blocks aligned whilst introducing the blouson effect at waist.

(2) Keeping the SG lines exactly on top of each other, push the block up towards the top of the sheet by the amount required for blouson effect — here 5 cm (remember the amount will appear halved in wear). Complete the block outline including the bust line.

(3) **To straighten side seams** thereby adding width to the elasticated waist — square down from bust line and U/A points to finished length which is 7 cm below crutch line. Squaring in this way will automatically add extra width at hip and leg level. Place balance marks on side seams for elastic casing position (lower casing level on basic waist, casing width = 2.5 cm).

(4) Square across to inside leg for finished length. Add turn-ups and hem allowance. Fold pattern into its turned up position to angle inside leg seam.

(5) **To shape neckline and armhole**
Square neckline for 7.5 cm from CF line, 5 cm up from bustline. Connect up to shoulder, 2.5 cm away from neck point. Strap width at shoulder = 5 cm. Re-shape the armhole keeping strap parallel in the shoulder area and sweeping down to a lowered U/A point.

(6) **For the top line of back playsuit**, place the straightened side seams together and continue the front armhole line into the back bodice, curving it slightly below the bust line.

(7) In order to continue the strap in the right direction onto the back bodice, place the front playsuit pattern against the back with shoulders touching and aim the strap towards and beyond the CB so that straps can be buttoned in a cross-over manner. It pays to mirror this image to see how it will look in wear. Cut front playsuit and strap in one, omitting shoulder seam. Plan button and buttonhole position on bodice and strap whilst patterns are so placed.

(8) **Add button and buttonhole wrap** beyond CF 1.5–2.5 cm wide depending on size of button, and about 15 cm below basic waist level. Mark in buttonhole positions.

(9) Cut a facing pattern for front edge, strap and front armhole in one piece. Cut a second facing pattern for top edge of back. Facing width should be sufficient to leave buttonholes sitting centrally. See Fig. 115.

(10) **For welt pocket**
Refer to the Bathrobe (Fig. 76) and accompanying text pages 130–33) for instructions but note that the pocket is smaller (see measurements on Fig. 114) to suit the proportions of the playsuit.

Note Other uses: this playsuit pattern, when extended to ankle can form the basis for dungaree and jumpsuit styles.

Playsuit

Fig. 114

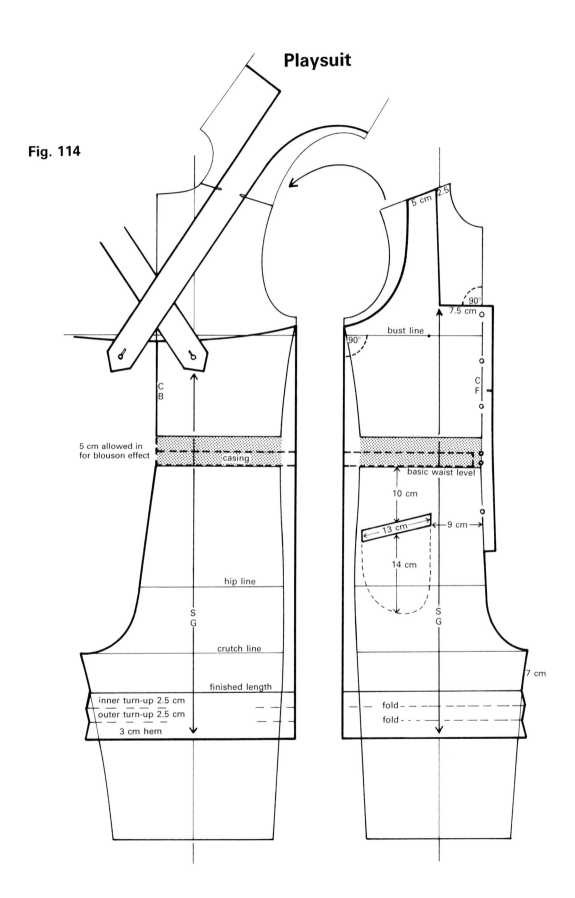

5 cm 2.5

90°

7.5 cm

bust line

90°

C B

C F

5 cm allowed in for blouson effect

casing

basic waist level

10 cm

13 cm

9 cm

14 cm

hip line

S G

S G

crutch line

7 cm

finished length

inner turn-up 2.5 cm

outer turn-up 2.5 cm

fold

3 cm hem

fold

196

Fig. 115

Facings for playsuit

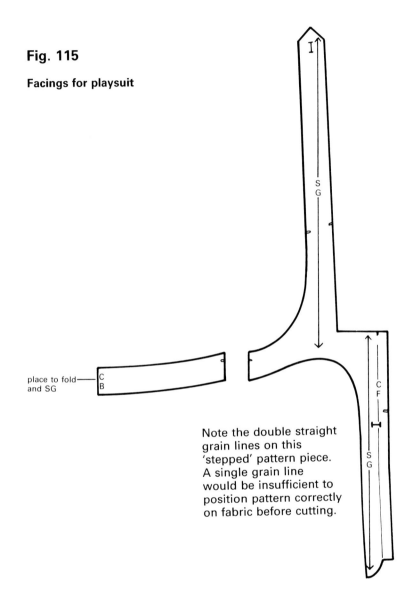

place to fold and SG

Note the double straight grain lines on this 'stepped' pattern piece. A single grain line would be insufficient to position pattern correctly on fabric before cutting.

BEACH-WRAP

A very useful garment to throw over a swimsuit, especially when bathing in the British Isles! They are particularly comfortable when cut in, or lined with, towelling or other absorbent fabrics. They vary in length according to fashion and benefit from such additions as large pockets and hoods.

Beach-wrap and bathrobe patterns are invariably interchangeable – the bathrobe pattern in this book could certainly be used to make a beach-wrap with the appropriate choice of fabric, such as a strongly coloured and/or boldly patterned towelling. Alternatively, thin transparent fabrics are often used to produce scanty, shirt-shaped beach-wraps of whatever length is fashionable at the time.

Easy fitting raglan sleeved beach-wrap

Firstly plan and prepare the raglan sleeve.

Refer to Fig. 116

(1) Outline the back and front Loose-Fitting Dartless Block (see page 30). Decide on the position of the front raglan seam. (When working with large loose-fitting blocks, raglan seams are best kept straight or nearly so, which suits the enlarged proportions of the block more than the curved raglan seams as used on more fitted styles.) Start the seam well down into the front neckline. From here draw a straight line into a point on the armhole where it will blend well into the underarm curve. This is the only part of the armhole which is not altered. It should be carefully measured (tape measure on edge) and the measurement transferred to the corresponding part of the sleeve.

(2) Repeat this procedure on the back bodice keeping the raglan points on the same level, but note the slightly smaller neck area of the raglan section.

(3) **Refer to Fig. 117(a)**

To correctly place the sleeve against the armhole, match the front raglan balance points and pivot from here until the sleeve head touches the shoulder point of the block. Outline the entire sleeve in this position. (When square shoulders are in fashion a gap of 1−3 cm can be left between sleeve head and shoulder point. See Fig. 117(b).)

(4) Bring the outlined back bodice against the sleeve in the same manner as the front. The raglan sleeve can now be seen superimposed on the raglan bodice. Place differing balance marks on front and back raglan seams and smooth off the inner points (dotted line).

If the three pattern pieces are recorded in this position you will have a good example for future reference.

(5) **Refer to Fig. 118**

Trace the raglan sleeve shape from the plan and deal with the space between shoulder points according to the design and fabric.

(a) For light to medium weight soft fabrics, a curved dart about 7 cm long can be formed on the shoulder which allows the sleeve to be cut in one piece. There are few problems sewing darts in such fabrics.

(b) For medium to heavy weight fabrics which are likely to result in darts that 'poke', a seam along the centre line would be preferable, making a two-piece sleeve.

If in doubt − use a seam.

Refer to Fig. 119(a)

(6) Lengthen the pattern as required. Add sufficient wrap-over beyond the CF (solid line) to suit your choice of fabric − add more for heavier weight fabrics than for lighter weights.

Place the front, sleeve and back patterns together in the neck area, and continuing up from the front edge of the wrap, draw the neckline curving into the original back block neckline.

(7) Draw the inner edge of the band 3 cm from the outer edge and parallel to it. Place balance marks on the inner and outer edges for accurate sewing. The whole band pattern is rarely cut in one piece (very wasteful of fabric) − the usual place for the join is on the shoulder. Trace this band pattern from the plan and add seams. Make the sleeve hem band similarly. To attach band see Fig. 119(b).

(8) For belt pattern
length = waist measurement × 3, plus seams
width = 3 cm doubled, plus seams
belt loop position − centre is 5 cm down from natural waist

(9) Pocket − top edge is banded as sleeve hem. Whole pocket is caught in with the side seam. Draw its shape, size and position on plan; trace from it and add seams.

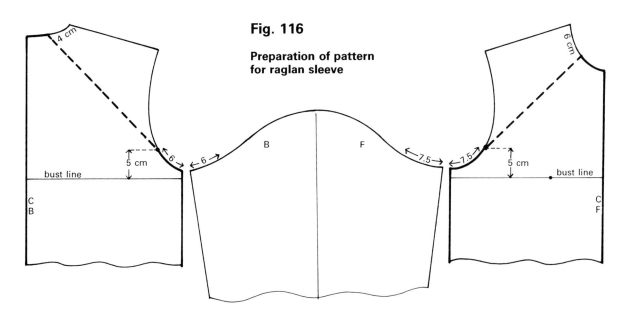

Fig. 116

Preparation of pattern for raglan sleeve

Fig. 117(a)

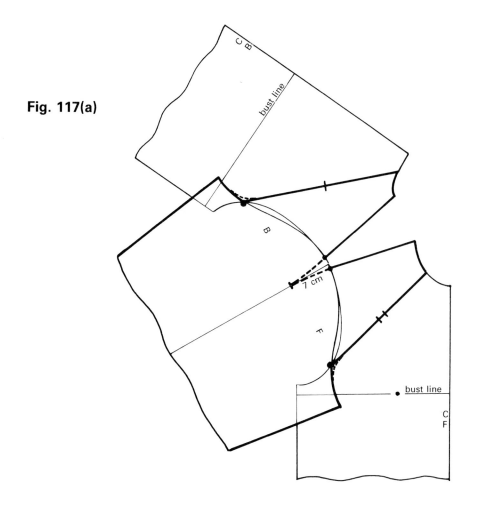

Fig. 117(b)

Square shouldered raglan sleeve

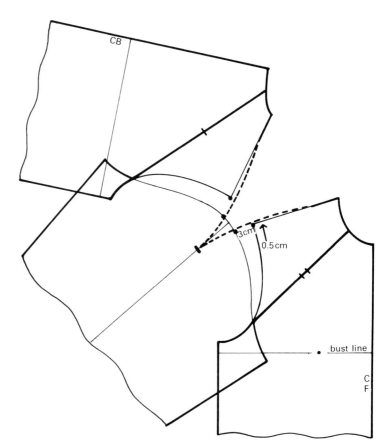

Fig. 118

Finished raglan shapes

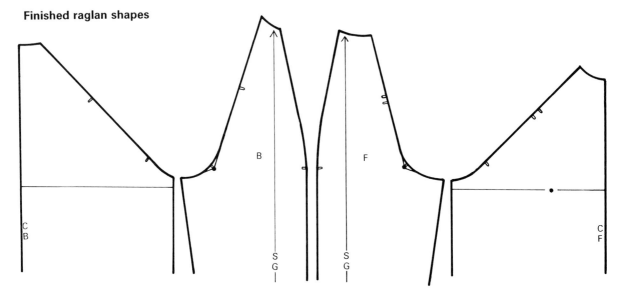

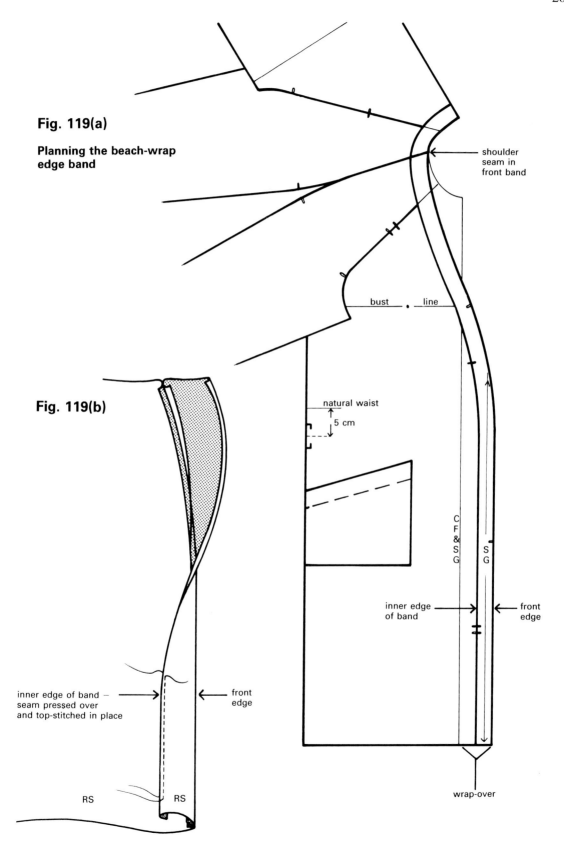

Fig. 119(a)

Planning the beach-wrap edge band

shoulder seam in front band

bust line

natural waist

5 cm

Fig. 119(b)

C F & S G

S G

inner edge of band

front edge

inner edge of band — seam pressed over and top-stitched in place

front edge

RS

RS

wrap-over

BEACH PYJAMAS

Beach pyjamas have an air of luxury about them, reminiscent of holidays in hot, faraway places where protection from the sun is often more important than exposure to it.

Styles vary according to fashion but loose, airy designs cut in lightweight, floating fabrics such as jap silk and cotton voile are the most comfortable. The trousers are generally simplified in shape and cut wide, either at the hem or hip or both. The tops are most often cut on the lines of a shirt.

Beach Pyjamas — short, shirty top and softly draped trouser with side pockets.

Suitable fabrics for this style:
jap silk, cotton voile.

TROUSER

Refer to Fig. 120

The following alterations have the effect of lowering and loosening the crutch and straightening the inside leg to suit a very loose style. Note that the overall trouser length from waist to hem, remains the same.

(1) Outline the Trouser Block (see page 23) including darts, hip and knee levels and SG lines. Drop the block 5 cm towards the hem (keep straight grains aligned) and re-draw the crutch area − dotted line.

(2) Add 2−3 cm width to these new crutch points. Using the inside leg of the front block to trace against, re-draw *both* inside leg seams down to the hemline. (The back block inside leg is too shapely to use for very loose styles and furthermore the stretching arrangement as described in Note 3 on page 24 − end of Trouser Block notes − is also unsuitable. Therefore the whole of the back inside leg seam needs adjusting and the simplest way is to use the front inside leg as a guide to the back.)

After re-drawing these seams, place them together matching the hem levels and raise the back crutch point level with the front. While the patterns are so positioned, re-draw the crutch seam checking for good continuity of the curve.

Draw curved 'drape' lines where required. Number the sections − they can get out of order when separated.

Refer to Fig. 121

(3) On a large sheet of paper, minimum size 120 cm wide × 130 cm long (joined if necessary), draw a vertical centre line and another at a right angle, about 15 cm down from the top. These lines will help maintain the balance between the back and front trouser when patterns are cut and spread.

To introduce the side drapes, cut on curved lines and spread the sections as shown in Fig. 121. The important points to watch are:

(a) Outside leg hem points must touch on the centre line. (Once final pattern shape is decided, round off points at (a) to keep a level hem. See dotted line.)

(b) Outside leg thigh points *and* side waist points must be equidistant from centre line.

(c) Side waist points must touch horizontal line.

(d) The darts are eliminated from the waist curve although in practice it may be necessary to retain a small dart in the front to allow the side waist point to reach the horizontal line. This may remain as a dart or alternatively be tucked, pleated or eased into the waist.

(4) The horizontal line now becomes the top of the 'side seam.' In-seam pockets are a useful addition − they may be cut in one with the trouser or cut separately and joined. If the latter, extend the seam into the pocket, away from view.

Place a bias straight grain line at 45° to the centre line.

(5) **Refer to Fig. 122**

The trouser is folded in half along the centre line and seamed from the side waist points to the fold.

For the trouser opening you could have a CB or CF zip but preferable to both of these is a buttoned side opening, via an extended pocket. The pattern shape is shown in Fig. 123 and details of how it works in Fig. 124. Note the shaped waist facing, used in place of a waistband in this style.

Cut a pattern for the sash − length = 2 m × 25 cm wide.

Beach pyjama trouser

Fig. 120

**Lowering crutch and loosening
inside leg seams**

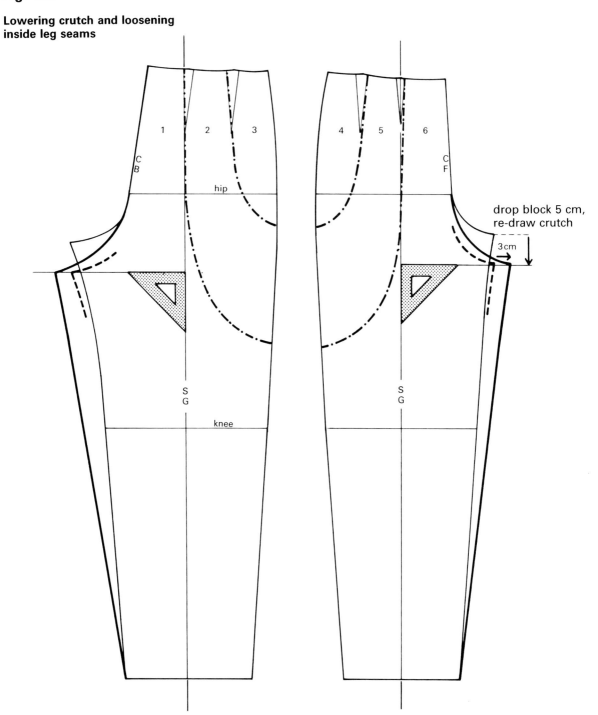

Fig. 121

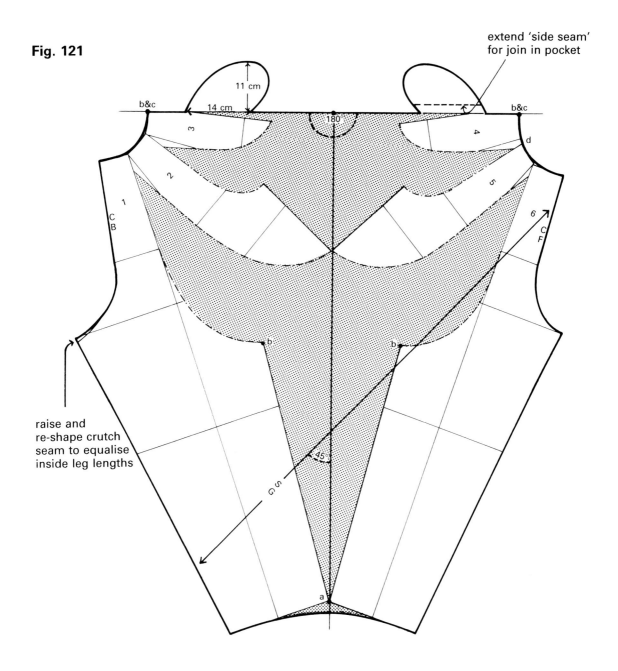

extend 'side seam'
for join in pocket

raise and
re-shape crutch
seam to equalise
inside leg lengths

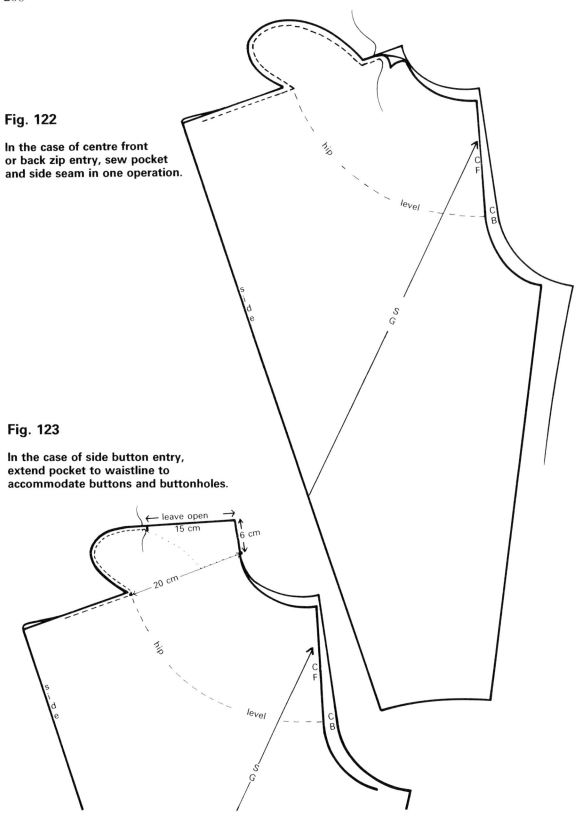

Fig. 122

In the case of centre front
or back zip entry, sew pocket
and side seam in one operation.

Fig. 123

In the case of side button entry,
extend pocket to waistline to
accommodate buttons and buttonholes.

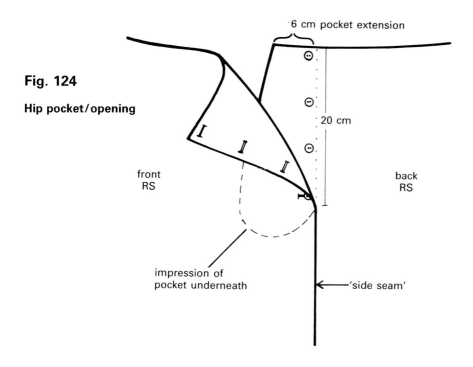

Fig. 124

Hip pocket/opening

6 cm pocket extension

20 cm

front
RS

back
RS

impression of
pocket underneath

'side seam'

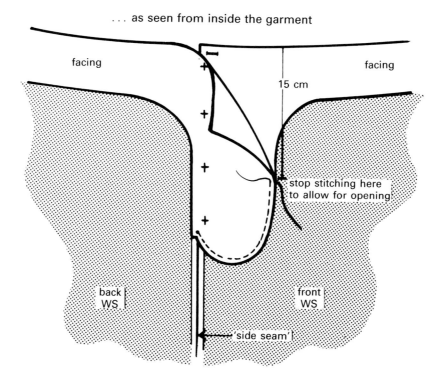

. . . as seen from inside the garment

facing

facing

15 cm

stop stitching here
to allow for opening

back
WS

front
WS

'side seam'

TOP
Refer to Fig. 125

(1) Outline the back and front Loose-Fitting Dartless Bodice Block to a level 3–4 cm below waist. Square across. To reduce the width around the waist, remove 8 cm at the side hem level – the maximum amount to avoid distorting the fit of the block. If a closer fit is required, darts will be necessary.

   Place new side seams together to round off the hemline.

(2) **Button and Buttonhole stand** – **Fig. 125**
   Add 1.5 cm beyond the CF. Double this for the back of the stand and double again for inside the band, which forms a self interfacing – particularly suitable for semi-transparent fabrics where other interfacings could be too evident.

   This type of button stand is very easy to assemble – simply press into position (see sketch in Fig. 125). The buttons and buttonholes will secure it without the need for any stitching. *Note* if you wish the button/buttonhole stands to fold over onto the right side of the garment (as in sketch) you must choose a fabric with identical right and wrong sides.

Beach pyjama top

Fig. 125

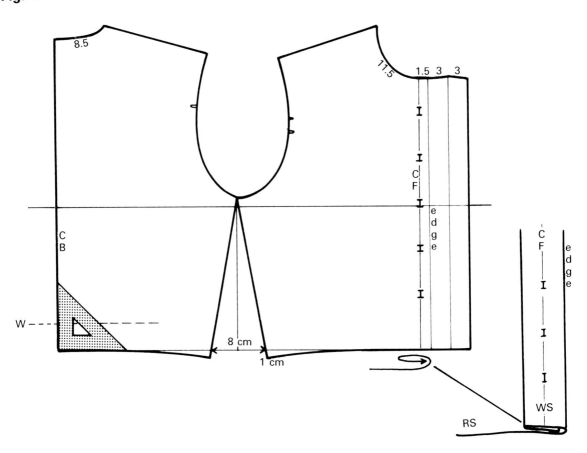

(3) Sleeve − **Fig. 126**

Outline the Extra Flat-Headed Sleeve Block. Square down from underarm line for a wider wrist and generous gathering. Shape the bottom as shown so that it will dip attractively towards the back.

Position for opening is midway between centre and new underarm seam. For lightweight fabrics 8 cm length is sufficient. Cut a narrow continuous strip for binding the slit. Size: 16 cm + 2−3 mm (a little extra is taken up when sewing corner).

(4) Cuff Size, e.g. size 12

Length:

wrist	= 16 cm
ease	= 4
button stand	= 1.5
buttonhole stand	$= \dfrac{1.5}{23\ \text{cm}}$

Depth: = 3 cm doubled

The underarm seam balance mark is positioned in proportion to the sleeve width − i.e. three quarters of the way along cuff.

Fig. 126

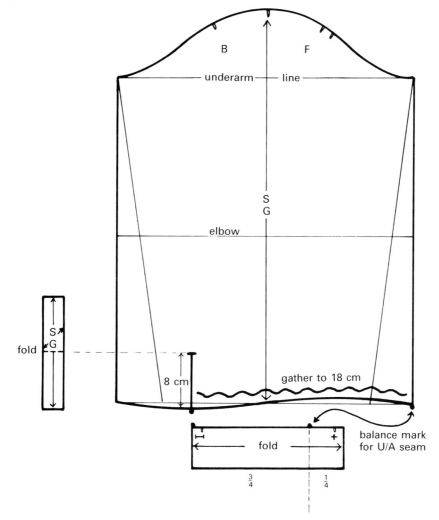

(5) Collar – small and neat, rather like a man's shirt collar.

Refer to Fig. 127

Neckband:

Square up and across from 1.

1–2 = Beach pyjama neckline measurement, from CB–shoulder.

Square up from 2.

2–3 = Beach pyjama neckline measurement, from shoulder–CF.

At 2, lower 0.2 cm.

Midway 2 and 3, lower 0.7 cm.

At 3, lower 0.5 cm.

Draw the neckline from 1 through lowered points in a smooth curve. Measure this curve from CB to check neckline size, marking CF neckpoint. Square up from curved neckline, mark point 4, 2 cm above.

1–5 = width of neck band – 2.5 cm.

Square across. For top seam of neckband where collar will attach, draw a curve parallel with neckline to just past shoulder level, then straight to 4 and beyond. Measure this line from 5–4 (i.e. CB–CF) and record amount for collar construction.

Add a buttonhole extension equal to that on shirt and parallel to CF. Round off top corner where it will sit under collar. Mark buttonhole from just beyond CF.

Collar:

5–6 = 1.5 cm. Square across

6–7 = Top of neckband measurement. Square up and down.

7–8 = 1.5 cm. Curve line from 6–8. Check measurement of top neckband along this curve adjusting 8 if necessary.

6–9 = Width of collar – 3.5 cm. Square across for fall edge of collar.

10 & 11 = 1 cm from squared corner. For point of collar, curve from fall edge through point 10.

8–11 = Connect for front edge.

Fig. 127

Shirt collar with separate band

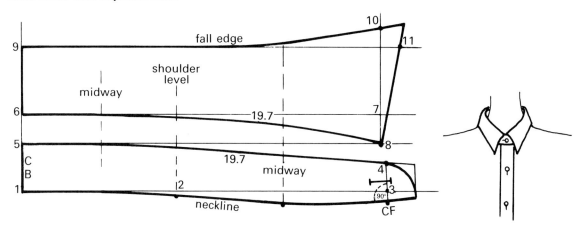

HOUSEDRESS

In this category of leisure clothing, style, cut and details are usually kept very simple and casual. Housedresses should be easy to get in and out of as they are meant as quick cover-ups and could even replace a dressing-gown in the summer months. As with all lounge/ leisurewear, large pockets are an advantage.

There are few restrictions on the types of fabrics that can be used but those that resist creasing will help the appearance of a garment used for lounging.

Housedress — with simple tie fastening for a loose, lounging cover-up

Refer to Fig. 128

(1) Outline the Loose-Fitting Dartless Bodice Block including bust and waist levels. Lengthen to 95 cm from the nape. Square across for hemline. Raise shoulder/armhole points 1 cm, connect back to neck points and extend for top sleeve seam.

(2) Add 2 cm on each side to bust level width (8 cm altogether). For hem circumference: measure one quarter of the *body* hip plus 1.5 cm, from CB and CF.

(3) Place new shoulder seams together, matching neckpoints.

Re-shape neckline

Lower 3 cm at CF, widen 2 cm at shoulder and lower 1.5 cm at CB.

(4) **For sleeve**

This is the simplest type of kimono and the method is recommended only for a short sleeve.

Square on new side seams 13 cm up from waist levels. Measure 10 cm for underarm sleeve length. Connect hemline of sleeve while patterns are still together at shoulder. (Sleeve in sketch is simply rolled up.)

Refer to Fig. 129

Round off back and front underarm seams with a gentle curve. See measurement for guidance.

(5) **For front opening** – measure down 50 cm from the new CF neckpoint. Square out 2 cm; draw edge of tie wrap parallel to CF up to bust level. Shape to 1 cm inside neckpoint.

Mark sewing positions of ties – at bust and waist levels, plus a strengthening box at base of opening. These will act as a guide to the width of the facing, needed to finish the shaped front edge. It should be wide enough to catch in with the tie stitching but narrower at neck and base to avoid unnecessary bulk. (Back facing not needed as collar will finish neck edge.)

Ties – cut pattern 2.5 cm wide doubled, × 30 cm long.

Collar – measure new neckline from CB to original CF neckpoint. Use this measurement to draft the collar band (for instructions see Beach Pyjama Top, Fig. 127 on page 212). Make it a little wider – up to 3 cm – and keep the front edge straight, not rounded. See Fig. 129.

Refer to Fig. 130

To shape the end of the collar in line with the dress front, place neck edge of collar against neck edge of housedress, at least near the CF. Continue the front edge shaping into the collar, discarding the end.

Pocket – large patch pockets sewn into the side seams and parallel to CF. Dimensions as in Fig. 129.

Side seams are slit from hem to base of pocket.

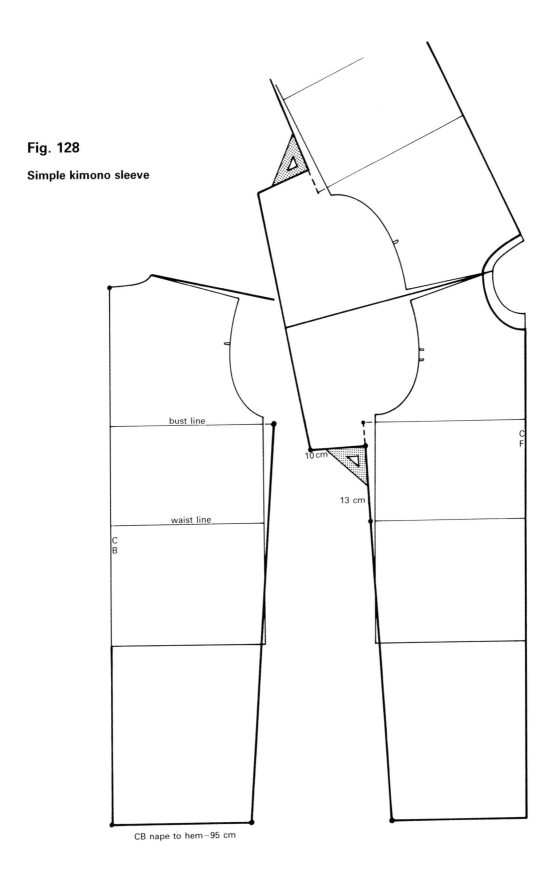

Fig. 128

Simple kimono sleeve

bust line

waist line

C
B

C
F

10 cm

13 cm

CB nape to hem—95 cm

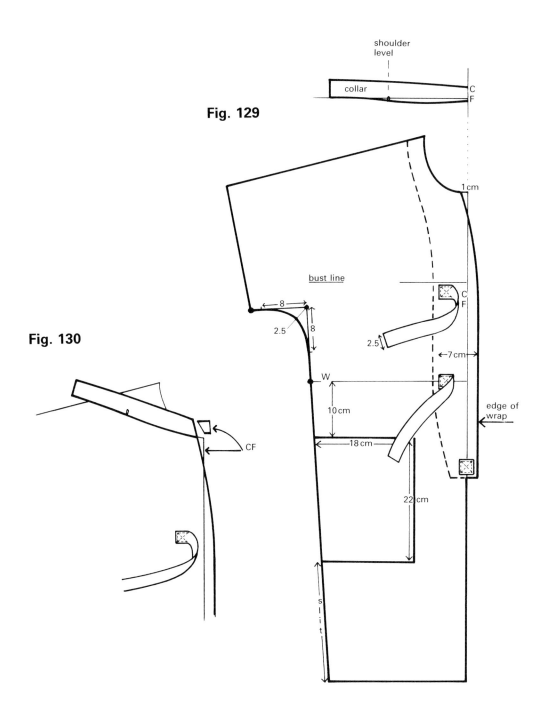

Fig. 129

shoulder level

collar

C F

Fig. 130

bust line

8

2.5

8

C F

2.5

W

1 cm

7 cm

edge of wrap

10 cm

18 cm

22 cm

CF

s l i t

5 BLOCKS FOR STRETCH FABRICS

BLOCKS FOR STRETCH FABRICS

It is unnecessary always to draft new blocks or patterns for use with stretch fabrics/knits. They can be adapted from patterns originally designed for woven fabrics, thus retaining the continuity of working with familiar, tried and tested shapes.

The ease incorporated into blocks designed for woven fabrics is superfluous when using those blocks for stretch knits. The inherent elasticity generally provides sufficient 'give' to replace this ease. Adjustments consist mainly of reducing the width (and sometimes the length) of the pattern and also partial or total removal of darts which may no longer be necessary. (Small darts may still be required for fabrics with minimum stretch.)

Exact adjustments can only be made when it is possible to assess the elasticity of the actual fabric chosen for the style. For more general purposes a set of 'stretch blocks' are extremely useful to the designer/pattern cutter.

The amounts used to reduce the blocks can be varied to suit the elasticity of the fabric. *Amounts used in the following examples will reduce the patterns to suit slight to moderate stretch.* (Refer to the stretch gauge on page 244.) Double these reductions for super stretch fabrics but if possible check the degree of stretch in the fabric against the stretch gauge before beginning as it can vary greatly. Consider also the degree of tightness needed for the style to have the right look. As always with close fitting, stretchy garments, the only way to be sure that the pattern will work exactly as you wish is to make a trial garment in a similar (less expensive) fabric.

The following set of stretch blocks have been adapted from the Basic Dress Blocks, i.e. straight skirt, bodice, sleeve and trouser as constructed in Chapter 1. These will provide a basis for almost any stretch garment, from head to toe. Once the basic blocks have been reduced in size they may then be used to produce patterns for stretch fabrics just as the ordinary blocks are used to produce patterns for non-stretch fabrics.

Skirt

Refer to Fig. 131

(1) Outline the Straight Skirt Block (page 11). Include the hip line and the waist darts lightly drawn. Consult the Size Chart (page 6) for the ease allowance over the hips. Divide this into quarters and apply between parallel lines starting on the outer dart lines.

(2) Measure the remaining front dart, transferring the amount to the side seam for removal. Mirror this on the back side seam, maintaining the original balance.

Blocks for stretch fabrics – Skirt

Fig. 131

Preparation

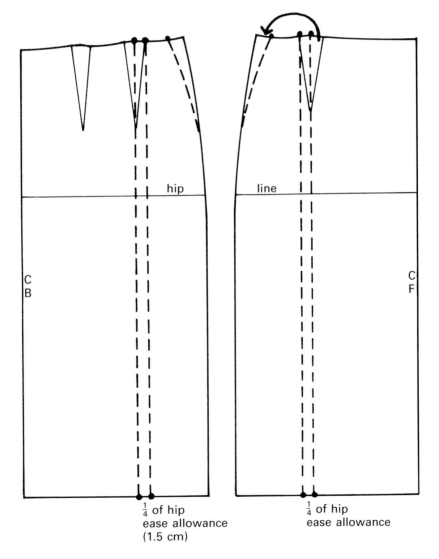

$\frac{1}{4}$ of hip ease allowance (1.5 cm)

$\frac{1}{4}$ of hip ease allowance

Refer to Fig. 132 – finished pattern shape

(3) Remove the parallel strips by folding or slashing. Part of the back dart allowance remains. This is best dealt with at the pattern making stage where it can be converted into easing or re-sited according to the style. Re-shape the waistline to suit the side seams – best done with the seams pushed together near waist. Lower the waistline 0.5 cm at CB and CF, curving back to side waist point.

Fig. 132

Completed skirt pattern

Example, size 12

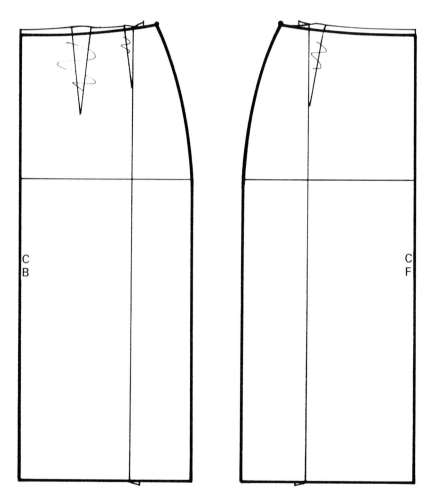

scale 1:5

Bodice

Outline the Bodice Block (page 13). Include the bust line, all darts lightly drawn and the armhole balance marks. Start with the front which needs additional alteration to the back on account of the bust shaping.

Refer to Fig. 133

(1) Transfer shoulder dart into the side seam using the bust line as the lower dart line. From a point halfway through this dart draw a horizontal (parallel) line to CF.

Refer to Fig. 134

(2) Remove this strip by folding or slashing, thereby shortening the CF neck to waist length. The remaining half dart will be eased into the back side seam at bust level.

Blocks for stretch fabrics – Bodice

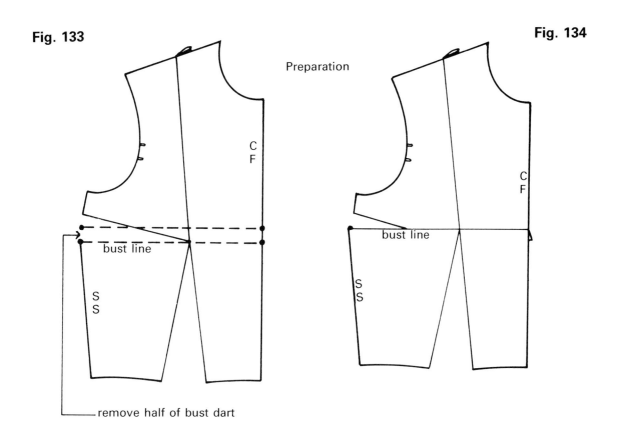

Fig. 133

bust line

C
F

S
S

remove half of bust dart

Preparation

Fig. 134

bust line

C
F

S
S

Ref to Fig. 135

(3) Place balance marks on side seams to control bust easing. The back and front bodices now receive the same adjustments:

To reduce through body width:

Mark 0.5 cm on shoulders ⎫ connect through to
Mark 2 cm on bustline ⎭ waistline and fold out

Note that back shoulder dart may be completely eliminated.

To reduce neck and armhole circumferences:

Mark 0.3 cm at neck ⎫ connect and
Mark 0.5 cm at armhole ⎭ fold out

Ref to Fig. 136

(4) To complete width reduction, trim 0.5 cm from back and front side seams.

To finalise the pattern shapes, smooth out neckline, armholes, shoulder seams and waist lines where pattern was folded or slashed. Re-draw the bust lines at right angles to CB and CF.

Fig. 135

Preparation

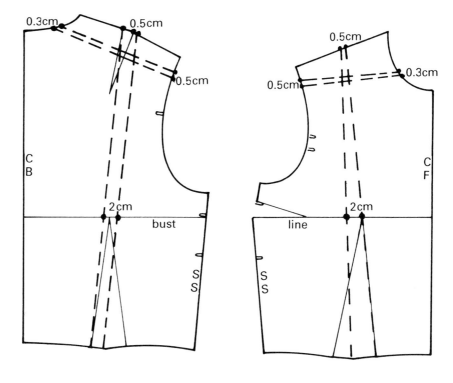

Fig. 136

Completed bodice pattern

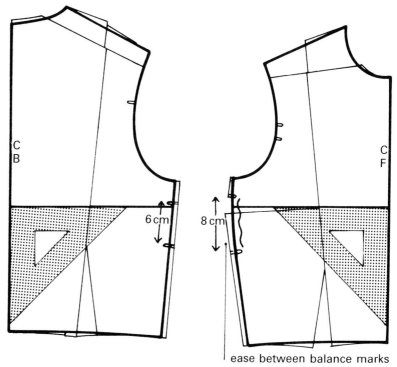

scale 1:5

Sleeve

Refer to Fig. 137

(1) Outline the Sleeve Block (page 16). Include the centre SG line, underarm and elbow lines and the sleeve head balance marks. Transfer the wrist dart into the back underarm seam. Remove half this dart by slashing or folding across to the opposite seam. The remaining half dart will be eased into the front sleeve seam at elbow level. Place balance marks accordingly.

Refer to Fig. 138

(2) Reduce sleeve head to fit adjusted armhole:

    (a) Remove a strip 0.5 cm wide horizontally through head (in a similar position to armhole adjustment).

    (b) Trim 0.5 cm from each underarm seam (to match side seam adjustment on bodice).

    (c) Set-in sleeves do not need the same amount of sleeve head easing when cut in stretch fabrics. Remove a strip 1 cm wide through vertical centre of sleeve. Re-mark SG line.

Completed sleeve pattern is shown in Fig. 139. Round off the elbow point. For a really tight wrist remove an extra 1 cm from each seam at wrist graduating off to underarm point (see dot-dash line). In this case remember to allow an opening for the hand.

Fig. 137

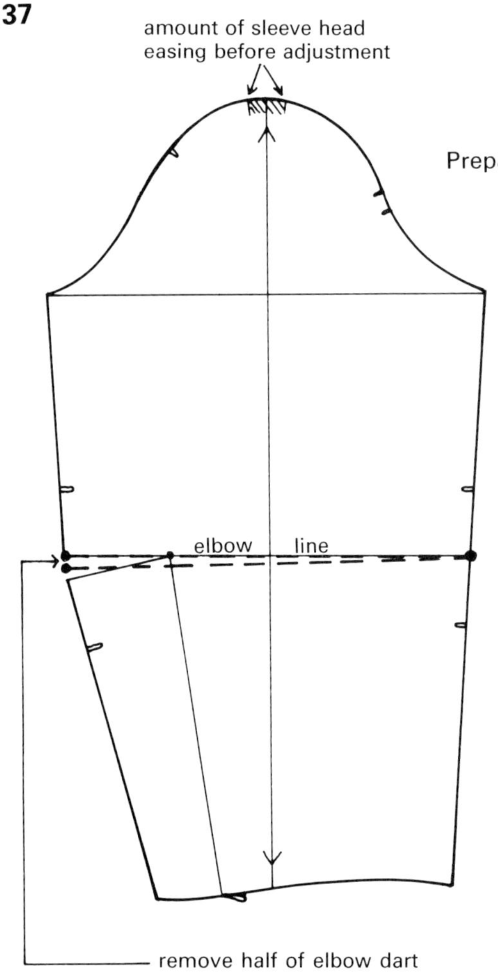

amount of sleeve head easing before adjustment

Preparation

elbow line

remove half of elbow dart

Fig. 138

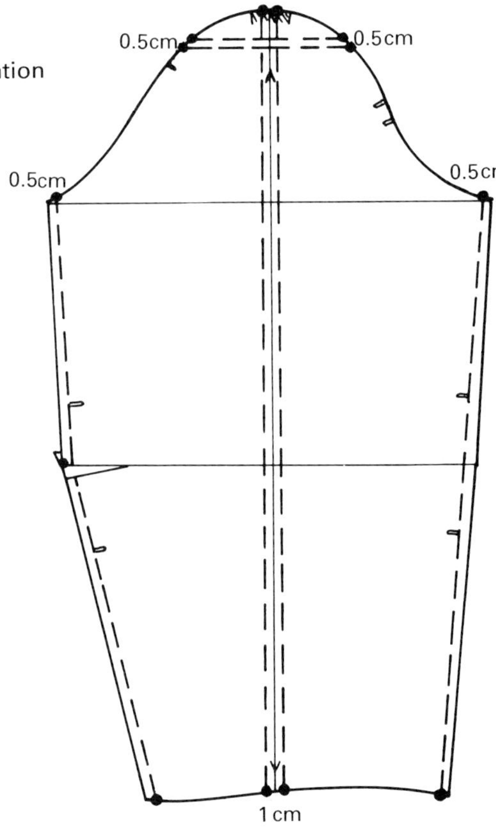

0.5cm 0.5cm

0.5cm 0.5cm

1 cm

Fig. 139

Completed sleeve pattern

Example, size 12

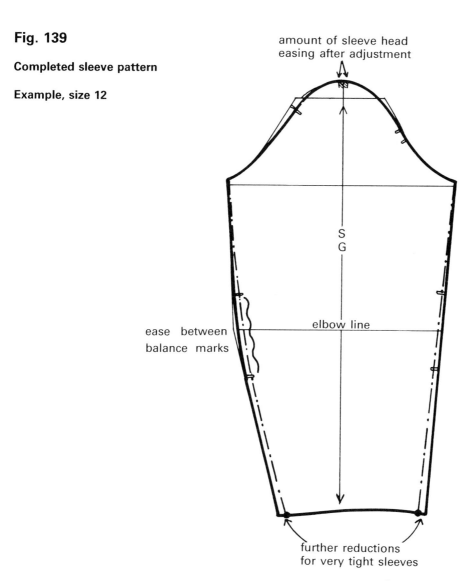

amount of sleeve head
easing after adjustment

S
G

elbow line

ease between
balance marks

further reductions
for very tight sleeves

scale 1:5

Trouser

Refer to Fig. 140

(1) Outline the Trouser Block (page 23). Include the hip, crutch and knee lines, the SG lines and the waist darts lightly drawn. The procedure is similar to that used for the skirt block but with additional adjustments.

(2) The following adjustments apply to back *and* front trouser. Mark one quarter of hip ease allowance between lines parallel with SG lines, positioned so as to include the waist darts nearest the CB and CF. These waist darts will disappear on removal of this strip.

(3) The remaining waist darts are transferred into the side seams, tapering off just above hip.

(4) The waist−crutch length may be shortened for a tight fit and when using fabric with two-way stretch; do this via a parallel horizontal strip removed at hip level, average amount 1.5 cm.

(5) The inside leg may be narrowed for a tighter crutch and thigh fit. Remove a parallel strip, average amount 1 cm.

(6) **Refer to Fig. 141**.

To complete the new trouser outline smooth off the old dart bumps at waistline and re-curve the crutch seams.

The ankle, knee and thigh circumferences may be further reduced for a closer fit. For amounts see Fig. 141, following dot-dash lines.

Note 1 When really tight trousers are in fashion reduce the trouser bottoms to suit the style but remember that the foot has to pass through. Think about ankle slits − perhaps buttoned, zipped, laced, buckled or left plain.

Note 2 Trousers cut in stretch fabrics (track suits etc.) are often elasticated at the waist. In this case disregard the fitted side seams above the hip, and straighten the pattern until it is parallel with the SG lines; the waist circumference should equal the body hip measurement plus 5−8 cm to pull on easily. Add a casing for elastic above the waistline; for method see paragraph 5 and Fig. 61 for Pyjama Bottoms on pages 110 and 111.

If the trousers are designed for active sports, lengthening the back crutch seam will allow more room for bending. See paragraph 3 and Fig. 60 of Pyjama Bottoms on pages 108 and 109.

Blocks for stretch fabrics − Trouser

Fig. 140

Preparation

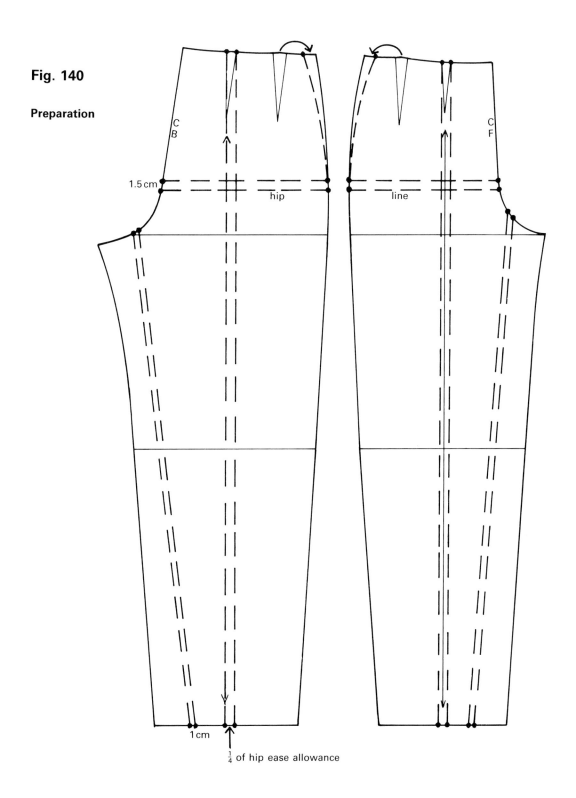

1.5 cm

C
B

hip line

C
F

1 cm

$\frac{1}{4}$ of hip ease allowance

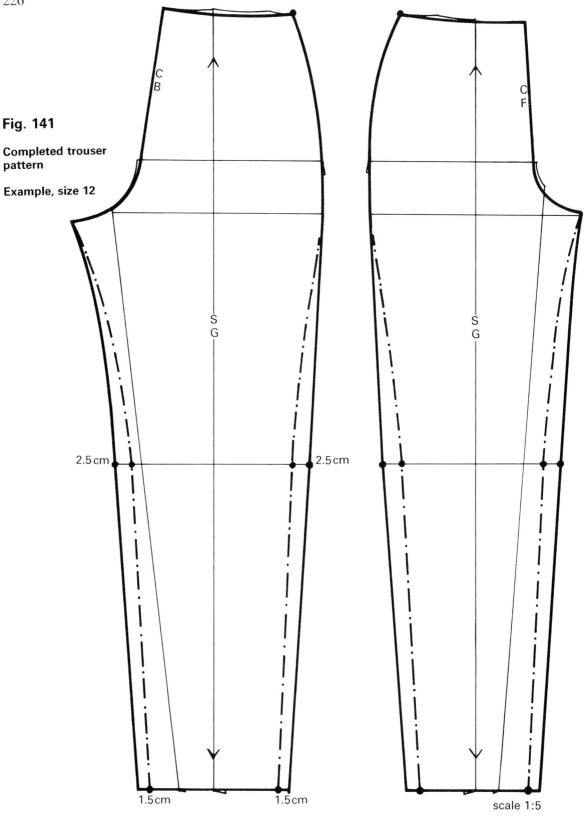

Fig. 141

Completed trouser pattern

Example, size 12

C
B

C
F

S
G

S
G

2.5 cm

2.5 cm

1.5 cm

1.5 cm

scale 1:5

—·—·—·— further reductions to fit leg closely
(while still allowing foot through without the need for an opening)

A COLLECTION OF STRETCHWEAR PATTERNS —

adapted from existing patterns

In addition to the stretch blocks and to save even more pattern cutting time it is invaluable to know how to extend the use of patterns already cut for styles in stretch fabrics, to other (similarly shaped) categories of clothing. The following ideas will show you how you can take existing patterns which you have tried and tested, and adapt them to produce other styles. This practice is widely adopted in professional design studios throughout the trade. It saves much time and energy in starting *every* pattern right from the beginning and allows you to take advantage of all the initial working out that had to be done first time around.

The art in this practice is that of being able to assess from the design sketch which pattern or block would serve as the best basis. This is to some extent a matter of common sense but it also helps to be familiar with your pattern shapes — to know how the two-dimensional flat pattern looks when made up in fabric and tried on the body. This kind of knowledge can only really be gained through experience but the following suggestions will give you a basic insight.

Tube dress, pull-on

Suggested fabrics: moderate to super stretch cotton jersey or lycra.

The Basic Swimsuit Block has been chosen as a basis for the tube dress because it comes closer to the size and shape required than any other pattern. There are alternatives:

(a) The One-Piece Dress Block (page 19) might seem the obvious choice but it would need much adjustment to reduce it to the close fit required.

(b) The Stretch Bodice and Skirt Blocks (pages 221 and 218) could be joined to produce the correct degree of fit, but you would then have to shape the neckline and smooth out the 'steps' at the side waist points which normally occur when joining bodice and skirts blocks into a one-piece pattern.

Most of this work has already been dealt with on the Basic Swimsuit Block and it therefore serves as a good basis.

Refer to Fig. 142

(1) Outline the Basic Swimsuit Block, Fig. 87 on page 157. Include the bust, squared waist and hip lines. Omit the darts.

(2) **Dress length**
Mark waist to knee level on CB (for measurements, see Size Chart on page 6) to help you decide how far above knee the hem should come. Square across for hem line.

(3) **Side seams**
Square up from hem line to side leg point of swimsuit. From here shape into the waist points, 2.5 cm inside swimsuit outline and up to UP in a body-like curve.

Important   Measure this suggested waist size − in this example for size 12, the whole pattern waist measures 75 cm. Check that 75 cm of your chosen fabric will stretch to the minimum required to pull the garment on over the shoulders, i.e. body bust measurement − 88 cm for size 12.

(4) **Neckline**
The front neckline is unaltered. Raise the back neckline 20 cm above bust line and draw a smooth curve into point (b). Note that this curve is parallel to the original Dress Block (dotted) neckline.

(5) Add narrow seams and hem allowance. Neckline and armhole edges may be simply overlocked, turned under and top-stitched into place, or these edges may be faced if preferred.

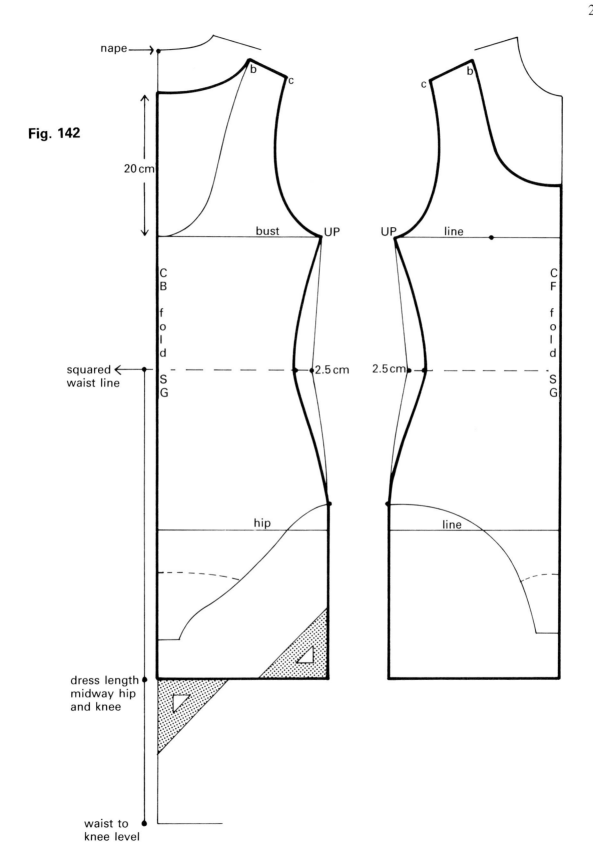

Fig. 142

nape →

20 cm

squared ← waist line

dress length • midway hip and knee

waist to • knee level

b

c

bust

UP

C B f o l d

S G

2.5 cm

hip

UP

line

C F f o l d

S G

2.5 cm

line

c

b

Thigh Length Swimsuit

Suggested fabrics: almost any slight to moderate stretch jersey (cotton is particularly suitable).

This is easily adapted from the Basic Swimsuit Block.

Refer to Fig. 143

(1) Outline the Basic Swimsuit Block, Fig. 87 on page 157. Include the waist and hip lines and the crutch reinforcement levels (dotted lines). Omit all darts and the pre-formed cup position, not normally included in this type of swimsuit.

(2) **Lengthen side seams** to 5 cm below hip line and parallel with CB and CF. Start thigh-top leg shaping at right angles to sides and then curve lines towards crutch reinforcement levels; add 2 cm width at back and 1.5 cm width at front. Widen crutch 1 cm. Remember to adjust reinforcement piece accordingly.

(3) Waist darts would rather spoil the long, lean look of this swimsuit. To compensate for their fit, *take in side seams 2 cm* on back and front at waist level, curving seams in line with body shape.

(4) The crutch seam may be centrally positioned, as at the lowest points of the pattern outline. When using thicker fabrics avoid uncomfortable bulk in that area: detach the back crutch section and replace it against the front swimsuit, eliminating the central crutch seam. For an example see Fig. 145.

Thigh length swimsuit

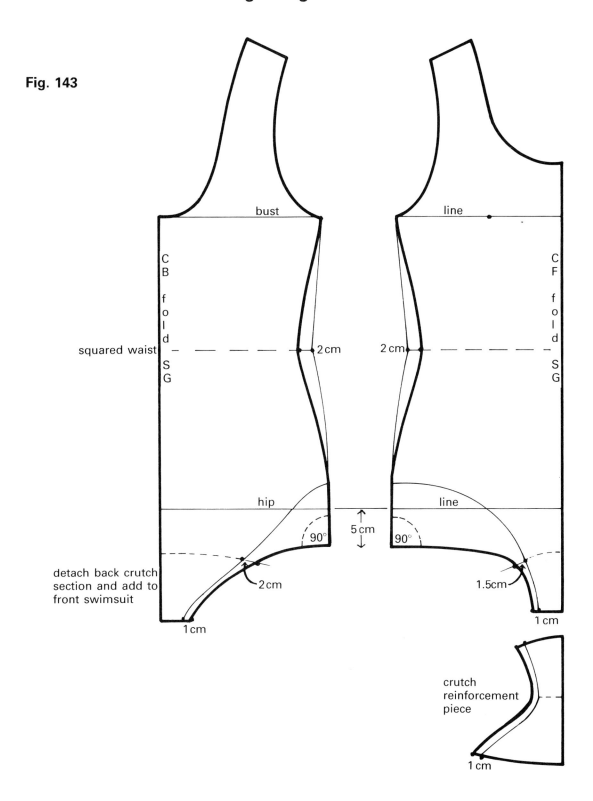

Fig. 143

Two-piece Bathing Suit

Suggested fabrics: moderate to super-stretch cotton jersey or lycra, or stretch knit.

Adapted from the Basic Swimsuit Block but with the leg cut higher and the top and bottoms fitted into midriff.

Refer to Fig. 144
(1) Outline the Basic Swimsuit Block, Fig. 87 on page 157, and include bust, waist and hip lines, the darts and the crutch reinforcement levels.
(2) **Raise side leg points** 10 cm above hip line and shape down to crutch levels as shown. Raise back neck in line with front. Decide on height of bottoms, measuring from waist. Draw a provisional line from CB to CF. Repeat with the top.

Refer to Fig. 145
(3) The midriff edge of top and bottoms must fit closely, *but without darts*, which are quite unnecessary if style is cut in suggested fabric: connect ends of darts to edges of pattern as shown in Fig. 144. Cut on these lines and overlap patterns to remove darts.
(4) Re-adjust leg curves if necessary. 'Waist' edges of both patterns will definitely need adjustment. Push patterns together, lower 1 cm at CB and CF on bottoms and at CF on top, and curve lines through side seam points.
(5) **To complete pattern**: detach back crutch section and add to front. Cut a reinforcement piece.

Two-piece bathing suit

Fig. 144

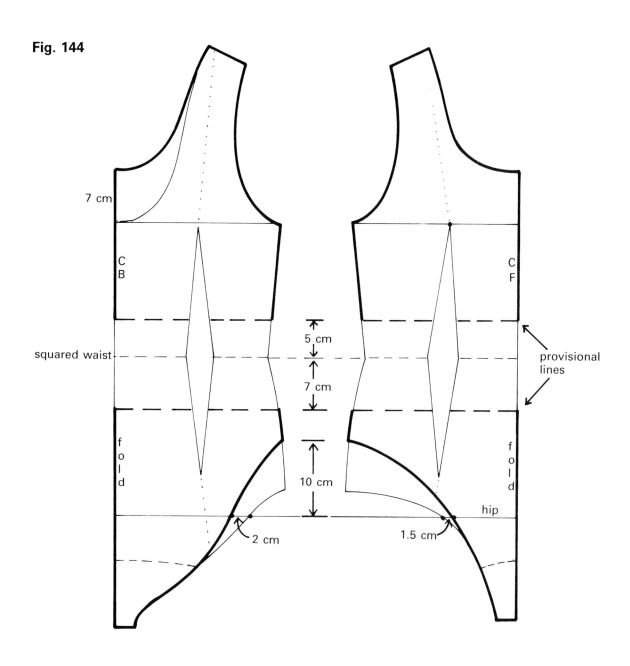

7 cm

C
B

C
F

squared waist

5 cm

7 cm

f
o
l
d

f
o
l
d

10 cm

provisional
lines

hip

2 cm

1.5 cm

Two-piece bathing suit

Fig. 145

Completing the pattern pieces

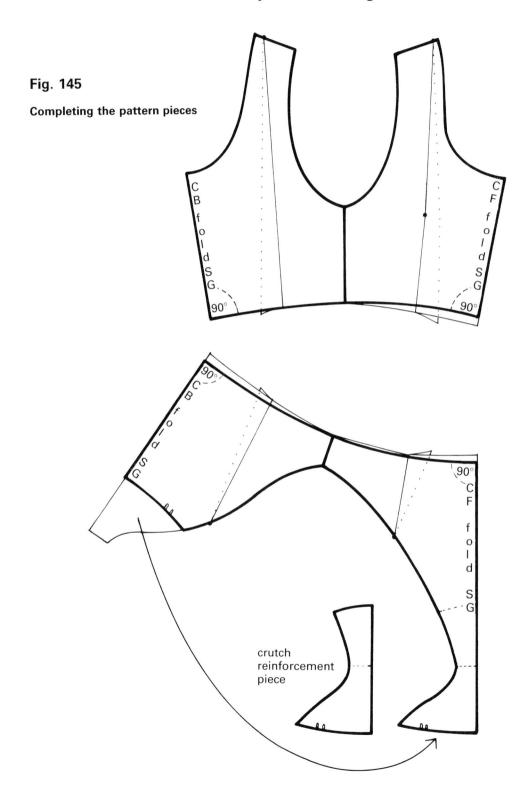

crutch
reinforcement
piece

Tube Top and Shorts in Stretch Knit

The most suitable blocks to use are the Strapless Swimsuit, Fig. 91 on page 165, and the Stretch Trouser Block, Fig. 141 on page 226. For the tube top, the

Strapless Bodice in Chapter 4 was also considered but dismissed as needing more adjustment.

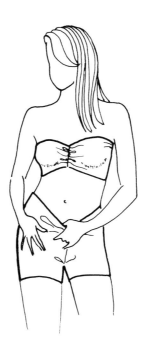

TUBE TOP
Refer to Fig. 146
(1) Outline the top area of the Strapless Swimsuit down to about 10 cm below bust line, drawing a provisional line across to CB. Include the chest line and the doubled bust dart.
(2) **Shape the top edge**: lower CF 5 cm, dip at CB into a right angled line.
   Shape the lower edge: make a right angle at CB, raise slightly at CF or leave line straight for extra gathering. Measure pattern at CF for a guide to length of gathering — here 12 cm.
Refer to Fig. 147
(3) **Transfer bust dart into CF to provide gathers**. Re-draw CF, either curved as pattern outline shows or, if knit is very stretchy, straightened between top and lower edge.

Check measurement of top edge against body chest circumference *and* with stretchiness of fabric in mind; overlap at side seams if necessary. Back and front may be cut in one piece (seam at CF). Place SG lines parallel with or at right angles to the CB, depending on the direction of greatest stretch.

SHORTS
Refer to Fig. 148
(4) Outline the Stretch Trouser Block using the *innermost lines for the closest fit*. Include hip line (for checking size of pattern against stretchiness of knit) and the SG lines. Decide on length of shorts — here 35 cm from front waist — square across using SG lines and push patterns together at side seams to judge hem curve. Repeat procedure on inside leg seams.

Tube top and shorts in stretch knit

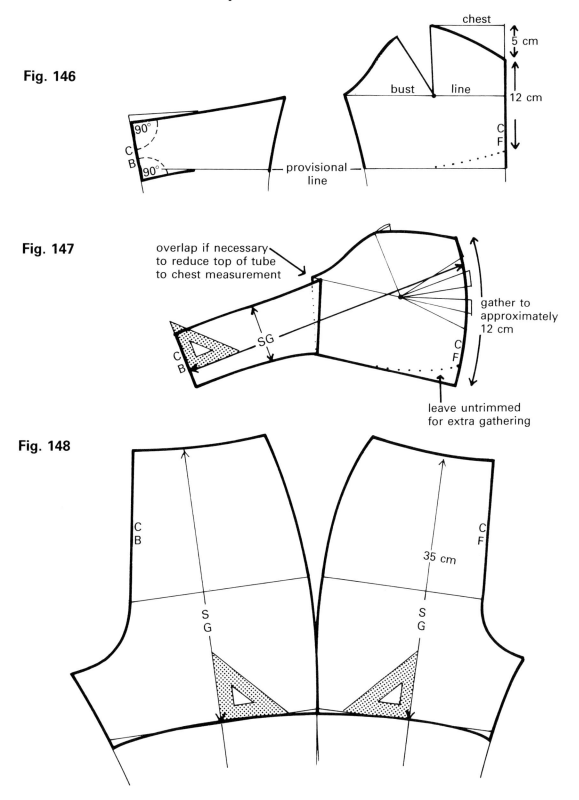

Fig. 146

chest
5 cm
bust line
12 cm
C F
90°
C
B
90°
provisional line

Fig. 147

overlap if necessary to reduce top of tube to chest measurement

gather to approximately 12 cm

SG

C B

C F

leave untrimmed for extra gathering

Fig. 148

C B

C F

35 cm

S G

S G

Long-legged Bodysuit (or Swimsuit)

Suitable only for super stretch fabrics or knits. The best patterns to use as a basis are the Stretch Bodice and Trouser Blocks specially joined at the waist for stretch fabrics.

Another possible base is the One-Piece Body Block in Chapter 4, but it would need much paring down in the width and a considerable adjustment to the trunk length which was specially designed for non-stretch fabrics.

Refer to Fig. 149

(1) Outline the back and front Stretch Bodice Block, Fig. 136 on page 221, with the CB and CF parallel and the bust lines on the same horizontal level. Extend the CB and CF lines well down the length of paper.

(2) Place the back Stretch Trouser Block, Fig. 141 on page 226, up to the back bodice waist, with its SG line parallel to the extended CB. The CB waist points of both patterns must align vertically and the side waist point of the trouser must touch exactly on the waistline of the bodice. (There will be a slight overlap in the CB area and a 'step' at the side.) Outline the trouser in this position down to required length − here it is 12 cm above knee level.

(3) Include the hip line on the back trouser and continue this line across the paper. Place the hip line of the front Stretch Trouser Block on the continued line; place CF trouser waist on CF bodice waist point. Check that trouser SG line is parallel with extended CF and outline trouser in this position. There will be a considerable overlap of waistlines near side seam − due to extra length on the bodice for bust easing. The extra length is unnecessary for this type of garment, provided a super-stretch fabric is used, and may therefore be removed by overlapping.

(4) Shape the neckline and armholes as shown to leave narrow shoulder straps centrally positioned along shoulder for optimum support and comfort.

(5) Re-shape CF, CB and side seams as shown for a more body-hugging fit. Push new side seams together at underarm to check armhole curve, and likewise at shoulder.

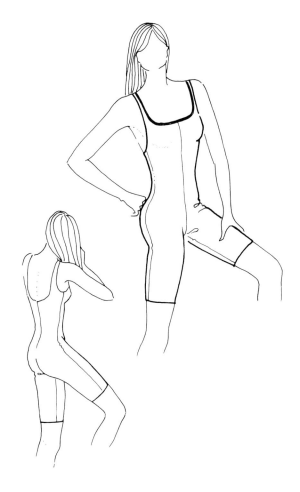

**Long-legged Bodysuit
(or Swimsuit)**

Long-legged Bodysuit
(or Swimsuit)

Fig. 149

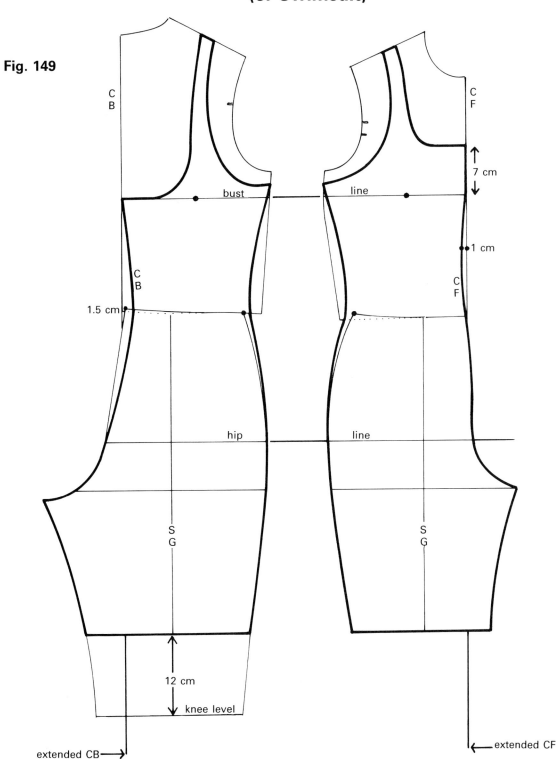

High-cut Bodysuit (or Leotard)

Suitable only for super-stretch fabrics or knits. The best patterns for developing this shape are the Stretch Bodice Block in Fig. 136 on page 221, and the bottom part of the Strapless Swimsuit in Fig. 91 on page 165.

Refer to Fig. 150

(1) Outline the lower half of the back and front Strapless Swimsuit. Omit the shaped CB line and use instead the straight CB. Include the squared waistline, the hip line and the crutch reinforcement levels. Extend the CB and CF lines upwards.

(2) Lay the back Stretch Bodice Block against the extended line with its *side waist point touching the squared waistline*. Outline the bodice in this position and include bust line and armhole balance marks.

(3) Lay the front Stretch Bodice Block against the extended line with the bust line level with that on the back bodice. The bodice waist will overlap the squared line. Outline and include information as on back bodice.

(4) **Re-shape the side seams as shown** (check waist size in the process — there should be just a few centimetres ease over the body size). The back and front side seams should be the same shape; check by laying patterns on top of one another.

(5) **Shape the neckline as shown**. Check the whole curve by pushing patterns together at shoulder.

(6) **Outline the Stretch Sleeve Block**, Fig. 139, to at least 10 cm below the elbow. Retain the slight easing over the elbow (useful for action garments) and shape the sleeve bottom as shown. The seam lengths below the lower balance marks must be equal. Check hem curve with seams placed together.

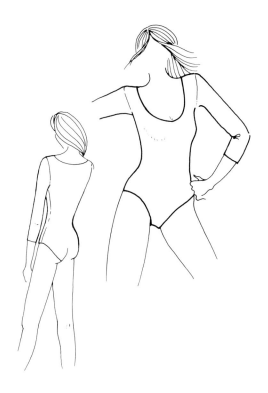

**High-cut Bodysuit
(or Leotard)**

High-cut Bodysuit
(or Leotard)

Fig. 150

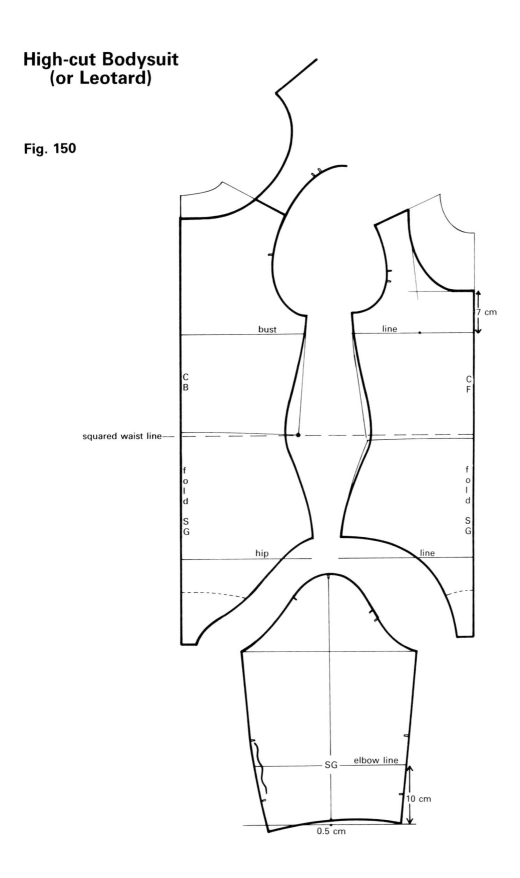

bust   line

7 cm

C
B

C
F

squared waist line—

f
o
l
d

S
G

f
o
l
d

S
G

hip   line

SG   elbow line

10 cm

0.5 cm

APPENDIX

STRETCH GAUGE

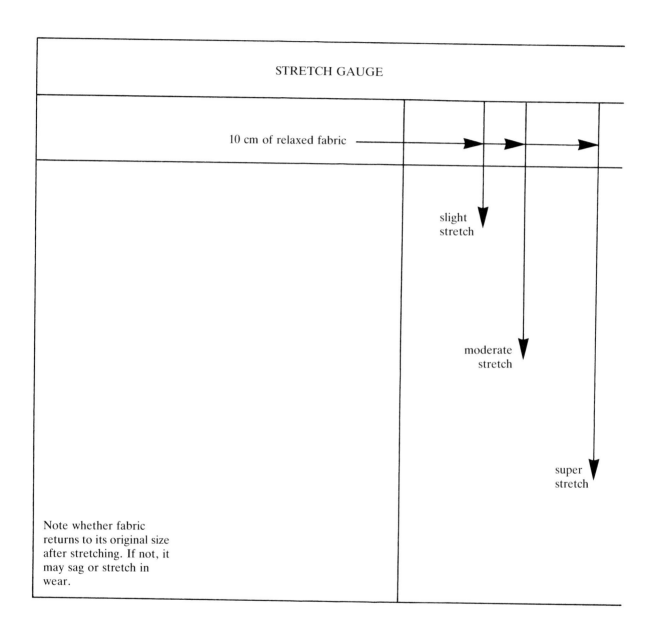

STRETCH GAUGE

10 cm of relaxed fabric

slight
stretch

moderate
stretch

super
stretch

Note whether fabric
returns to its original size
after stretching. If not, it
may sag or stretch in
wear.

LIST OF ABBREVIATIONS

B   – Back
BL   – Bust line
BR   – Body rise
CB   – Centre back
CF   – Centre front
F   – Front
FSS   – Forward side seam
H   – Hip
NP   – Neck point
RS   – Right side
SG   – Straight grain
SP   – Shoulder point
SS   – Side seam
U/A   – Underarm
UP   – Underarm point
W   – Waist line
WR   – Waist reduction
WS   – Wrong side

SEAM ALLOWANCE GUIDE

Collarless necklines
Sleeveless armholes
Bagged out edges of collars, cuffs
   and facings etc., non-fray fabrics   0.5 cm

Collarless necklines, fraying fabric
Collars−neckline
Sleeved armholes, non-fray fabric
Superlocked seams (closed overlocked seams)   1 cm

Side seams
Centre back seams
Shoulder seams
Sleeved armholes, fraying fabrics
Waist seams
Circular skirt hems, top-stitched hems   1.5−2 cm

Seams requiring alteration   2.5 cm

Normal hems   4−6 cm

Coat hems and fittings   7−8 cm

LIST OF PATTERN CUTTING EQUIPMENT

In order of necessity:

(1) Paper for patterns − plain white (marking)
    Card for blocks   − buff manilla
(2) Pencils for pattern work − 4H, 2H, HB
          for sketching   − 2B, 4B
(3) Rubbers
*(4) Grader's set square (perspex)
*(5) Tape measure − metric/imperial
*(6) Ruler, minimum length 1 metre − perspex or aluminium
*(7) Scissors or shears, minimum blade length 10 cm
    − two pairs are necessary: one for paper, one for cloth
(8) Dressmaker's pins − to pin patterns together
(9) Sellotape or drafting tape or dry glue stick
(10) Indicator or push pins, or weights − to hold patterns down ⎫
*(11) Tracing wheel − needle pointed ⎬ Will damage work surface. Linoleum topped tables are recommended for pattern cutting.
*(12) Awl − for making holes at dart points etc. ⎭
*(13) Dress stand
**(14) Ruler 15 cm long showing scale 1:5
*(15) Flexible ruler − for measuring curves
*(16) Pattern notchers
*(17) Pattern hole punch
*(18) Pattern hooks
*(19) Stanley knife
*(20) Felt-tip pens − for labelling patterns
*(21) French curves
(22) Compass − for circular patterns,
    e.g. skirts, capes/collars, frills and godets

*Specialist equipment available from:

R.D. Franks Ltd.,   Morplan,
Market Place,   56 Great Titchfield Street,
Oxford Circus,   London, W1P 8DX
London, W1N 8EJ   Tel. 071 636 1887
Tel. 071 636 1244/5/6

** Scale rulers manufactured by Rotring, Staedtler/Mars, etc.
Available from graphic equipment suppliers.

INDEX